VARIETIES OF RISK ANALYSIS IN PUBLIC ADMINISTRATIONS

This book sets out a novel conceptual and analytical framework to explain why risk analysis, cost-benefit analysis, and similar analytical tools have gained sizeable currency in public administrations, in comparative perspective.

Situated in critical interpretive policy analysis methodology, the book systematizes and innovates respective debates in three ways. First, it develops a novel typology of actors' appreciations of analytical tools as instrumental problem-solving, legitimacy-seeking, and power-seeking. It conceptualizes the latter two as "polity policies" with actors seeking to confirm or rework decision-making structures. Second, the book theorizes how executive fragmentation and the multiplication of coordination requirements – often treated as hindrances to substantial analytical turns in an administration – nourish actors' ideal typical appreciations of analytical tools in distinct ways. Lastly, it scrutinizes varieties of risk analysis across three risk-heavy policy domains in Germany (including the EU) and discusses the potential of risk analysis to stabilize or transform decision-making in multi-level settings.

This book will be of key interest to policy analysts and risk analysts, and scholars of European politics, comparative politics, policy studies, public administration, multi-level governance, EU studies, risk analysis, policy evaluation, and the political sociology of quantification.

Regine Paul is Associate Professor in Comparative Policy Studies at the Department of Administration and Organization Theory of the University of Bergen, Norway.

Routledge Studies in Governance and Public Policy

International Health Worker Migration and Recruitment
Global Governance, Politics and Policy
Nicola Yeates and Jane Pillinger

Challenges to Political Decision-making
Dealing with Information Overload, Ignorance and Contested Knowledge
Hubert Heinelt

Public Enterprise and Local Place
New Perspectives on Theory and Practice
John Fenwick and Lorraine Johnston

Public Administration in Central Europe
Ideas as Causes of Reforms
Edited by Stanisław Mazur

Middle Class and Welfare State
Making Sense of an Ambivalent Relationship
Marlon Barbehön, Marilena Geugjes, and Michael Haus

Localism and the Design of Political Systems
Rick Harmes

Varieties of Risk Analysis in Public Administrations
Problem-Solving and Polity Policies in Europe
Regine Paul

For more information about this series, please visit: https://www.routledge.com

VARIETIES OF RISK ANALYSIS IN PUBLIC ADMINISTRATIONS

Problem-Solving and Polity Policies in Europe

Regine Paul

Routledge
Taylor & Francis Group
LONDON AND NEW YORK

First published 2021
by Routledge
2 Park Square, Milton Park, Abingdon, Oxon OX14 4RN

and by Routledge
52 Vanderbilt Avenue, New York, NY 10017

Routledge is an imprint of the Taylor & Francis Group, an informa business

British Library Cataloguing-in-Publication Data
A catalogue record for this book is available from the British Library

Library of Congress Cataloging-in-Publication Data
Names: Paul, Regine, author.
Title: Varieties of risk analysis in public administrations : problem-solving and polity policies in Europe / Regine Paul.
Description: First Edition. | New York : Routledge, 2021. | Series: Routledge studies in governance and public policy | Includes bibliographical references and index.
Identifiers: LCCN 2020051518 (print) | LCCN 2020051519 (ebook) | ISBN 9780367141479 (Hardback) | ISBN 9780367767464 (Paperback) | ISBN 9780429030543 (eBook)
Subjects: LCSH: Crisis management in government. | Risk assessment—Government policy. | Public administration—Decision making.
Classification: LCC JF1525.C74 P38 2021 (print) | LCC JF1525.C74 (ebook) | DDC 352.4—dc23
LC record available at https://lccn.loc.gov/2020051518
LC ebook record available at https://lccn.loc.gov/2020051519

ISBN: 978-0-367-14147-9 (hbk)
ISBN: 978-0-367-76746-4 (pbk)
ISBN: 978-0-429-03054-3 (ebk)

Typeset in Bembo
by Apex CoVantage, LLC

CONTENTS

FIGURES AND TABLES

Figures

Tables

PREFACE AND ACKNOWLEDGMENTS

When I embarked on the journey toward understanding the role of risk analysis in public administrations, in early 2013, Michael Huber at Bielefeld predicted that the intense empirical engagement with this topic would generate enough puzzles and ideas to "fill a researcher's agenda until retirement". When we first met to discuss our collaboration on an international research project, I must have appeared visibly skeptical as to the ability of the ostensibly "dry" and "technocratic" domains of flood prevention, work safety inspections, or food safety controls to entice my enthusiasm after years of studying the more trendy migration governance. And yet, inspire it did, and it continues to precisely because the "political" in policymakers' analytical efforts is so often ambiguous or disguised and, unlike assumed in parts of policy and regulation studies, it seldomly relates to technical problem-solving alone. In line with one of the book's key claims, it is because risk analysis operates as a magic bullet for actors' visions of rational problem-solving *and* their attempts to (re-)position themselves in a policy domain that I could, indeed, study it until retirement. I hope that this volume may be a gateway into the fascinating and deeply political world of analytical tools for others, too.

I am especially grateful to the many interviewees for sharing with me not only their perspectives on risk analysis but also a whole library of – sometimes secretive – documents about how they use risk analysis in their day-to-day decision-making and how they coordinate their respective adoption of risk analysis with others. Some also graciously opened their professional networks to facilitate my learning about their field, others even took me with them on inspections. Attending a practitioners' conference on work safety in Düsseldorf in 2014 and spending days in a row listening to chief inspectors discussing how to best apply risk analysis in their domain and why this all matters was more informative than any one interview.

Individual thanks are due to several people. First and foremost: Michael Huber who has recruited me into the Open Research Area Project "How States Account for Failure" (HowSAFE), set me on a whole new research track and interpreted his roles as a mentor and colleague in a constructive and engaging manner. Michael is also the person who has read and provided feedback on most drafts of this manuscript. Thank you! I thank Henry Rothstein and David Demeritt at King's College London, Olivier Borraz at Sciences-Po Paris, and Frederic Bouder at the University of Stavanger from the HowSAFE project for creating a constructive environment for conceptual puzzling and empirical testing across a wide range of cases, for stimulating very useful, at times heated, debates about whether we can treat the British case as a benchmark for assessing other cases. Indeed, the project's implicit assumption that the British narrative of why risk analysis appeals would be a litmus test for the German case stood at the cradle of this monograph. Thanks for giving me the intellectual space to carve out my argument through discussions and collaborative work. These thanks extend to Anne-Laure Beaussier, Mara Wesseling, and Marijke Hermans, whose work on the British, Dutch, and French cases helped me strengthen my arguments about the German case. At Bielefeld, I thank Alfons Bora, Maarten Hillebrandt, Vera Linke, and Marc Mölders for engaging with my writing in the research seminar on law and regulation. Vera Linke, Marc Mölders, Detlef Sack, and Holger Straßheim at Bielefeld kindly read the whole manuscript and gave valuable feedback. So did Henry Rothstein over in London: thank you!

Just when I was sandwiched between the near end of my empirical research for HowSAFE and thoughts about whether I could (afford to) turn this into a book, I was lucky to meet Andreas Busch at Göttingen. He encouraged me not only to pursue the book idea but also to seek funding for a writing retreat. Some months later, I was endowed with a John F. Kennedy Memorial Fellowship for a year at the wonderful Centre for European Studies (CES) at Harvard. I thank the German Academic Exchange Service for the generous fellowship which allowed me to iterate reading, thinking, and writing for a whole year without other obligations, to engage in stimulating exchanges with other scholars on a daily basis, and to travel beautiful New England with the family. At the CES, some people deserve special thanks. Peter Hall, Andy Martin, Vivien Schmidt, Rosemary Taylor, and Kathleen Thelen offered generous feedback on draft chapters and it was an early career scholar's dream come true to discuss research with these eminent institutionalists. I thank the whole community of visiting fellows 2017/2018, some of which also read draft chapters: Başak Bilecen, Lukas Haffert, Christian Lybbe Ibsen, Ivana Isailovic, Ewa Kopcienski, Kerstin Martens, Steffen Mau, and Katja Möhring. In the academic bubble that is the Greater Boston Area, I also met Deborah Stone, who kindly shared her expert feedback and enthused me about her then ongoing book project on counting and how we use numbers to decide. I owe Deborah's work on interpretive and critical policy analysis much inspiration since doing my PhD, so discussing with her was especially dear to me. Thanks extend to Philippe Zittoun and participants of the IPPA workshop on "The hidden politics of solutions" in Pittsburgh (June 2018) for allowing me to test-run the book's basic argument. Next to Philippe, Gerry Alons offered extensive feedback on two draft chapters as a discussant. Closer to home, Holger Straßheim and Oliver Schwab organized a workshop on the Evidence-based Policymaking and the Politics of Evidence at the WZB Berlin (November 2018) and provided another floor for fine-tuning the argument. I thank Christina Boswell and Marc Geddes at Edinburgh University for inviting me to present the skeleton of the book in the SKAPE research seminar. Although the COVID-19 lockdown delayed our meeting by a year, previous exchanges with Christina, and her work on performance measurement in public administrations, have been a valuable source of inspiration. Last not least, I thank Andrew Taylor and Sophie Iddamalgoda at Routledge, who oversaw the production of this book from proposal to printing in highly professional, constructive, and always helpful ways.

I remain indebted to Emma Carmel for continuous exchanges on public policy governance and what might constitute a "critical" perspective, and to my family: Mathi, Moritz, and Rieke, for everything else.

ABBREVIATIONS

AEP	annual exceedance probability (probabilistic measure in flood prevention)
ASMK	Arbeits- und Sozialministerkonferenz (conference of the states' Ministries of Labor and Social Affairs, a horizontal coordination forum)
AVV RÜb	Allgemeine Verwaltungsvorschrift Rahmen-Überwachung (Federal level executive order on risk-based food safety controls)
BG	Berufsgenossenschaft (mutual trade association, in charge of sectoral work safety controls)
BSE	bovine spongiform encephalopathy ("mad cow" disease)
BVL	Bundesamt für Verbraucherschutz und Lebensmittelsicherheit (Federal Office of Consumer Protection and Food Safety)
CBA	cost-benefit analysis
EFSA	European Food Safety Authority
EU	European Union
FBO	food safety operators
FloRiAn	geo-information-system modeling software tool (flood risk analysis)
FRMP	flood risk management plans (as per EU Directive 2007/60/EC)
FVO	European Food and Veterinary Office
GAK	Gemeinschaftsaufgabe Agrarstruktur und Küstenschutz (joint task agrarian structure and coastal protection, a joint decision mechanism)
GDA	Gemeinsame Deutsche Arbeitsschutzstrategie (Joint German Work Safety Strategy)
HSE	Health and Safety Executive (British regulator for work safety issues)
ICPR	International Commission for the Protection of the Rhine
IFAS	software for documenting and planning work safety inspections

ILP	shorthand form my unified typology of analytical tools and their appeal, including the three ideal types of instrumental problem-solving, legitimacy-seeking, and power-seeking
IPA	interpretive policy analysis
LASI	Länderausschuss für Arbeitssicherheit und Sicherheitstechnik (inter-state working committee on work safety and safety technology, a horizontal coordination forum)
LAV	Länderarbeitsgemeinschaft Verbraucherschutz (inter-state working group on consumer protection, a horizontal coordination forum)
LAWA	Bund/Länder-Arbeitsgemeinschaft Wasser (inter-state working group on water issues, a horizontal coordination forum with an observer position for the Federal Ministry of the Environment)
NPM	New Public Management
OECD	Organization for Economic Co-operation and Development
OMC	Open Method of Coordination (EU governance tool)
RA	risk analysis
RIA	regulatory impact assessment
RSA	Rechnergestützte Steuerung der Aufsicht (computer-based steering of inspections)
SLIC	Senior Labor Inspectors Committee (EU level)
UK	United Kingdom
USA	United States of America

1

INTRODUCTION

Exploring the rise of analysis in public administrations

> *No effective central monitoring . . . [was] possible without standard, fixed units of measurement.*[1]

Analytical models usually work at the backstage of decision-making in public administration. They gained much public prominence in 2020, however, when EU efforts to harmonize member states' mobility restrictions in response to the COVID-19 pandemic culminated in "Corona risk maps" (Commission of the European Communities, 2020). The maps categorize the whole continent into weekly updated dots of red, orange, green, and grey[2] (see Figure 1.1). Their inventors hope that they will engender differential executive decision-making: the Council of the European Union (2020) proposes that "member states should *not restrict* the free movement of persons travelling to or from green areas" (my highlight) and travel bans only apply to orange and red risk areas. The EU's central monitoring of pandemic risks with a common analytical tool may serve, it seems, as a device both for effective crisis management and for rescuing free movement as a constitutive element of what the Union is about.

While unusually publicly visible and debated, Corona maps are only a recent addition to a much wider trend. For some decades now, governments and public administrations across the globe have invested heavily in stocking up their analytical tool sheds as a basis for their decision-making. They promote keenly what a recent volume on policy formulation calls "policy-analytical methods": analytical tools designed to generate and pre-select options for subsequent decision-making (Turnpenny et al., 2015). Three examples illustrate the rise of analytical tools in administrative decision-making:

- Potentially the most debated, *cost-benefit analysis* (CBA) gained momentum when US President Ronald Reagan, in 1981, mainstreamed it as a legally

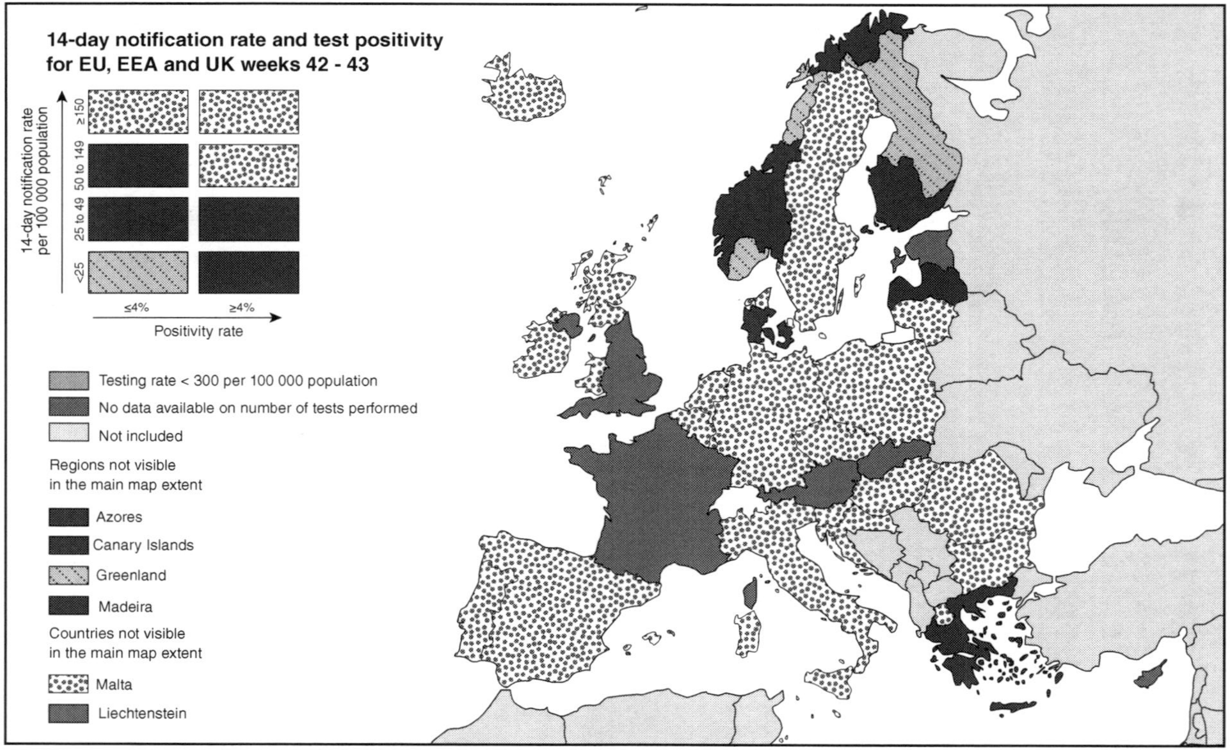

FIGURE 1.1 EU Corona "Risk Map" of October 29, 2020

Source: European Centre for Disease Prevention and Control (www.ecdc.europa.eu/en/covid-19/situation-updates/weekly-maps-coordinated-restriction-free-movement; accessed: October 31, 2020) prescribed method for *all* regulatory decision-making in the country with his Executive Order 12291. Despite an initial wave of criticism by the Democratic opposition, all subsequent US governments kept and even strengthened regulatory oversight by CBA (Posner, 2001). It made headlines more recently, during the 2020 COVID-19 pandemic, when some economists demanded the lives saved by lock-down measures be counted against the costs of shutting down the economy (Stone, 2020, p. 232).

- In a similar manner, the EU Commission introduced, in 2002, an integrated single template to assess the impact for *any* pending decision-making within its bureaucracy (Dunlop and Radaelli, 2015). Such *regulatory impact assessment* (RIA) is a form of prognostic policy analysis which appraises the likely effects of regulatory proposals in terms of their administrative and societal costs before an actual policy decision is made. In 2008, for example, the independent Impact Assessment Board set up for this purpose issued 135 impact assessments as well as 182 opinions on the Commission's impact assessment reports (Commission of the European Communities, 2012). In the United Kingdom (UK), roughly 180 RIAs are conducted per year (Dunlop et al., 2012, p. 29).
- A third example – the one which this book will scrutinize in depth – concerns *risk analysis*. In the UK, for example, an increasing number of regulatory agencies have adopted an explicit risk-analytical framework since a review (Hampton, 2005) promoted risk analysis as a foundation for *all* enforcement decisions in the administration (Black, 2005; Hutter, 2005; Black and Baldwin, 2010). Similarly, risk analysis became a principle of decision-making in the EU with a 1997 communication on Consumer Health and Food Safety (Delogu, 2016). The EU has since imposed risk analysis as baseline for regulatory decisions in numerous other domains including air quality, cosmetics, medical devices, pharmaceuticals, pollution, but also counter-terrorism, flood prevention, macro-prudential regulation, and migration and border control (Neal, 2009; Micklitz and Tridimas, 2015). Corona risk maps are just the most recent and publicized addition.

So, what explains the appeal of analytical tools for public administrations across the OECD and EU world? This question may seem surprising: wasn't the birth of policy analysis as a discipline itself heavily shaped by policymakers' wish to advance their analytical tools for the sake of improving administrative decision-making? Indeed, scholarly elaborations on planning, programming, and budgeting system models (PPBS) – an analytical approach designed to decide how to spend public money – stood at the cradle of a mushrooming policy-analytical industry in the US (prominently: Lasswell, 1971; cf. the recent overview in: Turnpenny et al., 2015). In this tradition, contemporary scholars depict CBA, RIA, and risk analysis as "policy-analytical methods", or *analytical tools* (I adapt the term from Turnpenny et al., 2015, p. 4). As "option assessment" tools they render different policy solutions comparable, through numerical assessment, *before* decision-making

(Turnpenny et al., 2015, p. 51). As Michael Howlett notes, analytical tools have become crucial in policy-making because they can "[generate] options about what to do about a public problem" (Howlett, 2011, p. 29). They *objectify* decisions, it seems, by running them through numerical analysis first.

And yet scholars disagree over (1) the extent to which the rationalization of policy-making is the sole or even main target of analytical efforts and, interrelatedly (2) whether and how variation in policy-making structures shapes a higher or lower appeal of analytical tools. While some scholars of analytical tools tend to claim that the pursuit of more rational executive decision-making meets severe obstacles in multi-level and fragmented decision-making settings (Radaelli, 2005; Rothstein, Borraz and Huber, 2013), others have highlighted that analysis can be central to finding consensus (and even building a collective identity) among disparate actors (Black, 2010; Paul and Huber, 2015). This both extends Howlett's decision aid logic to analysis-based coordination and offers a more optimistic account of analytical tool's allures in multi-level settings. Yet others suggest that analysis helps actors defend or expand their relative positions of power in a domain, providing further reason to expect analytical tools to matter specifically in complex decision-making settings (prominently for CBA in the US, Porter, 1995).

Such controversies about the appeal of analytical tools, which receive more detailed attention below, are shaped by divergent (yet often implicit) assumptions about (1) *what it is* that administrations seek to rationalize through analysis and (2) how what they seek to solve with analysis is shaped by their distinct contexts of decision-making. As respective arguments surface unsystematically in and across rather isolated silos of research – for example on policy change, public administration reform, policy tools, the politics of instrumentation, and the politics of evaluation, risk regulation, the sociology and political history of quantification, or multi-level governance – accounts of why analytical tools appeal and how context shapes such attractions remain partial at best. And this is where the book's aims and contributions unfold.

1.1 Aims and contributions of the book

The first aim of the book is to systematize the debate by bringing together scattered accounts of why (and under which institutional conditions) analytical tools appeal in one conceptual-analytical framework. Rather than excluding any explanation from the outset, I want to understand the variety of attractions that analytical tools offer to policymakers, from their own viewpoint. I take the cue from existing typologies of policy tools and evaluation methods (Hood, 1983; Weiss, Murphy-Graham and Birkeland, 2005; Boswell, 2008; Radaelli, 2010; Capano and Lippi, 2017), which highlight the multidimensionality of their respective allures, to develop my own three-fold typology of analytical tools' appeal (Chapter 2). At its basic, this suggests that policymakers can variably vest hopes of *instrumental problem-solving*, *legitimacy-seeking*, and *power-seeking* in an analytical tool.

I elaborate this general categorization for risk analysis (Chapter 2), an increasingly widespread tool of administrative decision-making, by exploring how exactly it may serve instrumental problem-solving, legitimacy-seeking, or power-seeking purposes. As there is no coherent body of research on why and how exactly risk analysis appeals in public administrations, one additional contribution of the book is a synthesization of existing accounts through my typological lens. This specification grounds my subsequent study because it helps investigate how policymakers' attractions to an analytical tool interact with the specific calculative and representational abilities ascribed to this particular form of analysis.

Overall, my typological work rests on a systematic integration of the highly interdisciplinary and thus far rather unconnected silos of research from the vantage point of interpretive policy analysis (IPA). It stresses that a narrow focus on instrumental problem-solving – often featuring in accounts of *analytical* tools – is misleading, because it underestimates actors' appreciation (and use) of analysis as a means to defend or expand their respective role and influence in a domain. The book thus builds on Heinelt's claim (2016), among others, that any form of knowledge provision in the policy realm – including ex-ante policy analysis – is never merely concerned with finding "optimal" policy solutions but with enabling coordination and supporting actors' strategic (re-)positioning in the decision-making setting. At the same time, the typology does not throw instrumental appeals overboard. Rather, being methodologically situated in IPA (see Section 1.3), my typology acknowledges – and renders accessible for systematic comparative exploration – the co-existence of multiple, and perhaps ambivalent or even contradictory, orientations in actors' individual and collective meaning-making about analytical tools.

The second aim of the book is to explore how different contexts of administrative decision-making shape the variable appeal of analytical tools. I advance existing accounts in three ways. First, I expose how dominant assumptions of what analysis holds for policymakers essentialize the experience with analytical tools in countries which pioneered their adoption: the UK and US. While a strong commitment to the New Public Management (NPM) agenda and a focus on managing principal-agent relationships favored the appreciative interpretation of analysis in the forerunner cases, the absence of such conditions ought not be taken as a measure for the lower attractiveness of analytical tools elsewhere. Second, therefore, I take a fresh look at insights on decision-making structures in multi-level administrations, drawing on a close review of the prototypical German case, to theorize how and why analytical tools might appeal in such contexts *in their own right* (Chapter 4). I elaborate how, rather than inhibiting the diffusion of analytical methods in policy-making, executive fragmentation nourishes actors' appreciation of analytical tools in distinct ways. In particular, as the German multi-level administration provides strong requirements for policy coordination between interdependent actors and a need to constantly confirm or rework (if ever so incrementally) the balance between legal-administrative unity and autonomous subnational decision making; it should also favor:

- an instrumental appreciation of analytical tools as enablers of *collective* problem-solving and keys to rational consensus-seeking between interdependent actors,
- legitimacy-related attempts to showcase analysis-based coordination to *collectively* defend subnational decision-making powers against unitarization demands, and
- analysis-based efforts to tilt decision-making structures from autonomous subnational actors toward the center, formally or informally.

The third aim of the book is to offer a comparative account of the rise of analytical tools beyond national essentialism. My theorization of how structural conditions for decision-making in multi-level administrations shape the appeal of analytical tools requires a shift of methodological strategy. As I propose in Chapter 4, perceptions of collective action problems, the severity of coordination requirements and legitimacy pressures, and actors' relative appetite and ability to tilt decision-making structures vary considerably across different cases of "executive federalism", as does the specific constellation of actors and their respective influence at different levels. My interpretivist and critical governance approach, charted in Section 1.3, understands context not as fully determining policy-making but as "context-in-use" (Wagenaar, 2011) which actors mobilize or immobilize in their "strategically-selective" (Jessop, 2016) meaning-making around an analytical tool.

Broad-brush cross-national comparisons seem rather futile from this perspective. To fully account for the appeal of analytical tools in multi-level administrations, instead, I turn toward ideographic within-case analysis through a small-n cross-sectoral comparison in the same country. Within-case analysis enables me to explore interactions of different actors' appreciative orientations in any one case – within and across administrative levels – and to chart dynamic development in how the promotion of an analytical tool travels through a policy domain and across its decision-making structures. Cross-sectoral comparison allows me to look beyond national essentialist answers and to develop, inductively through the analysis, conclusions about why structurally similar policy domains, featuring strong executive fragmentation, differ in their appreciation and uses of risk analysis (more in case selection in Section 1.4). Overall, the book contributes a more nuanced account of the varied – but patterned – appeals of analytical tools beyond monolithic assumptions of national "essences".

In the reminder of this Introduction, I will set the scene for this study as follows: (Section 1.2) I review existing accounts of analytical tools and explore key controversies, (Section 1.3) set out a conceptual-analytical approach, building on IPA, (Section 1.4) introduce the empirical focus and methods of this study, the comparative adoption of risk analysis in three policy domains in Germany's multi-level administration, and (Section 1.5) detail the structure of the book.

1.2 Controversies over why analytical tools appeal: rationalizing *what* exactly?

Vantage point for this book's arguments and analysis is the diagnosis that scholars disagree over why and how analytical tools appeal to actors in public administrations. While respective accounts will receive more detailed scrutiny in the conceptual work of subsequent chapters, a cursory review of controversies over who seeks to rationalize what exactly through CBA and its cousins, and with which perceptions of the merits of such tools, helps situating this book in a wider field of research.

1.2.1 Rationalizing problem-solving in unitary or concentrated executives

Analytical tools have become prominent in research – once again – with the influential NPM debate in public administration studies since the late 1980s. Among other foci, NPM highlighted the merits of novel (or newly mainstreamed[3]) analytical approaches borrowed from the business world for effective public administration reforms (cf. Hood, 1991; Osborne and Gaebler, 1992). The revived empirical relevance of analytical tools provoked studies on the role of CBA and RIA in administrative transformation processes (e.g., Atkinson, 2015; Radaelli, 2005, 2010; Dunlop and Radaelli, 2016). The renewed interest in studying analytical tools is certainly also related to how international and supranational organizations promote their adoption as universal methods for rationalizing administrative decision-making in the sense of cost-effectiveness (e.g., for risk analysis: OECD, 2010). For example, a contemporary staff working document in the EU Commission airs the hope that RIA can lead to "better" regulatory decisions and implementation and mentions cost-effectiveness and transparency in this context (Commission of the European Communities, 2015). Risk analysis seems to serve a similar rationalization strategy in the EU. The hope is that by an ex-ante assessment of the likelihood and impact of a potential adverse outcome, administrators can target resources toward the riskiest events and save money and efforts elsewhere. Such a more "rational" approach seemed desirable after the bovine spongiform encephalopathy (BSE) crisis in Europe – in the 1990s and early 2000s – had indicated a massive political tainting of food safety regulation in member states (e.g., Krapohl, 2003).

Rational choice scholars of public administration and regulation follow that lead from policy practice and situate analytical tools in a wider debate about bureaucratic control and principal-agent relationships (cf. Dunsire, 1978). Rather than simply helping identify optimal policy solutions, analysis helps enforce these by engendering commitment to analytically informed decision-making across the bureaucracy – be it in the shape of local government or regulatory agencies (cf. recent summary of these expectations, from the perspective of performance measurement: Boswell, 2018). For example, CBA has been discussed as a response to the expanding regulatory activities of the Environmental Protection Agency, which President Reagan and his Republican Party viewed skeptically at the time. Scholarly proponents of CBA hoped that "poor priority setting, excessively costly tools, and inattention to the unfortunate side-effects of regulation" could be avoided (Sunstein, 2000, p. 1660). As for RIA, scholars describe a "rational-synoptic model"– at least for the US forerunner and OECD blueprint – according to which economic analysis of a planned piece of regulation helps identify the most cost-effective among probed alternatives (Radaelli, 2005, p. 931). This fits with parts of the policy studies literature which associate policy tools at large (and analysis in particular) with instrumental problem-solving (e.g., Hood, 1983; Hall, 1993; Turnpenny et al., 2015; Margetts and Hood, 2016), and in the literature on risk and regulation where risk analysis counts as a tool for less biased, more objective, and thus more "rational" forms of regulatory decision-making (e.g., Viscusi 1983; Majone, 2010; Wiener, 2010). I will detail and operationalize these assumptions in the coming chapters. Their common expectation is the following: administrations adopt analytical tools to inform and enact onto agents a more rational problem-solving approach (cf. for a recent summary and problematization of that debate; Boswell, 2018).

This (shorthand) perspective on the appeal of analytical tools comes with specific ideas about the macro-institutional conditions that favor their adoption. Research on comparative public administration and policy reform discusses the structure of states and their decision-making processes as a key variable for divergent adoption patterns. Christopher Pollitt and Geert Bouckaert's (2011) seminal stocktaking of public management reforms suggests that relatively unitary and centralized administrative regimes such as the British one – in which devolution is countered by strong central regulatory agencies and majoritarian institutions – have witnessed far-reaching turns to analytical (and other NPM) tools. David Demeritt and colleagues specify that

> contexts in which management responsibilities are concentrated will promote the use of risk analysis [. . . because this] creates both budgetary and accountability pressures that make risk instruments appealing for prioritisation and rationalising how far to go in pursuit of policy goals.
>
> *(Demeritt et al., 2017, p. 6)*

By contrast, federal polities with strong interdependencies in decision-making count as late comers in the adoption of new analytical tools. Unlike more unitary administrations – or indeed federal polities with a clear division of powers and/or strong regulatory agencies at Federal level, such as the US – they would introduce reforms in an incremental and patchy manner (Pollitt and Bouckaert, 2011; for risk analysis: Rothstein, Borraz and Huber, 2013; Demeritt et al., 2017). The fragmented competencies in such multi-level administrations would impede the adoption of a common analytical toolbox across a whole country as lower level governance actors cannot easily be constrained in their autonomous decision-making. This control problem is aggravated, from this perspective, where the multi-level polity does not distribute powers to legislate and enact policies to one level of governance – federal or states – or to a strong regulatory agency like in the US, but cross-allocates them in complex forms of interdependent decision-making. Eventually, scholars of analytical tools assume that where "the regulatory process is highly fragmented, with multiple points of contact between politics and administration, and between different logics and criteria", the proclivity to adopt shared analytical frameworks for executive decision-making is rather low (Radaelli, 2005, p. 933). In their study of risk-based decision-making, Rothstein, Borraz and Huber (2013) have initially been equally pessimistic about fragmented administrations' turns to analysis: "horizontal and vertical fragmentation of policy responsibilities and accountabilities" would impede the development of a comprehensive analytical template for all and resist formulaic uses of analysis in decision-making (p. 227). Even if these accounts do not explicitly state so, their line of argument goes with the grain of the literature on "joint-decision making" in interdependent systems of multi-level governance (Scharpf, 1988, 2006). This eminent work on German federalism – and its lessons for multi-level policy-making in the EU – highlighted how mixed competencies and the institutional requirement to coordinate across and between levels of government produces incremental "least common denominator" policy change and, in the worst case, deadlock in problem-solving endeavors (for a recent review, see Benz, Detemple and Heinz, 2016, pp. 19–31).

1.2.2 Rationalizing collective decision-making (structures) in multi-level settings

Three historical accounts of the role of analytical tools, models, and standards in the making of modern states inform a rather different interpretation of the perceived merits of analytical tools and reappraise their likely appeal to decision makers in multi-level settings. They depict how shared analytical models and measurement can rationalize not only *collective* decision-making in fragmented settings but also the underlying decision-making structures themselves.

- A first is Ken Alder's *The Measure of All Things* (2002) which details the erratic journey toward the metric system by the two French astronomers Delambre and Méchain, who set out, in 1792, to measure the meridian arc between Paris and Barcelona. It shows how this enlightenment project got heavily entangled with (and almost failed because of) struggles over legitimacy: the metric project was hard to sustain until a globalizing economy made the existence of commensurable measures seem useful, appropriate, and fair from the perspective of locals wary of governments playing favorites (pp. 133–168). At the same time, the project also prospered because it seemed to support French politicians' pursuit of diplomatic and economic influence in a world dominated by Anglo-American measurement standards (p. 248).
- A second is reported in James Scott's *Seeing Like a State* (1998). He, too, discusses the introduction of the metric system in Napoleonic France, in less detail but with a more political-scientific interpretation than Alder. Scott

argues that, as the meter replaced the locally highly fragmented measurement practices with a common standard, it not only induced a more effective common market but also enabled far-reaching administrative centralization: "The academicians of the revolutionary Republic . . . saw the meter as one of the intellectual instruments that would make France 'revenue-rich, militarily potent, and *easily administered*'" (Scott, 1998, p. 31, highlight added). Scott may be less explicitly concerned with analytical models than others; yet, his insights on how the "homogenization of measures" (p. 32) targeted and – at least in some cases[4] – enabled administrative homogenization are revealing.

- A third is Alain Desrosières' (2002) The *Politics of Large Numbers*; a history of statistical reasoning in Europe and the US. One of his core claims is that "statistics is one of the mechanisms that sustains a state when its stability is problematical" (p. 180). With the German case of early *Statistik* in mind, Desroisières claims that "uncertainty in regard to the state's consistency and legitimacy" help explain the rise of common assessment models (p. 178). In a highly fragmented administrative setting – *Statistik* in Germany emerged at a time when the territory was split up into over 300 individual states – comparative analyses were perceived as a chief requirement for the creation of a common market which could eventually also advance economic and policy harmonization.

These historical episodes hold important lessons for present-day appeals of analytical tools. Most importantly, they depict forms of rationalization which focus less on policy substance and the cost-effectiveness of decision-making than on enabling and even tilting (forms of) decision-making in fragmented administrations. Alder, Desroisières, and Scott thus chart the historical precursors of a wider literature on policy-making in complex, multi-level administrations. While this literature does not, to my knowledge, normally engage with analytical tools per se, its interest in how coordinated decision-making comes about and how analytical frameworks play out in this context offers a crucial conceptual vantage point for the arguments developed in this book.

Scholars of EU policy-making have underlined the importance of shared analytical frameworks for enabling decision-making in a complex multi-level setting, including in domains where the EU lacks a de jure mandate for regulation. A prominent starting point is Giandomenico Majone, who argued that, as the growing complexity of policy problems and decision-making structures in the EU has disabled the routine use of coercive tools, European regulation has increasingly relied on "information and persuasion, rather than on command and control" (Majone, 1997, p. 269, for the more general argument, see 1989). Analytical approaches have become crucial in this context, he argues, as they give credibility to the information provided, avoid the impression of "political expediency", and may thus transform data into policy-relevant knowledge (ibid., p. 271). For Majone, the information provided through the ex-ante analysis of policy options *enables* decision-making in "an increasingly complex and interdependent world" (ibid., p. 269). Importantly, Majone's interpretation of information in the policy-making process relaxes ideas about its strictly instrumental rationality: rather than identifying the optimal path for achieving a pre-defined policy goal – Majone rejects "the theoretical optimum" as "either unknown or practically unobtainable" (1989, p. 8) – analysis provides a wealth of information from which persuasive arguments about suitable policy goals and paths emerge (Majone, 1989).

Work on comparative policy styles confirms this assumption when prescribing a unifying effect to (analytical) expertise in fragmented settings. Germany's "rationalist consensus" orientation (cf. Richardson, 1982; Howlett and Tosun, 2018, p. 7) suggests, for example, that actors involve analytical expertise in multi-level consensus-seeking processes to stimulate harmonized decision-making and enforcement across fragmented jurisdictions. A study on work safety regulation found, for example, that risk analysis injected mutual trust and a consensus-orientation in corporatist actors' negotiations of a common approach toward carcinogenic substance management (Paul and Huber, 2015).

These accounts imply that analytical tools may appeal because they promise to rationalize *collective* problem-solving processes by building an accepted foundation for consensus. This perspective is also mirrored in interpretivist accounts of the enabling role of knowledge in policy coordination. Before political negotiations about policy options can even start, they argue, actors need to engage in knowledge-based arguments about the causes of a policy problem and the effects specific solutions might wield (Heinelt, 2016). In this context and contrary to what the orthodox literature on analytical tools claims, scholars expect multi-level settings with fragmented competencies but coordinated forms of decision-making to be even more likely to develop "shared problem definitions and causal assumptions" about how world and society work than those marked by pluralist competition (Heinelt, 2016, p. 44).

But even where consensus is not to be obtained, analysis may entice policy harmonization. Research on the EU's Open Method of Coordination (OMC) has detailed how shared analytical frameworks may engender policy harmonization in weakly integrated domains (Kropp, 2010, p. 155ff). OMCs are benchmarking exercises in which member states agree to regular reporting to, and comparative numerical and qualitative assessment of their policy approaches by, Brussels. Research on OMCs shows that their analytical frameworks have considerably shaped the autonomous policy-making of member states and their sub-central enforcement entities (e.g., Dehousse, 2004; Heidenreich and Bischoff, 2008; Tholoniat, 2010). Indeed, while OMCs count as tools of "soft law" without legally binding effect on member states, it has become common sense to expect voluntary coordination around benchmarking, league tables, naming and shaming and (publicly available) policy recommendations to unfold "considerable political pressure" for the formally autonomous member states to adapt (Kropp, 2010, p. 157). Such pressure can also engender policy harmonization where there are less formal benchmarking structures than the OMC. My own research on the EU's flood risk mapping (Paul, Bouder and Wesseling, 2016) – also to be discussed in this volume – and Frontex' "common integrated risk analysis model" in border control (Paul, 2017a) depicts processes of analysis-based harmonization.

Beyond the EU, scholars of the OECD have described similar dynamics when they associate the much-discussed example of the organization's common evaluation of education policies – the Programme for International Student Assessment (PISA) ranking – with a strong potential to induce soft harmonization "by numbers" (Grek, 2009; more generally: Martens and Jakobi, 2010). For example, the scandalization of the relatively poor German PISA ranking has set in motion a process of "performance-oriented output steering" *within* the country's multi-level administration (Benz, Detemple and Heinz, 2016, pp. 241–245). The attempt to harmonize performance has been surprising in so far as legislative and executive prerogatives in the policy domain have been jealously guarded by the German Länder and horizontal policy coordination has traditionally been weak. Overall, like in the historical case of policy harmonization through shared statistical reasoning among Germany's 300 states, analytical tools seem to appeal as instruments for engendering policy harmonization where not only coercive powers of central level actors but also a formally coordinated policy consensus between actors in the multi-level setting are missing.

Scholars of international bureaucracies, often also with an EU focus, take the argument even further. More than informing consensus-seeking or voluntary policy harmonization among autonomous actors at subcentral governance levels, analytical frameworks can also tilt decision-making structures toward a respective center, both strategically so and as an unintended effect. Tholoniat (2010) argues, for example, that the infrastructure created with the OMCs – in particular, related to central reporting requirements and comparative analytical capacity-building – has increased the decision-making capacities of EU institutions vis-à-vis member states *precisely* in policy domains where the EU has a limited mandate to act. Work on RIA equally indicates that the EU administration uses analytical innovation very strategically to change processes of decision-making in areas where consensus on policy substance is hard to come by, with the effect of strengthening the Commission Secretariat General (Radaelli and Meuwese, 2010, p. 136). Research on the better regulation framework highlights how analysis-based forms of self-evaluation contribute to the "strategic actorness" of the EU Commission, arguing that such analysis contributes to "better coordination and interest alignment within the Commission and enhance[s] its ability to justify its own initiatives vis-à-vis the member states" (Jankauskas and Eckhard, 2019, p. 695). My research on border control also argues that the EU Commission uses common risk analysis strategically to establish itself as a high-risk regulator against member states' sovereignty concerns (Paul, 2017a). These arguments also find support in work on the incremental build-up of "core state powers" in the EU, which highlights that central administrative capacity-building in the EU Commission over the last 60 years was driven by a horizontal integration of organizational forms, including regulatory agencies at EU level, and administrative procedures in member states (Heidbreder, 2013; Trondal, 2013).

Again, these accounts sound rather familiar against the historical episodes of central administrative influence-wielding in Napoleonic France or amidst Germany's multiple *Kleinstaaten*. While not centrally concerned with the appeal of analytical tools per se, they imply a need to expand scholarly understanding of what it is that policymakers seek to rationalize when they adopt CBA, risk analysis, and so on. Next to finding optimal policy solutions through analysis, enabling "rationalist" consensus, and engendering harmonization among autonomous jurisdictions, analytical tools can serve to negotiate the very decision-making structures in which policies come about. If anything, these interpretations of analytical tools certainly boost expectations about their appeal to actors in multi-level settings.

1.3 Accounting for analytical tools' multiple appeals: the book's conceptual approach

As the review in Section 1.2 highlights, the question of who seeks to rationalize what and why through analytical tools depends very much on how narrowly we conceptualize actors' perceptions of "rationalization" and its targets but also on the structural and institutional conditions which shape such perceptions. To account more fully for the appeal of analytical tools, this book synthesizes existing explanations in two ways as follows:

- it conceptualizes their appeal in relation to *both* the rationalization of policy solutions *and* the rationalization of the underlying decision-making structures and
- it systematically reappraises the related appeals of analytical tools in multi-level administrations.

As I detail next, I develop these contributions with an interpretive approach to policy analysis (Yanow, 2000, 2007; Yanow and Schwartz-Shea, 2006). I also borrow from critical governance analysis and its view on how actors' actions both are shaped by and re-work institutions and structures in selective ways (Sum and Jessop, 2013; Jessop, 2016; Carmel, 2019a).

1.3.1 IPA and critical governance analysis

One core argument of this book is that the perspectives charted briefly in Section 1.2 are not mutually exclusive but co-exist – and interact in contingent ways – in policymakers' perceptions of analytical tools. This view ties the book – just as much of my earlier work in policy studies (Paul, 2012, 2013, 2015, 2016b) – to a decidedly interpretivist approach to policy analysis (Yanow, 2006, 2007; Wagenaar, 2011; Stone, 2012). Interpretivists assume that policies do not entail objective meaning but are projection surfaces for actors' ambiguous, complex, contradictory, non-linear, and always unfinished sense-making about the world around them, their role in this world, but also their future vision of both. As Yanow argues (2000, p. 4), there can be no generalization about the meanings actors vest in policies – appeals of analytical tools in our case – but only case-specific subjective interpretations. Policies, and by extension policy tools and analytical tools, "mean" not of themselves but because actors vest specific sets of meaning in them during contingent processes of sense-making (see review in R. Paul, 2015, p. 34f). Yanow (2000, p. 5) continues: "as living requires sense making, and sense making entails interpretation, so too does policy analysis". It is therefore that "the effort to exclude meaning and values from the work of the policy analyst cuts the very heart out of political inquiry" (Fischer, 2003, p. 216; cf. Fischer and Forester, 1993; Yanow and Schwartz-Shea, 2006).

When we consider *analytical tools*, interpretation matters in at least three ways: first, though numbers count as objective, numerical analysis is impossible without prior judgment about what one should count, why and how (red fish or blue fish, small fish or big fish, weighted by size or all counting equal?) (Stone, 2020, p. 12); second, once numbers are in the social world, they regularly become subject to deliberate fudging by social actors; third, beyond fudge, decision makers attach numerical analysis to most different political projects, from highly diverse approaches to problem-solving to the confirmation or redistribution of power in a domain. While this book is mostly concerned with the third level of interpretation, Chapter 3 on risk analysis will detail how the first- and second-level interpretations of risk numbers get inscribed into and support instrumental, legitimacy-seeking, and power-seeking interpretations of risk analysis.

Taking up the interpretivist lead, I treat the appeal of analytical tools as a multifaceted, potentially ambiguous, and contingent assemblage of meanings which actors in a specific policy-making setting have vested in these tools in a policy domain. Importantly, such assemblages include the various meanings any individual actor associated with an analytical tool but also the combinations of meanings which different actors across administrative levels attach to it. The typology I develop in Chapter 2 provides clear ideal-typical yardsticks for exploring such assemblages: it enables me to chart patterns of interactions between (different) actors' various interpretations of an analytical tool in a domain and thus renders highly complex processes of meaning-making accessible for comparative scrutiny.

More than merely highlighting the plurality of meanings vested in policies, the interpretive paradigm also acknowledges that policy-related sense-making never solely relates to problem-solving but also includes positional struggles over power and authority in policy-making. Such struggles are at the heart of the analysis, for example, in EU studies, which explore how the Commission expands its "strategic agency" through analytical frameworks, or accounts of the OMCs as forms of "soft governance" through which Brussels secures influence over autonomous member state decision-making (Section 1.2). Critical governance analysts capture such efforts well when they portray public policy governance as a mutual co-constitution of *policy substance* and *positional struggles* in a policy domain. For example, Jessop's neo-Gramscian approach to the state highlights that governance "cannot be reduced to questions of how to solve issues of a specific techno-economic, narrowly juridico-political in character, tightly focused social-administrative, or otherwise neatly framed problem" (Jessop, 2016, p. 178). This is because all governance efforts always also modify decision-making processes in a domain and "change the balance of forces" in its wider socio-economic and socio-political context (ibid., p. 177). Others explicitly take up that critical cue from Jessop when arguing that any form of policy-related knowledge provision never merely concerns the finding of optimal policy solutions but also speaks to actors' strategic (re-)positioning in the decision-making setting as the very foundation for knowledge-based policy coordination (Heinelt, 2016). Critical governance analysis "synthesizes the discursive conditions of what actors think is possible with the material social action of creation that can challenge these conditions of possibility, even accidentally" (Carmel, 2019c, p. 25). A critical perspective on governance, as Carmel argues, therefore requires us to understand public policy as contributing "to the creation and reproduction of governance regimes over time" in the sense that policies always *also* "generate new – or confirm existing – inequalities of power", both with respect to "who is subject to which aspects of public policy" and with regard to "who has access to decision-making" (Carmel, 2019b, p. 7).

I argue that to adopt an analytical tool is a powerful act of interpreting (and re-interpreting) not just how a policy problem is best understood, counted, and solved in a specific context, but also how the socio-political world around this policy problem is to be governed and by whom. From this perspective, analytical tools move away from mere decision aids in Howlett's sense and closer to what scholars of public administration have called *polity policies* (cf. Janning, 2006): interventions which seek to negotiate the ways in which collectively binding decisions come about within the administration and who is included in decision-making; "deliberate changes [or strategic defence] of organizational structures and procedures in public administrations aimed at redrawing [or confirming] the 'institutional logistics' of public policy making" (Kuhlmann, Bogumil and Grohs, 2008, p. 851). In this book, I adopt the term "polity policy" prominently, albeit in a more interpretivist reading than intended by its inventors, because it explicitly expands the concept of policy from narrow problem-solving to include positional struggles over the distribution of power and authority in a policy domain.

As the review in Section 1.2 charted, polity policies also involve attempts of actors to govern the autonomous decision-making of others in domains where they lack the formal capacity to steer and/or to formally change decision-making structures. The wider discussion of *meta-governance* in critical state theory captures this idea as follows: "the organisation of self-organisation, the regulation of self-regulation, the steering of self-steering, the structuring of game-like interactions within networks" . . . "with a view to influencing parameter changes to the overall system" (Jessop, 2016, p. 169). As states – or central state governments – have lost competencies to govern hierarchically through direct intervention and have delegated decision-making powers to markets and networks, they have increasingly elaborated techniques for influencing the conditions for the self-governance of others (Jessop, 2016, pp. 164–185, cf. the author's earlier reflections in: Jessop,

2009). While the notion of meta-governance originally focused on how the state seeks to govern the output of autonomous actors *outside* the classic public administration (cf. review for German governance: Sack, 2013, pp. 93–104, 167f), it is also useful for capturing the appeal of analytical tools within *multi*-level administrations, where central level actors adopt analysis with the goal of shaping the autonomous actions of lower level administrative actors.

1.3.2 Contextualization and strategic selectivity

Next to systematizing the debate about why analysis appeals from a distinct IPA perspective, the second aim of the book is to explore how different contexts of administrative decision-making shape the variable appeal of analytical tools. My conceptualization of context draws on IPA and critical governance analysis, once more.

At its basic, the book agrees with the historical and sociological institutionalist paradigm in social sciences research insofar it understands cases as complex configurations shaped by cultural proclivities and historical paths of policy development (cf. seminal summaries of the approaches in Hall and Taylor, 1996). To overcome essentializing accounts of analytical tools, the book aims to explore how policymakers' appreciative perceptions of analytical tools *interact with institutional contexts* in empirically specific ways. Institutions are understood here as both formal and informal rules of interactions in a given context, including legacies and norms of state intervention, but also the key markers of "politico-administrative regimes" (Pollitt and Bouckaert, 2011) such as constitutional relationships between actors, degrees of centralization or decentralization, and formal relationships of accountability and competition. I explore how these contextual features shape contemporary interpretations of analytical tools, both conceptually (Chapter 4) and empirically (Chapters 5–7).

However, unlike institutionalists, I do not treat formal and informal rules as absolutely constraining. From an interpretive perspective, actors' sense-making is always also *constitutive* of new relationships in a domain, especially where their formal authority lends them high levels of symbolic capital and therefore underscores the relevance of their meanings in collectively binding decision-making (Bourdieu, 1991; Paul, 2015, pp. 27–40). I take inspiration from Ngai-Ling Sum and Bob Jessop's foundational work in critical political economy who insist on the explanatory benefits of integrating (1) a sound analysis of the material structures and institutional ("extra-semiotic") conditions of a field and (2) the ways in which the logics of the institutional environment are being mobilized (or indeed muted or reworked) in actors' meaning-making processes ("semiosis") (Sum and Jessop, 2013; detailed discussion of cultural political economy in Paul, 2015).[5] Sum and Jessop speak of the "selection, variation and retention" of both semiotic and extra-semiotic provisions through actors' sense-making. Jessop's older notion of *strategic selectivity* already worked around the dichotomy of structure and agency when proposing that, while structures constrain actors' sense-making processes in governance, "scope exists for actions to overwhelm, circumvent, or subvert structural constraints" (Jessop, 2016, p. 55, in most depth: Jessop, 2008). The joint venture of Jessop's "strategic-relational approach" to the state – drawing on Poulantzas and Gramsci – with Sum's Foucauldian discourse perspective has been most fruitful for explorations of how actors' meaning-making is structured by context all while strategically re-shaping it (Sum and Jessop, 2013). Indeed, it is by conceptualizing context as strategically selective that we can fully grasp analytical tools' appeal in instances of polity making – attempts to re-work decision-making structures – in the first place.

It is clear then that any typology of analytical tools cannot (and does not want to) offer a predictive model of how types of appeal vary by context. Rather, context provides a dynamic infrastructure which can be mobilized or immobilized, amplified or muted in meaning-making processes (Carmel, 1999; Yanow, 2007, 2014; Wagenaar, 2011). As Wagenaar (2011, p. 110f.) suitably notes, "meanings are actualized in a specific context-in-use, depending on the particular historical circumstances and the specific intentions, challenges and possibilities that actors face". So, while the institutional environment shapes the proclivity of specific instrumental, legitimacy-oriented and power-oriented perceptions of an analytical tool in a setting, this context does never fully prescribe such interpretations. Rather, I understand the adoption of an analytical tool as a *process of institutionally filtered but strategically selective meaning-making* during which administrative actors come to activate variable combinations of meanings against specific contextual conditions while ignoring (or even trying to circumvent) others. An ideographic comparative design is most suited to explore the interaction of context and meaning-making around analytical tools (Section 1.4).

Last, not least, the interpretivist paradigm also implies that turns to analytical tools need not be depicted as intentional[6] or, as often done in the policy tool literature, as lucid and self-aware moments of actors' strategic "tool choice" (Capano and Lippi, 2017). Rather, to situate the ILP framework in an interpretivist and context-sensitive methodology requires analytical openness to the potentially complex, ambivalent, potentially contradictory, non-linear, and endogenous patterns by which analytical tools emerge in different settings. This seems especially relevant in multi-level administrations where the number of relevant actors and venues is multiplied and where decision-making does not tend to follow an overall chronology or strategic orchestration. I therefore prefer to speak of *adoption patterns of analytical tools* rather than of tool "choice". Adoption patterns are unlikely to be determined by any one actor's intentions in problem-solving and/or polity policies. Instead, their relative proximity to the ideal-typical poles of instrumental problem-solving, legitimacy-seeking, or power-seeking will be the result of the empirical specific intermeshing of different actors' perceptions and their variable ability to mobilize them (or not) in not necessarily linear, hierarchical, or otherwise systematic processes of collective meaning-making.

1.4 Risk analysis across Germany's multi-level administration

To examine the appeal of analytical tools in multi-level administrations, I compare the adoption of risk analysis in three policy domains in Germany's multi-level setting: food safety, flood prevention, and work safety. I justify these methodical choices next.

Risk analysis is a good case for examining the appeal of analytical tools for two reasons. First, it is a rather recent, highly prominent but under-researched addition to the analytical toolbox, particularly in multi-level settings. While CBA and RIA have been virulent since the 1980s and 1990s, respectively, wider-spread administrative uses of risk analysis by the EU or in Continental Europe (beyond the British forerunner) only appeared in the late 1990s. Indeed, a rather underreported wave of measurement efforts has taken grip of public administrations in Europe under the banner of risk analysis over the last 15–20 years.

For example, a search in the EU's legal database EUR-Lex indicates an exponential rise of risk analysis as featuring in regulations and directives (see Figure 1.2), especially so in the past two decades. Of roughly 18,300 pieces of legislation passed or amended between 2006 and 2015, more than 15,400 invoked risk analysis – a steep rise from the initially 28 occurrences in 1956–1965 but also a multiplication by the factor five since the mid-1990s. Beyond its much wider contribution to scholarly debates about analytical innovation, the book's empirical illustrations are thus also an opportunity to contribute to a nascent field of comparative research on

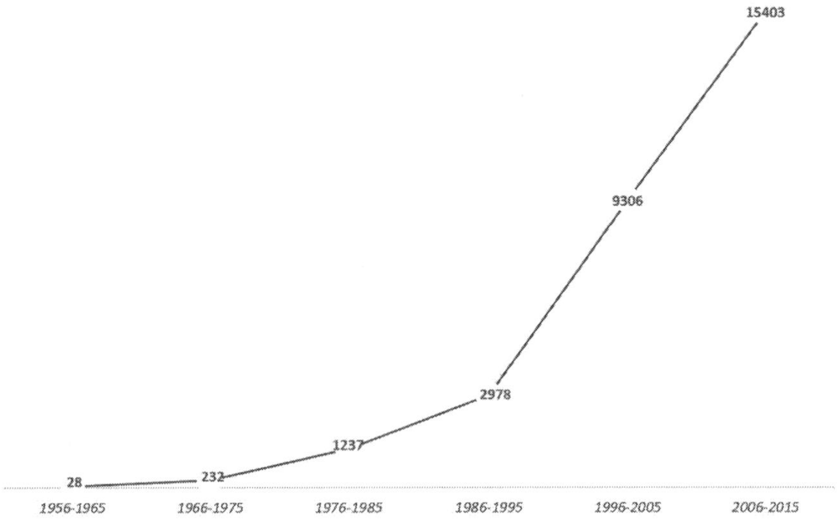

FIGURE 1.2 The rise of risk analysis in EU legislation

Source: eur-lex.europa.eu (search term "risk analysis", search conducted on May 23, 2018)

risk-based forms of decision-making in which political scientists have so far been rather absent (while there is a large sociological literature on risk perception and much work on risk regulation in general, a recent conceptual discussion rightly bemoans the lack of comparative accounts of administrative uses of risk analysis; Döhler and Wegrich, 2010).

Second, while being strongly attached to a scientific-empiricist model of regulation, risk analysis comes with less normative baggage than CBA and RIA. Risk analysis has certainly been attached to a deregulatory agenda, too (Tombs and Whyte, 2013; Demeritt et al., 2015; Paul et al., 2017), but it does not prescribe such an agenda by itself. This also makes risk analysis less suspicious, from the viewpoint of administrative actors, to be nothing more than a NPM fancy. This is different with CBA and RIA where a focus on cost saving and value for money involves a clearer normative bias toward "lean" government (most explicitly in Osborne and Gaebler, 1992). A focus on risk analysis can hence expose a wider variety of attractions among a wider set of actors.

Germany is a *representative*, in some respects also *prototypical case* of a multi-level administration. Both a stereotype and role model of a multi-level administrative setting – with its strong embedding in the EU and equally strong subnational administrations at state and municipal level – the case can shed light on the appeal of analytical tools outside the well-studied Anglo-American world more widely. The assumption, in parts of the literature, that fragmentation impedes the spread of analytical tools in administrative decision-making, also makes Germany a *least likely case* for the analysis. Against these predictions, risk analysis has been increasingly mainstreamed in the German public administration much beyond locally contained trials over the last 10–15 years, a development that has so far remained unexplored (see critique in Döhler and Wegrich, 2010; Paul, 2016a). Findings will thus help assessing the potential for analytical turns in other EU member states with federalist or quasi-federalist polities (Austria, Belgium, and Spain), but also strongly devolved states (Italy). They also matter more generally for the EU and any of its member states, first because its multi-level administration is itself often modeled after German executive federalism (Scharpf, 1988), and second, because analytical efforts in Germany regularly shape EU policy-making. For example, the EU's flood risk mapping requirements – to be analyzed in depth in this book – draw on promotional work by the German Rhine states. Equally, the EU Commission's 2020 Corona risk map uses, and expands, an analytical approach first used to coordinate differentiated lock-down decisions among municipalities and states within Germany.

One aim of the study is to chart variation in the attractions ascribed to analytical tools *within* a polity. On the one hand, this requires examination of the interactions of actors (and their individual and/or collective promotions of risk analysis) across different levels in the multi-level administration and thus a shifting up of analytical attention to the EU and down to state and municipal actors. Rather than having to present broad-brush claims about a country – as often the case in cross-national research – the multi-level analytical focus allows this book to offer more nuanced insights about who exactly, within a country, pushes or impedes the rise of analytical tools and why. On the other hand, we need to insert some systematic theoretical variety in our material to fully account for the appeal of analytical tools. As the exact institutional conditions for multi-level decision-making –with respect to both the coordination of problem-solving and polity policies – will vary by policy domain, a *cross-sectoral analysis* within the German multi-level administration seems most fruitful (John and Cole, 2000; Heinelt, 2007; cf. methodological recommendations on cross-sectoral policy analysis by: Döhler, 2015). In particular, the study compares risk-analytical turns in EU-Germany across three policy domains: *food safety controls*, *flood prevention*, and *work safety inspections*.

Four criteria determine the selection of these domains (cf. Table 1.1):

TABLE 1.1 Overview of cases in the comparative study

Cases	*Food safety controls*	*Flood prevention*	*Work safety controls*
Country-wide adoption of RA ("positive" cases)	In 2004 with EU Regulation on *food safety inspections*	In 2007 with EU Directive on *flood risk management*	In 2014 with a guideline on *inspection* principles by Länder working group
Federalist structure and coordination requirements ("least likely" cases)	Communal inspectorates coordinated by Länder Central administrative decrees Major incidences coordinated by task forces within Federal Authority (BVL) Länder working group (LAV) coordinates implementation	Communal responsibility for (limited) protection, partly delegated to self-regulated bodies Länder and Bund co-fund communal protection and prevention measures Bund-Länder working group (LAWA) coordinates implementation	Communal inspectorates coordinated by Länder Additional inspections conducted by corporatist actors (tightly coupled with social insurance) Länder working group (LASI) coordinates implementation
Legacy of mandate and collection action pressures	Strong and stable mandate; early and strong collective action pressure	Vague mandate; recent and strong collective action pressure	Historically weak and contested mandate; weak collective action pressure
Level of EU coercion	Strong	Medium	Weak
Role of Federal level	Strong administrative unitarization	Recent introduction of centralized funding	No strong role in enforcement

Source: Author's compilation (details in Chapters 5–7)

- First, they all are cases of strong executive federalism which, according to some scholars of analytical tools, creates adverse institutional conditions for the comprehensive appeal of analytical frameworks across a country. And yet, all three domains have seen a streamlining of risk analysis across the territorial borders of Germany's municipal and state administrations over the last 5–15 years.
- Second, case selection ensures a requisite theoretical variety in the sample, allowing for the observation of interesting diversity of risk-analytical turns in contemporary Germany. While cases are similar as to their high degrees of executive fragmentation, they vary with respect to their specific patterns of multi-level administration, legacies of statutory action, and collective action pressures (cf. Table 1.1, details in Chapters 5–7). These factors matter because they shape actors' relative appetite and imperatives for policy coordination as well as positional struggles in the domain and might thus influence the types of hopes and promises actors vest in risk analysis.
- Third, the density of empirical observations required for case-sensitive comparisons necessitates a pragmatic view on the accessibility of the domain and its actors (Blatter and Haverland, 2012). In my three cases, accessibility was aided by the fact that the adoption of risk analysis is a rather recent phenomenon (adopted in 2004 for food safety, in 2007 for flooding, and in 2014 for work safety) with the relevant actors still in charge and able to recall the situations and goals that have shaped their perceptions of risk analysis. In addition, none of the domains involve secretive data that would hamper data gathering. In general, field access was rather straightforward and greatly facilitated by generous funding by the Open Research Area Programme for the Social Sciences in the international project "How States Account for Failure in Europe".[7]
- Last, the selected cases are practically relevant. The policy domains jointly cover two important everyday life risks of all citizens (food-borne and work-related illnesses and deaths) as well as one major natural disaster which has repeatedly produced catastrophic harms over the last decades and is predicted to increase its destructive potential with climate change (flood prevention). The relative appetite of actors to engage in risk analysis for coordinated problem-solving and a negotiation of decision-making powers – to be mapped and explained in the book – thus has a direct societal impact, too.

1.4.2 Data and methods

I adopt a mixed-methods design to increase the number of observations from a wide array of sources and heighten the internal validity of explanations. To replicate the variable institutional contexts for analytical tools and their appeal, the study relies on five types of qualitative data sources (see the Appendix):

- *Secondary literature* formed the basis for gaining initial familiarity with key developments, issues, and debates in the three policy domains. This concerns mainly works that reconstruct the historical context for statutory interventions, the genesis of the regulatory mandate, and the emergence of a specific constellation of actors in multi-level administration (e.g., work safety: Simons, 1984; Hennock, 2007; flooding: Allemeyer, 2006; food safety: Hierholzer, 2010).

- *Official documents* on risk analysis models and their formation, as well as on the application of risk analysis in administrative decision-making, were identified in online searches of the websites of relevant authorities. This entailed internal documents on the prioritization strategies of respective enforcement authorities, which were shared by interviewees. Such documents include laws, decrees, risk models and indicators, best practice guidelines by the respective Länder working groups, and reports (e.g., on annual inspection strategies). In total, between 12 and 15 documents were gathered per policy domain.
- To reconstruct the goals which administrators vested in analytical tools, I conducted an extensive set of *semi-structured expert interviews* (details in Appendix 1) between 2014 and 2017. Interviewees were targeted to cover the multiple levels of decision-making including representatives at the EU, Federal, Länder, and communal level for each domain. As time and budgetary constraints of the study did not allow for interviews in all 16 Länder, let alone all municipalities, I sampled sub-national experts according to their political relevance (e.g., leading role in the respective inter-state coordination forum when risk analysis was adopted). All interviews followed a semi-structured topic guide with open-ended questions on the institutional context, goals, motivations for, and issues with adopting risk analysis. They were transcribed and anonymized for analysis.
- In the food safety domain, I gathered additional data via a *standardized qualitative questionnaire* on the implementation of risk-based inspection planning. This followed mainly pragmatic considerations of time and cost saving, seizing a unique opportunity to access the field via the Director of the professional association of food inspectors in Germany, that had arisen during an expert workshop with food safety inspectors at Sciences-Po Paris in May 2015. Fifteen Länder heads of the professional association responded (almost full response rate) with detailed answers and partly also additional internal documents. The questionnaire thus balances out a comparatively lower geographical diversity of interviews for this domain (five Länder in work safety and flooding, and two in food safety).
- Finally, I conducted *participant observations* in expert workshops in all domains (2013–2015) to access more tacit knowledge – expressed in field notes – about how relevant experts perceive their domain, where they see critical motivations for risk-analytical innovation, and how risk analysis has been used in administrative decision-making since its adoption.

Data analysis followed IPA methods to reconstruct from textual raw data the variable meanings administrators vested in the adoption of risk analysis (cf. Yanow,

2000 and details on IPA above; Yanow and Schwartz-Shea, 2006). Documents, interviews, open-ended survey responses, and field notes have been coded with MaxQDA software in an iteration of deductive assumptions and inductive insights from the field with respect to three broad coding categories: (1) the instrumental, legitimacy-related, and power-seeking orientations vested in risk analysis (following theorization in Chapters 2 and 3), (2) the specific uses of risk analysis in practice (drawing on the operationalization in Chapter 3), and (3) the institutional conditions that policy-makers describe as underpinning these orientations and uses (based on my conceptual work in Chapter 4).

1.5 Organization of the book

The book is organized in two main parts: (1) conceptual framework and (2) the comparative analysis of risk analysis across three policy domains in Germany. Part 1 develops the conceptual and theoretical approach of the book in three chapters. Chapter 2 introduces the analytical framework for examining the appeal of analytical tools. I argue that administrative actors can ideal-typically vest three types of interpretations in analytical tools (and policy tools more generally speaking): its merits for instrumental problem-solving (I), its ability to enhance the legitimacy of administrative mandates (L), and its potential for advancing an actor's relative position of power in decision-making (P). While the former is a classic case of policy-making, the latter two are cases of *polity policies* as they target the confirmation and transformation of decision-making structures. Chapter 3 specifies this general analytical framework from the perspective of risk analysis. As risk can be viewed both as a manageable event and as a decision-making heuristic (Paul, 2017b, p. 61; cf. Bora, 2007), it offers a highly versatile analytical entry point for policymakers needing to engage with *both* problem-solving and polity policies. Risk-based differentiation semiotically connects seamlessly to hopes of rational problem-solving (societal risk management) but also to actors' attempts of rationalizing their own (institutional risk management) and others' relative positions in the policy domain (governance by risk). To operationalize the ILP framework for comparative analysis, the chapter identifies key indicators for the empirical scrutiny of risk-analytical orientations. Chapter 4 contextualizes assumptions about why analytical tools more generally, and risk analysis in particular, appeal. It reviews the well-researched Anglo-American "benchmark" cases and sets their dominant interpretive patterns around the merits of analytical models against the less well-known case of highly coordinated multi-level administrations. The chapter filters the more abstract insights from Chapters 2 and 3 through the lens of the formal and informal coordination requirements (e.g., norms of legal-administrative-unity and equal living conditions), and the related tensions between central level steering and subnational executive autonomy, in Germany's multi-level administration. It thus develops novel theoretical expectations about the appeal of analytical tools to be assessed in Part 2 of the book.

Part 2 of the book presents the empirical analysis in four chapters. Chapters 5–7 scrutinize the adoptions and appeal of risk analysis in German food safety controls, flood prevention, and work safety controls. Each chapter focuses on (1) the portrayal of the legacies and evolution of dominant problem perceptions (including collective action problems), statutory mandates for intervention, and patterns of multi-level decision-making in the domain; (2) a description of the domain-specific adoption pattern, including the respective design and actual uses of risk analysis in decision-making; and (3) an IPA which explores administrators' respective semiotic orientations alongside the ILP framework. Chapter 8 discusses findings in comparative perspective. It maps and explains variety in administrators' turns to risk analysis across the three domains. Each of the three cases involves significant (sometimes rather subtle or hidden) interaction dynamics between instrumental, legitimacy-seeking, and power-seeking orientations toward risk analysis. These interactions range from the effectiveness-oriented reinforcement of long existing patterns of central steering of food safety controls, via the ongoing negotiation of the "right" allocation of decision-making powers in flood prevention in the slipstream of soaring collective action desires, to the rather existential legitimacy-seeking efforts in the case of statutory work safety inspections. I discuss implications of comparative findings for our understanding of analytical tools in multi-level settings.

The conclusion summarizes the book's findings and develops ideas for future research. It does so in three steps. First, it discusses the implications of the inescapable co-existence of actors' problem-solving orientations and their valuation of analysis in polity policies for our understanding of analytical tools. Second, it reappraises the proclivity of multi-level administration to adopt analytical tools. That they flourish in Germany not "against the odds" of fragmented executive powers but, in fact, because of these odds has significant implications for other multi-level decision-making contexts, too. Third, the conclusion illuminates the material effects of actors' meaning-making around analytical tools. They can wield both stabilizing and transformative effects on decision-making structures in multi-level administrations. A brief final reflection on contemporary efforts to coordinate European member states' approaches to fight the COVID-19 pandemic with the help of common Corona risk maps (cf. Figure 1.1) illustrates that the relevance of analytical tools and their perceived merits *and* material effects in problem-solving and polity policies reaches much beyond scholarly spheres.

Notes

1 (Scott, 1998, p. 30)
2 For details on the measurement, see www.ecdc.europa.eu/en/covid-19/situation-updates/weekly-maps-coordinated-restriction-free-movement
3 Theodore Porter (1995) rightly notes that cost-benefit analysis was not invented by the US Federal government but by the US Army Corps of Engineers as early as in 1830 and was only mainstreamed with Reagan's Executive Order in 1981.
4 Much of Scott's empirical work goes on to highlight the failure of utopian state projects of central level planning and calculating.

5 This also resonates with critiques of the concepts of policy transfer or policy diffusion by which a policy or analytical template is copied and pasted from a setting A to a setting B. Rather than understanding such processes as "rationally selected best (or better) practices moving between jurisdictional spaces . . . [they involve] hybrid mutations of policy techniques and practices across dynamized institutional landscapes" (Peck, 2011, p. 774).

6 I thank Michael Huber, Marc Mölders, Rosemary Taylor, and Phillipe Zittoun for highlighting the need to address intentionality.

7 HowSAFE, 2013–2016, ESRC Grant Number ES/K006169/1.

PART 1

Concepts and theory

Contextualizing the appeal of analytical tools

2

FROM PROBLEM-SOLVING TO POLITY POLICIES

Three interpretive frames for analytical tools

Taking an interest in instruments must not in any way justify the erasure of the political.[1]

The controversies about why analytical models are on the rise across public administrations, charted in the introduction to this book, can be resolved – to some extent – when we avoid bias on the "dependent variable". Indeed, if we expand and systematize conceptual assumptions about the kind of rationalization that tools such as CBA, RIA, or risk analysis pursue, our empirical analyses will become both richer and more accurate. In particular, narrow foci on analytical tools as instrumental in *problem-solving* – by their capacity to help identify cost-effective policy options before decision-making and/or coerce irrational bureaucrats to implement policies in a targeted manner – obscure the importance of analytical models in *polity policies*. The latter perspective focuses on how actors' interpretations and uses of policy tools in general, and analytical tools in particular, relate to their attempts to legitimize, stabilize, or even expand their mandate to collectively bind decision-making in a policy domain.

The interpretive approach of this book (Introduction) suggests that the aforementioned perspectives are not mutually exclusive but co-exist, and interact in specific ways, in policymakers' understandings of the likely merits of analytical frameworks for policy-making. Rather than assuming instrumental problem-solving to be a dominant interpretation of analytical tools, analysts must deconstruct its empirical relevance in a multidimensional semiotic space through interpretive analysis. This does not require abandoning instrumental perspectives altogether. Rather, rational choice type interpretations of analytical tools constitute one of several interpretive framings for why CBA, RIA, or risk analysis gains currency among policymakers (this follows critical policy scholars' proposition that rational choice may be a useful "heuristic" for understanding public administration; Hay, 2004). Conceptual acknowledgment of a wider set of interpretations of analytical tools, including but not limited to instrumental problem-solving, is also the first step toward developing context-sensitive explanations for why these tools appeal in specific settings, including in fragmented polities to which parts of the literature attribute little inclination to adopt analytical tools in any comprehensive manner (Chapter 4).

To conceptualize analytical tools and their appeal to policymakers from an interpretivist perspective, this chapter reviews existing typologies in the literature on policy tools and policy change, the politics of tools and instrumentation, and the politics of evaluation. These inconsistently portray policy (-analytical) tools as rational problem-solving, symbolic action and legitimacy-seeking, or (less explicitly and less often) power-seeking within existing structures of decision-making. While the typologies jointly highlight the multidimensionality of analytical tools, their limited cross-fertilization and consistency have hindered research advances (for similar critique of the "polyhedral nature of the concept of policy instruments", see Acciai and Capano, 2020). Therefore, I provide a systematic integration of insights from across these so far unconnected silos of literature and explain the increasing use of analytical tools as related to *both* problem-solving endeavors and polity policies. I propose a *unified typology* of the appeal of analytical tools, arguing that actors have three distinct orientations in mind when they promote an analytical tool: instrumental problem-solving (I), legitimacy-seeking (L), and power-seeking (P).

While the first of the semiotic orientations in my ILP typology is related to *policy-making* in a more traditional understanding and considers how actors seek to rationalize problem-solving based on a pre-defined policy goal (guided by the logic of consequentiality), the other two display instances of *polity policies* – either because actors interpret and use analytical tools to stabilize their mandate for decision-making (through a logic of appropriateness) and/or as an attempt to expand their own decision-making powers in a policy domain (logic of influence) (cf. Figure 2.1 in the summary section of this chapter). Thus, the typology also builds on scholarly work on knowledge and policy-making, arguing that any form of knowledge provision in the policy realm is never concerned with finding "optimal" policy solutions alone but also enables policy coordination and actors' strategic (re-)positioning in the decision-making setting (Heinelt, 2016).

2.1 Typologies and the multiple meanings of policy (-analytical) tools

As highlighted in the Introduction, *analytical tools* are widely understood as precursors for policy formulation because they offer methods to analyze policy problems *before* decision-making. While the literature so far provides only limited attempts to conceptualize analytical tools beyond this narrow problem-solving focus (see Claudio Radaelli's work on RIA, cited later), existing typologies of policy tools and evaluation methods help identify relevant additional perspectives as well as highlight research silos and the need to develop an integrated conceptual-analytical framework. The review informs my own multidimensional conceptualization of analytical tools in the reminder of the chapter.

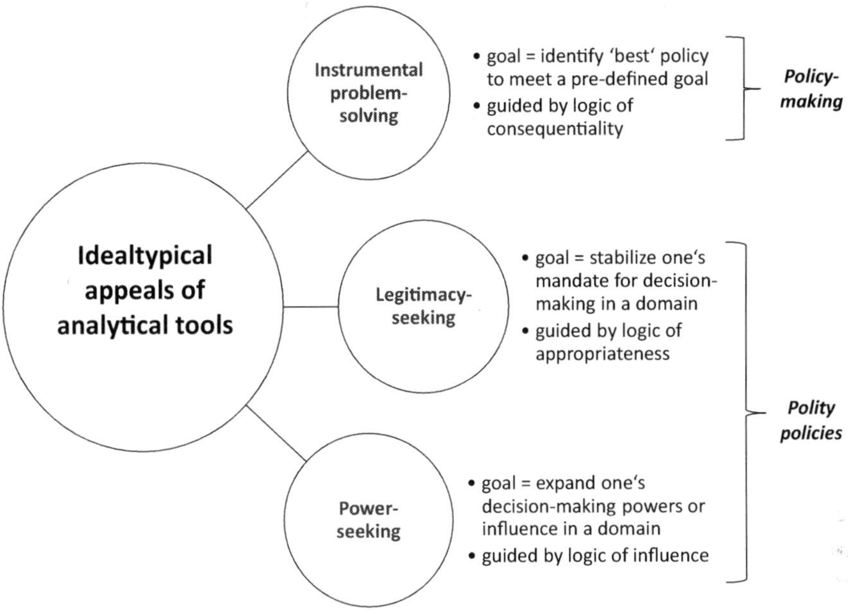

FIGURE 2.1 Unified typology of analytical tools' appeal

Source: Author's own compilation

Within the policy tools literature, typologization has long focused on different resources and tools that can achieve a nominal policy goal (Acciai and Capano, 2020). This is exemplified in the discussion of "carrots, sticks, and sermons" (Bemelmans-Videc, Rist and Vedung, 2011) as well as Christopher Hood's (1983) NATO typology with four different vantage points for behavioral change (nodality, authority, treasure, and organization). These typologies – discussed in more detail in Section 2.2 – assume that civil servants within the public administration have rational views of how a specific type of tool can achieve a policy goal at the lowest cost and with the least visibility and most effective targeting of regulatees (e.g., incentives for self-regulation vs. sanctioned prohibitions). While the specific role of analytical models is not of concern in these studies, they propose an instrumental reading of tools which fits the definition of analytical tools as optimizers of policy decisions.

Several typologies go beyond such an instrumental perspective of tools. A more recent typology of "tool choice" (Capano and Lippi, 2017) systematizes decision makers' perception of tools in an attempt to balance between its expected instrumentality and perceived legitimacy. The authors thus adhere to wider claims in political science that policymakers, in order to justify their policy-making power, need to showcase *both* the effectiveness (as the ability of policies to meet specific policy goals) and legitimacy (as their appropriateness, in terms of normative standards) of their decisions (Heinelt, 2016). Critical evaluation scholars also propose typologies, such as how policymakers use evaluation methods, that include legitimacy and instrumental considerations. They argue that evaluation methods[2] can be used "(a) *instrumentally*, to give direction to policy and practice; (b) *politically or symbolically*, to justify pre-existing preferences and actions, and (c) *conceptually*, to provide new generalizations, ideas, or concepts that are useful for making sense of the policy scene" (Weiss, Murphy-Graham and Birkeland, 2005, p. 13; emphasis added). Their third interpretation of evaluation uses, that is, the conceptual type, points toward an additional dimension for policymakers' assessments of how analytical tools appeal. Arguably, from my perspective, the process of "making sense of a policy scene" through conceptual debate may involve not only considerations of what a problem is about and how well policy approaches are suited to respond to it. It also involves reflections on how well the structures and processes of a policy domain are suited to instrumental problem-solving and different actors' positional struggles over legitimacy and influence in a domain.

Radaelli's study on four images of RIA (2010) systematically considers variable perceptions of *analytical* tools: alongside rational policy-making (instrumental) and symbolic action (legitimacy related) – the two well-known motivations for tool adoption based on previous discussions – he distinguishes "control of the bureaucracy" to "public management reform". Control of the bureaucracy-type images of RIA suggests a power-political dimension: central level actors in an administration; see RIA as a tool to reduce the gap between central-level policy decisions and local implementation decisions (Radaelli, 2010, pp. 169, 172f). Similar expectations surface in the debate about CBA, as discussed in Chapter 1 (Sunstein, 2000; Posner, 2001). It is unclear, however, if such control foci only focus on the extent to which an assumed principal can push through an instrumentally oriented policy against irrational and unruly decentral actors (the implication of control of the bureaucracy type arguments) or if "control" extends to more general questions on navigating or transforming decision-making structures in a polycentric setting (as the OMC debate and research on international bureaucracies, charted briefly in Chapter 1, would suggest). It also remains less clear how "public management reform" forms a distinct ideal type; arguably, the goals of such a reform have been shown to connect other ideas of rational problem-solving, control of the bureaucracy, and legitimacy action (Pollitt and Bouckaert, 2011).

Considering a more explicitly power-related interpretation of tool choice, Peters (2002, p. 554) argued that, next to problem-solving foci, tools imply expectations about "whose ox will be gored and whose nest will be feathered". In a similar vein, Capano and Lippi acknowledged that a tool "allocates opportunities and duties, creates values or symbols, as well as stakes, and also distributes costs and benefits" (2017, p. 279). In fact, they explicitly extend their own definition of what is "instrumental" in a decision maker's tool choice to include a tool's "impact on the distribution of power within the policy field" (ibid.). However, their decision to conflate actors' problem-solving perceptions with power distributional concerns under the heading of "instrumentality" obscures investigation of the relative weight of both framings in empirical situations – their potential conflict with one another, such as when a tool efficiently solves a problem but seems to weaken a specific actor's strategic position, or the respective institutional conditions that inform either perception. Overall, while recent typologies of policy tools and evaluation methods are united by a focus on instrumental promises of problem-solving and a legitimation of policymakers' actions, these accounts discuss the role of positional struggles over decision-making powers in a domain implicitly at best.

Read jointly, the existing typologies highlight the *multidimensionality* of policymakers' perceptions of policy tools, evaluative frameworks, and analytical tools. While some focus on how instrumental perspectives justify policy tool adoption, others highlight how legitimacy-related goals interact with instrumental perceptions. Beyond some generic nods to the power distributional politics of tools (Peters, 2002; Capano and Lippi, 2017), a systematic integration of power-related appeals of analytical tools – that is, policymakers' perceptions of how tools may help in struggles over their own and others' decision-making powers – is missing in the existing typologies. However, such an extended conceptualization of analytical tools seems central if we want to understand analytical frameworks' role in actors' attempts to shape decision-making processes and structures along the lines set out by scholars of European integration, international bureaucracies, or the socio-economic history of quantification (cf. Chapter 1).

Thus, this chapter is focused on systematizing insights from across the existing disconnected literature on policy tools and policy change, instrument constituencies, and the politics of "instrumentation" and evaluation into my own unified typology. Three ideal types of actors' meaning-making about policy (-analytical) tools emerge from this systematization effort:

- *instrumental problem-solving* where policymakers seek to rationalize policy decisions by the help of analytical models (Section 2.2);
- *legitimacy-seeking*, where actors seek to use analytical frameworks to present their actions as appropriate (Section 2.3); and
- a *power-seeking* perspective, where analytical tools count as utile in actors' attempts to influence decision-making structures in their favor (Section 2.4).

2.2 The appeal of policy (-analytical) tools as instrumental policy-making

I start this review by specifying the role of analytical tools – and policy tools in general – in those parts of the literature that focus on "rational" problem-solving credentials. Even though I do not buy into a rational choice ontology as a guide for my own research in this book (see the chapter introduction), I agree with Colin Hay's observation that rational choice can nonetheless serve as a "stylized heuristic" for scholarly analysis of decision makers' own meaning-making about a tool (Hay, 2004). Interpretivist scholars of policy-making highlight that although perceptions of policy problems and goals vary considerably and feature ambiguities, even for the same actor, policymakers need to reflect and communicate upon the effectiveness of their actions (e.g., Heinelt, 2016, p. 12ff). In a similar vein, several scholars of policy analysis interpret the adoption of analytical tools as process guided by policymakers' hopes of rationalizing policy decisions. I situate this rationality claim in conventional readings of policy change in which policy tools generally play an ancillary role in the fulfilment of politically inaugurated policy goals. This literature helps detailing widespread, albeit not always explicit, expectations about the dominance of instrumental considerations in administrators' analytical efforts, in line with Howlett's view that their role is to "generat[e] options about what to do about a public problem" and to thus enable rational policy choice (2011, p. 29).

2.2.1 Policy tools as auxiliary to policy change

Scholarly policy analysis often focuses on processes of change writ large, that is, changes in the norms and ways of thinking about a policy domain at large. Within these frameworks, policy tools often play an ancillary and supportive role in the instrumental fulfilment of policy goals, without a political life of their own. They thus offer an important starting point for specifying instrumental accounts of analytical tools.

Two of the most influential theories of policy change – in terms of citations and research applications – are offered within the framework of policy paradigm change (Hall, 1993) and in the advocacy coalitions framework (ACF) (Sabatier, 1988; Sabatier and Jenkins-Smith, 1993). As common starting points, both have shaped the ways in which scholars think about policy tools. The approaches are ontologically and epistemologically different, mainly because the latter adopts a methodological individualism which the former rejects, all while the former operates with a coherent notion of ideas relaxed by the latter (Cairney and Weible, 2015). Yet, an important observation for the purpose of this book is that both operate with a hierarchically ordered and linear heuristic of change, which suitably considers ideational variation at higher levels of abstraction but, further down the ladder of abstraction, assigns a marginal and unpolitical role to policy tools (and does not explicitly consider analytical tools).

Hall famously adapted the framework of Kuhn's scientific revolutions for the explanation of policy change. He developed a three-tier structure of policies consisting of coherent sets of ideas about a policy (such as paradigms), policy tools, and policy settings or calibrations. Within this model, the re-calibration of tools and the choice of new tools for policy-making are "cases of 'normal policymaking', namely of a process that adjusts policy without challenging the overall terms of a given policy paradigm, much like 'normal science'" (Hall, 1993, p. 279). First order change concerns calibration of the tool settings, for example, the adjustment of an interest rate in monetary policies in Hall's field of research. This is likely to be incremental, satisficing, and routinized. The second order change of tools themselves may "move further in the direction of strategic action", but only the third order of change will open up opportunities for more radical change through "experimentation with new forms of policy" (p. 280). This will only happen when a new set of somewhat coherent ideas (a paradigm) is available and can gain ground over the existing one due to shifts in policy authority and a concurring sense of failure for the old paradigm to explain anomalies.

The ACF operates with the idea of a three-tier belief system consisting of (rather stable) deep core beliefs, core policy beliefs, and secondary beliefs. As Weible and Sabatier (2007, p. 128, highlights added by author) explain, "secondary beliefs include policy participants' preferences for specific *government tools* for achieving objectives". The basic idea is that through strategic alignment of their (individually derived) policy preferences, actors who share core beliefs can come together in so-called advocacy coalitions to change policies within a policy subsystem according to their preferences. Their success depends on the role of policy brokers, the extent to which they can mobilize different resources, their ability to exploit different venues for decision-making, and external events and shocks (summary in Weible and Sabatier, 2007). The ACF was first used to explain changes in the water quality policy for Lake Tahoe Basin in the US and the involvement of actors with competing views.

Both approaches suggest that smaller-scale adaptive changes within or of policy tools (first or second order change in Peter Hall's terms, secondary policy change conceptualized as change of "secondary" or "empirical" beliefs in the ACF) range behind transformations of whole "policy paradigms" (Hall) or "policy core beliefs" (ACF). At the same time, they also argue that smaller-scale changes of policy tools are relatively easy to achieve, rather apolitical, and irrelevant in terms of their potential to transform a policy domain. Generally speaking, the conventional assumptions about hierarchies of policy change – with tools ranging near the bottom and having little political implications of themselves – can be linked back to the discipline's classic concept of policy cycle. As promoted by early policy analyst Harold D. Lasswell, the cycle metaphor suggests that policy change happens in distinct and hierarchically linked stages: first, problem definition and agenda setting set the framework for discussing policy solutions; second, policymakers design and adopt policies which are functionally linked; third, they implement these solutions – using policy tools in a functional way; and lastly, policy outcomes are evaluated (Lasswell, 1970, 1971, 2003). Overall, parts of the policy change literature portray the adoption of a (new) policy tool as a politically neutral process that is hierarchically subordinated to larger scale changes – much more openly political – of policy paradigms and goals (and, therefore, also less interesting a subject of analysis). It is in this sense that they can be associated with a "logic of consequentiality" (see critical debate by March and Olsen, 1989).

2.2.2 Policy tools as instrumental problem solvers

The assumptions of a hierarchically ordered process of policy change in which policymakers adopt new policy tools from an instrumental mindset have been carved out further by scholars of policy tools. They propose a neat alignment of tool choice with pre-set goals and consequently conceptualize policymakers' adoption of tools as an instrumental matching exercise guided by their desire to rationalize problem solving. This view certainly dominates Hood's seminal The *Tools of Government*, wherein he writes that "it is by applying its tools that government makes the link between wish and fulfilment" (Hood, 1983, p. 8). Hood argues that administrations choose from a wider "tool shed" when trying "to shape our lives", and that they do so "in many different combinations and contexts, to suit a variety of purposes" (Hood, 1983, p. 2). Importantly, while Hood acknowledges here that policy purposes vary considerably – and are shaped by political struggles – tool adoption does not involve political rationalities of its own.

Following this line of argument, many policy analysts after Hood have depicted a unidirectional and instrumental relationship between policy purposes (ends or goals) – the normative decisions about what a policy should aim to achieve – and the means selected to achieve an end. A recent study on policy tool change in the EU notes, "policy instruments are means and techniques in order to achieve policy goals" (Bähr, 2010, p. 15). Such definitions share basic assumptions of the hierarchical structure of policies which feature in the ACF's belief system and as policy components in Hall's paradigm change approach. They imply that once decided, overarching ideational "prisms through which policymakers [see]" (Hall, 1993, p. 279) aspects of the social world trickle down to determine choices of tools and their calibration. As a recent textbook on public policy-making summarizes, "goal rationality[3] as the guiding principle affects the way policy instruments are perceived" in the rational choice perspective (Bekkers, Fenger and Scholten, 2017, p. 46). Therefore, the policy tool debate by Hood and others invokes a specific concept of rationalization as policymakers' pursuit of rational problem-solving through (optimal) tool choice, shaped by pre-defined policy problems and goals.

To account for the empirical and theoretical "variety and variability of government's policy instruments" (Hood, 2007, p. 128) and the focus on "optimal" choice from within the "tool shed", several authors have highlighted the *specific* instrumental appeal of policy tools (Hood, 1983, 2007; Margetts and Hood, 2016; cf. Capano and Lippi, 2017). This implies that any one tool comes with a set of abilities, giving it an advantage in achieving some goals over others. Thus, instrumentality "concerns the decisionmakers' perception of an instrument as useful and effective in achieving given ends" (Capano and Lippi, 2017, p. 278). Administrators' instrumental considerations of a policy tool are hence likely to vary with respect to perceptions of the specific policy problem meant to be solved and the goal meant to be achieved. Put simply, if I want a hole in the ground (my goal), it would be irrational for me to pick a saw over a driller (tool choice). Importantly, the variation in tool choice is not interpreted as a matter of context here (unlike for tools' role in polity policies, as discussed later) but as a matter of how problem definition by itself narrows the types of solutions suitable to achieve the goal. For example, Hood's (1983) cybernetic typology of policy tools ascribes to tool-inherent characteristics, which work as control levers for gathering information (detecting) and modifying behavior (effecting). This way, they help explain their various appeals to governments. Hood's related typology of tools (NATO for nodality, authority, treasury, and organization) assumes civil servants within the public administration have a rational view on how a specific type of tool can achieve a policy goal at the lowest cost, least visibility, and most effective targeting of regulatees (e.g., incentives for self-regulation through "nodality" vs. sanctioned prohibitions through "authority").

Unfortunately, the studies discussed earlier do not offer a specific theorization of the role of pre-decision analysis in policy-making. However, when synthesizing the more general accounts of policy change and policy tools presented so far with insights on the role of analytical tools, the potentially decisive role of the latter becomes obvious. In situations where the choice of policy tools and paths is unclear, in instrumental terms, analysis can help establish the likelihood of a tool to *actually* fulfil policy goals. Indeed, rational choice scholars of CBA, RIA, and risk analysis propose that their respective adoption may help avoid "poor priority setting, excessively costly tools, and inattention to the unfortunate side-effects of regulation" (Sunstein, 2000, p. 1660; Majone, 2010; Wiener, 2010). Within this framework, analytical tools would lay the groundwork for rationalizing decision-making about optimal problem-solving alongside pre-established policy goals. Where ambiguity over policy tool choice prevails, the instrumentalist's answer would be to establish, perhaps through CBA, the tool or combination of tools that are likely to best achieve a pre-defined policy goal while using the least resources (more on these assumptions for the example of risk analysis in Chapter 3). Such rational choice interpretations also surface in evaluation research, as critically reviewed in the case of international organizations by Raimondo (2018, p. 33):

> *evaluation systems' raison d'être is [seemingly] to enhance formal rationality, such as efficiency, effectiveness and ultimately social betterment. Whether it is through organizational learning, or external accountability, the rationale for evaluation in International Organizations is to optimize development processes, and then find the 'best' possible way forward.*

The "paradoxical structuralism" of rational choice (Hay, 2004) implies that there is not much of a choice for an organization – a straightforward utility function would help establish one (or, at best, a few) equilibrium solution(s) to then be "selected" without much agency for the actors involved across different levels and sites. From this perspective, analysis is instrumental in finding "the 'best' possible way forward". In Chapter 3, I detail policymakers' perceptions about how exactly analysis can help rationalize decision-making in that sense and how such interpretative framing translates into analytical templates and their institutionalization for the case of risk analysis.

2.3 Beyond narrow concepts of policy-oriented rationalization

The instrumental perspective on policy tools has been problematized for its rather narrow perception of policy tools, and analytical tools, as technocratic and apolitical instruments of rational problem-solving. This section briefly summarizes key arguments in this debate to carve out the book's broader conceptualization of analytical tools as oriented, from the perspective of policymakers' meaning-making about such tools, *both* toward the effectiveness of policies (problem-solving) and toward legitimacy and the distribution of power in the decision-making setting (polity policies). I thus expand the question of *what* actors seek to rationalize when they adopt analytical tools from immediate policy decisions to the structural conditions under which they come about.

Several policy scholars – including Peter Hall himself – acknowledge that "many policies are not supported by anything so grand" as a coherent set of core ideas or beliefs (Hall, 1993, p. 291; see also Baumgartner, 2014, p. 476; Hogan and Howlett, 2015). The analytical link between ends and means as a normative choice vs. an operational enactment of that choice would thus involve a considerable leap of faith. Indeed, several scholars have criticized the rational choice undertones in instrumentalist conceptualizations of policy (-analytical) tools and argue that "making the link" between policy goals and tools is usually neither as straightforward nor as politically neutral as conventional theories of policy change suggest (e.g., Linder and Peters, 1989; Béland and Howlett, 2016; Capano and Lippi, 2017). Peter Hall suggests, more specifically, that change at the level of tools does most likely operate somewhere *in between* routinized organizational behavior and strategic political decision-making. Indeed, his study of British macroeconomic policy-making after World War II – passing over to the question of paradigm change which interests him the most – offers an interesting diversion on the instrumentality of tool change as he discusses the dynamics of introducing cash limits. This resulted, as he argues, mainly from "growing dissatisfaction" with expenditure controls among "senior civil servants at the Treasury" who had to implement the policies (Hall, 1993, p. 282), who had already grouped around the alternative tool (cash benefits) for a while, and who then embraced the opportunity to introduce it when an appropriate problem arose. There is, however, no systematic theorization of the conditions under which policy tools (or analytical methods) change in pursuit of instrumental means-ends-logics or because they seem to support the strategic power-related efforts of public administrators. Equally, Hood acknowledges diversion from his strictly instrumental tool adoption pathway when asking "why some particular method . . . comes to be seen or argued to be the 'one best way' and which possible alternatives are 'framed out'" (Hood, 2007, p. 141). He does not, however, specify the factors that shape such framing processes, nor does he theorize the conditions under which potentially more distinctly political perceptions of tools shape their adoption.

These clarifications open the floor for critique of instrumental perceptions of analytical tools. Wider scholarly debates in political sciences, public administration, and sociology about the relative independence of means and ends in policy-making warrant doubt as to any exclusive influence of instrumental means-ends relationships on perceptions of analytical tools. They demand, or at least imply, an expansion of the analytical canvas to include administrative actors' meta-level concerns over the structures and processes of decision-making. More specifically, ever since the publication of "A Garbage Can Model of Organizational Choice" (Cohen, March and Olsen, 1972), scholars have proposed that organizational decision-making is usually not rational in the sense of goal-oriented linear courses of action. Instead, as March and Olsen (1989, p. 12) note in their later work, "In pure form, garbage can models assume that problems, solutions, decision makers, and choice opportunities are independent, exogenous streams flowing through a system". A policymakers' perception of a policy tool might depend less then – or not at all – on its instrumental fit with a pre-defined policy problem, but on the highly contingent attachment of a preferred policy solution to perceived problems by policy entrepreneurs (cf. Kingdon, 1984).

In the spirit of the garbage can model – but focusing more on the endogenous identity-building features of the joint promotion of a policy tool – a growing number of studies in the literature relate the emergence of specific solutions to the influence of so-called "instrument constituencies". These would gather around the elaboration and promotion of policy solutions, such as emission trading certificates or funded pension schemes, and seek opportunities for installing them as suitable problem solutions (Voß and Simons, 2014; Béland and Howlett, 2016; Simons and Voß, 2017). Scholars in this camp suggest that policy tools – and analytical tools by extension – appeal for reasons that operate in relative independence from actors' perceptions about a specific policy or administrative problem, or at least *in addition to* problem-solving perceptions. The literature on instrument constituencies in particular concurs that actors may consider policy tools as attractive because (1) they seem normatively appropriate and therefore *legitimate* and/or (2) because they advance their *power* over *decision-making* in a domain (Voß and Simons, 2014). Others concur that any tool implies specific regulatory concepts which can help (re-)structure (strategically or unintendedly so) both the accountability relationships between administrators and regulatees and the allocation of decision-making authorities in a policy domain (Lascoumes and Le Galès, 2007). To the authors, this warrants a need to "move beyond the division of politics and policies" in our analyses of policy tools (p. 8).

This perspective on legitimacy and power-seeking also echoes the attempt of (some of the) existing typologies of policy tools and evaluation uses, reviewed in Section 2.1, to address the multidimensionality of actors' perceptions of why policy (-analytical) tools appeal. To provide a unified analytical framework for examining policymakers' turns to analytical tools, I therefore detail legitimacy-related and power-distributional interpretations of policy (-analytical) tools next.

2.4 The legitimacy-related appeal of policy (-analytical) tools

Legitimacy-seeking purposes have, as discussed earlier, long been established as an important – often the guiding – ingredient of organizational action. In Raimondo's (2018, p. 33) words, this is where we let go of the assumption that "everything in organizational life is reducible to purpose and function". By drawing on accounts of policymakers' legitimacy-seeking in policy analysis and organizational studies, this section identifies how the adoption of analytical tools may relate to legitimacy considerations.

2.4.1 Policy tools and the logic of appropriateness

Legitimacy claims in policy analysis and evaluation studies draw on the sociological variant of neo-institutionalist thinking (cf. Hall and Taylor, 1996). Establishing the general relevance of legitimacy considerations, March and Olsen have argued that a "logic of appropriateness" tends to guide decision-making within organizations as they attempt to legitimize, and thus sustain, their mandate. This suggests that, when taking decisions (including about policy tools), administrative actors engage in endogenous sense-making about their identity and the appropriateness of different paths of action, given what the situation seems to be about (March and Olsen, 1989, p. 23). This argument was developed in explicit opposition to what March and Olsen saw as an excessive dominance of rational choice explanations for organizational behavior, summarized in their terminology as a "logic of consequentiality".

Neo-institutionalist theories of isomorphism stress that the search for legitimate policy or organizational templates can follow three distinct patterns of institutional isomorphism: (1) external coercion to adopt specific templates, for example, if a supra- or international body prescribes the adoption (coercive isomorphism); but also emulation processes in which actors adopt templates either (2) because they seem well-tried and successful in other jurisdictions (mimetic isomorphism), and/or (3) because of their good fit with deeply held professional norms within the adopting organization (normative isomorphism) (DiMaggio and Powell, 1983; Powell and DiMaggio, 1991). This means that the source of legitimizing a new tool can be external (coercion) or internal (mimetism and normative convictions), depending on the specific context in which legitimacy considerations emerge.

Organizational legitimacy-seeking has featured widely in sociological interpretations of policy tools. Correspondingly, the emerging literature on so-called "instrument constituencies" (Voß and Simons, 2014; Béland and Howlett, 2016; Voß, 2016; Simons and Voß, 2017) assumes that actors elaborate policy tools, analytical models, and technical solutions (e.g., specific risk algorithms, emission trading certificates, or funded pension schemes) and promote them as both *efficient* and *appropriate* problem solution, without "consideration of the merits of policy means from goal definitions" (Béland and Howlett, 2016, p. 398). The focus of such research is on how actors become advocates of specific tools, how they develop infrastructures to support the theoretical elaboration and practical adoption of "their" tool, as well as on how collective identities form and stabilize themselves around policy tools. As this view straddles the boundary to power distributional perceptions of tools, I will come back to it in Section 2.5.

The literature on the politics of instrumentation argues specifically that any policy tool implies specific regulatory concepts, which affect (strategically or unintendedly so) accountability relationships between administrators and regulatees and the ascription of authority in a policy domain (Lascoumes and Le Galès, 2007). In other words, tools come with distinct ideas about who is to be held accountable by whom, affecting the perception of legitimacy of an administration as well as ideas about who should legitimately hold the power to take collectively binding decisions in a domain. Reflexive strategies of shaping (others') ideas about one's own accountability feature prominently in research on the politics of evaluation. Scholars in this field argue that "political pressures" tend to taint any purely instrumental conceptualization or use of evaluation frameworks (Weiss, 1973). Policymakers can adopt evaluations selectively and strategically, they argue, to "provide support for policies decided on the basis of intuition, professional experience, self-interest, organizational interest, a search for prestige. . . [or] to buttress an existing point of view" (Weiss, Murphy-Graham and Birkeland, 2005, p. 13f). This general point has been illustrated in a more recent study on performance measurement. Rather than being concerned with rational problem-solving, such forms of self-analysis would highlight the legitimacy functions of analytical tools as "symbols of modernity"; "By initiating evaluations, organizations picture themselves as modern and efficient organizations which are open towards criticism, changes, and efficient problem solving [. . .] doing what is appropriate" (Bjørnholt and Larsen, 2014, p. 403).

These cursory illustrations highlight that legitimacy-seeking, in the sense of indicating the appropriateness of actions, relies on an organization's ability to present itself as "modern", "efficient", and focused on rational "problem-solving". It is in that context that the debate on legitimacy-seeking focuses on "symbolic" action (see the overviews from a policy analysis perspective by: Radaelli, 2009, 2010) where there is a strong detachment of "talk" about being modern, efficient, and so forth, and actual "action" (Brunsson, 1989). The role of policy tools, in that context, is hence one of supporting the impression that an organization or decision-making body uses its powers appropriately.

The use of analytical tools can be a way to signal one's commitment to engage in rigorous analysis, modern methods of evaluation, and critical self-reflection even where such commitment may be weak(er) in instrumental problem-solving terms. A study on international benchmarking exercises, for example, proposed that national regulatory authorities' voluntary partake in such performance measurement frameworks may hardly change their policies in response to negative benchmarking results but rather reflects "the importance of being modern" (Lodge, 2005). Comparative scrutiny of RIA confirms similar symbolic – or legitimacy-related – uses of analytical tools in EU member states (Radaelli, 2005, 2010), as does Boswell's analysis of uses of expert knowledge as "a source of legitimation, or as a way of substantiating their policy preferences" (2008, p. 471).

Chapter 3 details the specific mechanisms, such as "trust in numbers" and "blame-shifting", through which the adoption of risk-analytical frameworks unfolds such legitimacy-enhancing power. Importantly, for now, legitimacy-oriented studies of benchmarking, RIA, and expert knowledge highlight a close link between the (symbolic) display of the instrumental merits of analytical frameworks and their role in substantiating the legitimacy of an organization. This strengthens the book's argument that actors hold multiple interpretive frames as to the merits of analytical tools and that these may interact to mutually support each other.

2.4.2 Policy tools as stabilizers of mandates for decision-making

Although there is much talk of "norms" and normative orientations' in this branch of the research, the pursuit of "appropriate" action, from the perspective of sociological neo-institutionalism, does not necessarily operate from a moral high ground. Rather, it responds to a perceived necessity to ensure organizational survival through actions perceived as legitimate by those who could threaten such survival. The "importance of being modern" lays not so much in collective assumptions about the superiority of "modern" analytical techniques (this would be an instrumental frame), but in how showcasing one's own "modernity" shapes one's legitimacy to (retain one's mandate to) act. This is what Weiss, Murphy-Graham and Birkeland (2005) imply when they speak of "self-interest" and "organizational interest" in the context of legitimacy uses of evaluation.

Indeed, Peters' early attempt to politicize policy tool choice highlighted interpretations of tools as a means to further an organization's institutional self-interest in its own stability (Peters, 2002). This framing concurs with (interpretivist) political scientists who have highlighted that, next to evidencing the effectiveness of their actions in an instrumental cause-effect interpretation of policies, policymakers always also need to consider – and showcase in communicative processes of collective sense-making – the appropriateness of these actions to justify their (continued possession of) political or administrative power positions (Heinelt, 2016, p. 12ff). In the policy tools debate, Capano and Lippi (2017) have systematized the claim that *next to* instrumentality considerations, policymakers who adopt a new policy tool always also seek to legitimize their mandate and actions through perceptions of the appropriateness of this very tool. Based on the Weberian definition of legitimacy as justifying the use of power, the authors argue that, due to their relation to the execution of governmental powers, tool choices always also need to be made considering how each tool performs in relation to the legitimacy of the administration (cf. on this point: Heinelt, 2016, p. 12ff). Voß and Simons (2014, p. 737) offer an example for such a self-defense pattern in the context of instrument constituencies; for example, when claiming that "instruments may provide a 'productive illusion' of public agency and thus orientate collective action and legitimate authoritative ruling".

While I will detail the sources of legitimacy claims in the coming chapters (as specific logics of risk-based rationalization in Chapter 3 and as related to decision-making dynamics in multi-level settings in Chapter 4), we can arrive at some basic assumptions about how actors seek to rationalize their own legitimacy and mandate through analytical tools. Within a legitimacy-seeking framework, analytical tools are perceived as instruments for rationalizing not so much any one policy decision but the more general orientation of actions of a decision-making body as appropriate. This view on legitimacy-seeking as an organization's – or in our case, administrative body's – attempt to stabilize its own mandate for "legitimate authoritative ruling" certainly matters in all contexts of collectively binding decision-making. However, multi-level settings imply a constant need for actors at lower levels of governance to not only justify their substantial policy actions but also to demonstrate their ability to coordinate policies without central state intervention, as is discussed in Chapter 4.

2.5 The power distributional appeal of policy (-analytical) tools

To be clear, when highlighting the power distributional appeal of analytical tools as a third ideal type, I do not argue that conventional policy analysis disregards power in policy-making. Rather, as the Introduction and Section 2.2 highlighted, parts of the literature treat policy tools and, particularly, analytical tools as rather apolitical and instrumentally subordinated to the outcomes of political struggles over policy goals. Others acknowledge that tools have an "impact on the distribution of power within the policy field" (Capano and Lippi, 2017, p. 279) but conflate actors' perceptions about such an impact with their rational problem-solving intentions under a more general notion of "instrumentality". Yet other scholars of policy tools have, however, considered more systematically how the design, choice, and use of tools are embedded in positional struggles over "whose ox will be gored or whose nest will be feathered" (Peters, 2002, p. 554). It is to these accounts that I turn last.

2.5.1 The "structural promises" of policy tools

The instrumentation literature argues that policy tools always also (re-)define roles and relationships in a domain. This is because they imply, at their very core, specific theories about the "relationship between the governing and the governed" as well as a "condensed form of knowledge about social control and ways of exercising it" (Lascoumes and Le Galès, 2007, p. 1). Not only do policy tools have unintended structuration effects from this perspective but can also be promoted for how they promise to (re-)structure a policy domain and the relationship of actors within it. As Simons and Voß (2017, p. 8) put it, instruments entail "structural promises" that concern "structural features of a future world that an instrument is expected to bring about, especially regarding the *roles and positions* this world offers *for different actors*" (emphases added). This means that a decision maker's meaning-making of a policy (-analytical) tool can include rationalization of their own position and decision-making powers in a policy setting relative to others. It is secondary for the interpretivist focus of this book that the "structural promises" that actors had envisaged when adopting a tool may often be disappointed in practice.

In elaboration of their basic argument, Lascoumes and Le Galès refer to examples around the rise of statistical analytical tools in 18th-century Germany (p. 8). They highlight that these had the initially unintended structural implication of creating conceptual divisions among various populations, which were later on used more strategically to target policies, related to taxation, social insurance, or the governance of the mentally ill, among others (cf. also: Rose, 1991). This draws explicitly on the seminal work of Desrosières (2002), introduced as one of the intellectual prompters for my perspective on polity policies in the Introduction. His social history of statistics stresses the mutually constitutive relationship between governmental authority and the growth of mathematical artifacts as tools for governing populations and subnational state entities. A good example of how implied regulatory concepts within a policy tool purposefully re-structure relationships in a policy field is offered in a study on the introduction of "partnership" instruments in British social policies (Carmel and Harlock, 2008). This examines the implications of partnership contracts for voluntary and community organization providers of social care services. The study highlights that contracts serve as a new procedural tool for operating service provision, enabling the government to "carve out a newly governable terrain, – the third sector – which is to be organized through the operational governance mechanisms of procurement and performance" (Carmel and Harlock, 2008, p. 155).

From a slightly different entry point, scholars of instrument constituencies describe processes of collective identify formation as well as the strategic advancement of supportive infrastructures for their preferred policy tool. Once a policy tool has been able to "attract and generate agency" (Simons and Voß, 2017, p. 9) for contingent initial reasons, a reinforcing process is set in motion: actors gather around the tool, develop a shared identity through tool-related interactions, jointly and individually seek opportunities to advance, and promote their tool as efficient and appropriate. They also – and this is most explicitly related to positional struggles over influence – create "infrastructures" that allow the tool and its constituency to flourish (cf. Simons and Voß, 2017). This focus on constituency and infrastructure formation around a tool perceived as "appropriate" by some actors straddles the boundary between legitimacy-seeking and power-distributional interpretations of policy tools. Thus, it usefully specifies a notion of strategic agency in relation to analytical tools. Such agency, for scholars of instrument constituencies, is endogenously strategic in the sense of a dedicated promotion of the tool (rather than the promotion of the tool relating to one's own strategic position in a domain). Indeed, the notion of instrument constituencies

1 cuts across formal decision-making structures and unites actors from across levels, from most diverse organizations (government departments, international organizations, NGOs, interest groups and social movements, scientific associations, the media, etc.), and with potentially conflicting ideas about their "interests" in a domain, and

2 informs a distinctly *endogenous* process of generating new collective identities (= constituencies) around and through the joint promotion of a policy tool and the joint strategic effort in keeping the tool "alive both as a model and as an implemented practice" (Béland and Howlett, 2016, p. 397, cf. Voß and Simons, 2014).

2.5.2 Policy (-analytical) tools as sites of "power politics"

In addition to highlighting endogenous identity formation and strategizing, the cited literature also offers a more explicit interpretation of how actors perceive and use the "structural promises" of policy (-analytical) tools in instances of "power politics" (Voß and Simons, 2014, p. 739). Indeed, studies on the "politics of instrumentation" suggest that the allocation of control over decision-making in an administration can itself be under negotiation with the emergence of a new policy tool. For example, contributions gathered in the special issue on the politics of instrumentation by Lascoumes and Le Galès (2007) highlight the structuring effects of tools for whole policy domains. They depict, for example, how the adoption of new tools such as funded pension schemes have incrementally transformed the French pension system – against resistance – and changed the relationships of state vs. private actors in the domain (Palier, 2007). While Lascoumes and Le Galès treat such changes mainly as "unintended structuring effects" (2007, p. 10f), Voß and Simons consider more intentional *power distributional politics* in processes of policy tool change. As instrument promotion inherently entails actors' (constituencies') envisioning of "shift[s] in responsibilities between governmental agencies or organizational departments", the adoption of a new tool may well become "a site of power politics in which expectations towards structural positions are negotiated" (Voß and Simons, 2014, p. 739). Research on the politics of evaluation agrees with this view of strategic power politics when assuming analytical models become a site for actors' attempts to further their positions of power and influence in a domain. Evaluation frameworks' appeal to actors, they argue, who are "manoeuvring for advantage and influence" and seeking to enhance "the influence of a particular division or department" (Weiss, 1973, p. 180f.). In a later contribution, critical evaluation scholar Carol Weiss (1993) specified her view on power politics, arguing that such "interagency and intraagency jockeying for advantage and influence" (p. 95) concerns both

1 abstract questions of relative power within and between public administration bodies and
2 substantial questions about whose values and normative premises get inscribed into an evaluation framework (p. 99).

Both readings of power distributional struggles through analytical tools – as meta-level struggles over decision-making powers as well as specific policy-related struggles over whose ideas shape policies (and their evaluation) – have also shaped actor-centered analysis of specific evaluation and benchmarking projects in international bureaucracies. Indeed, the understanding of analytical frameworks as tools through which actors advance their strategic positions in a policy domain is at the heart of the literature on European integration and international bureaucracies. For example, a recent study on the EU Commission's 2015 Better Regulation Reform concludes that, even if sold as a technical device for instrumental problem-solving and increased accountability, "the reform has contributed to the strategic actorness of the Commission as an international bureaucracy" (Jankauskas and Eckhard, 2019, p. 683). Along similar lines, Tholoniat (2010) argues that the infrastructure created with the OMCs – particularly related to central reporting requirements and comparative analytical capacity-building – has increased the decision-making capacities of EU institutions vis-à-vis member states *precisely* in policy domains where the EU has a limited mandate to act. Studies on RIA confirm that analytical tools may tilt the balance of power toward seemingly technocratic actors within the EU, such as the EU Commission's Secretariat (Radaelli and Meuwese, 2010). Rather than such dynamics being the "unintended structuring effects" of a benchmarking exercise, other studies have highlighted the EU's explicit wish to gain coordinating powers in weakly integrated policy domains (Paul, Bouder and Wesseling, 2016). Furthermore, research on EU border control policies indicates that the EU Commission embraces common risk analysis strategically to expand the supranational influence over member states' administrative decisions *de facto* in a *de jure* weakly integrated domain (Paul, 2017a) and that Frontex's risk-analytical capacities were central in claiming a more powerful executive mandate for the agency (Fjørtoft, 2020).

Based on these reflections, in addition to the more widely discussed logic of consequentiality and appropriateness, I expect administrations to pursue a logic of (expanding their) influence. Following this logic, they will conceive of analytical tools not only as means for rationalizing problem-solving and for legitimizing and in turn stabilizing their mandates. Administrative actors and policymakers may also adopt analytical tools where such tools – in their view – promise to facilitate their own power-seeking strategies and especially their wish to expand their mandate for and influence over collectively binding decision-making.

2.6 Conclusion

Through a review, critique, and systematic synthesis of disparate fields of research (on policy-making and policy change, public administration and policy tools, but also the politics of instrumentation and instrument constituencies), this chapter conceptualized analytical tools as socially constructed artifacts in which policymakers vest multiple meanings. I systematized the existing conceptualizations about these meanings from across so far unconnected silos of literature and thus forged one unified typology of analytical tools (cf. Figure 2.1). My typology proposes that actors' appreciative meaning-making about analytical tools has three distinct orientations: instrumental problem-solving (I); legitimacy-seeking (L); and power-seeking (P).

This implies that the appeals of analytical tools can be reconstructed with a threefold heuristic about the various logics guiding policymakers' interpretations: a logic of consequentiality, a logic of appropriateness, and a logic of influence.

With its re-focusing from policy-related problem-solving to polity policies, the ILP brings together so far disconnected ways of explaining why analytical tools appeal. In particular, public administration and public policy studies often treat analytical tools unidimensionally from an I, L, *or* (much less often) P perspective. This is also true of accounts that do not themselves adopt a rational choice ontology of policies but do, nonetheless, treat policy tools as instrumentally subordinated to the fulfilment of politically struggled over and ideationally situated policy goals (see Sections 2.2 and 2.3). Others have highlighted the multiple meanings vested in tools but remained silent or have not been explicit enough on their power distributional implications and motivations (cf. Section 2.1). Rather than ruling out any of these explanations from the outset or favoring one over others, an interpretivist account of analytical tools requires conceptual openness as to the expected weight of any of the three orientations in meaning-making processes. Indeed, the extent to which they matter in explaining policymakers' proclivity to adopt analytical tools remains, to a large extent, an empirical question.

Notes

1 (Lascoumes and Le Galès, 2007, p. 9).
2 A specific category of analytical tools which, unlike risk analysis or CBA, operate to assess policies ex-post rather than ex-ante.
3 This is not to be confused with the classic Weberian idea of Zweckrationalität as a structural feature of bureaucracies. Weber's notion concerns a type of decision-making in political-administrative systems that is structured by legally derived authority and subordination (rather than tradition or charisma, for example) (cf. the excellent discussion in Breuer, 1990). It does not focus on goal-rationality as the rationalisation of policy-making with the view of achieving a pre-set goal in an optimal manner.

3

RISK ANALYSIS AS A SEMIOTIC MAGIC BULLET

Societal risk management, institutional risk management, and governance by risk

> *Risk analysis . . . purports to be a science and to provide objective answers to problems of security that all rational people can agree upon.*[1]

Risk analysis has been with humans since ancient times – even the Athenians were familiar with the idea of assessing future consequences of policy actions and favored taking chances when major societal (or individual) benefits could be expected from a choice that may incur some harm (Aven, 2003). More recently, key social institutions such as mutual funds or insurance schemes, hence the modern welfare state itself, were born out of advances in risk assessment techniques (Ewald, 1986; O'Malley, 2004; Di Palma, 2013). Some researchers claim that to think systematically about risk is the essence of modernity, as the use of risk analysis in the development of policies, business management, and technology has not only replaced a pre-modern trust in the acts of Gods and fate but also provoked unprecedented waves – for better or worse from the respective accounts – of reflexive innovation (for the worse: Beck, 1992; for the better: Bernstein, 1996). However, the remarks on the exponential rise of risk analysis requirements in the EU (cf. Figure 1.2) suggest we live not only in a risk society but also in a *risk-analytical state* with risk analysis increasingly informing public decision-making.

At its basic, risk analysis examines "the likelihood of something bad happening, expressed as a percentage, as in '25 percent chance of rain'" (Stone, 2012, p. 131). Risk analysts combine calculations on how bad we expect an adverse event will be with how likely it is: the expected value of a danger (ibid.). As this chapter will argue, this kind of actuarial risk analysis resembles a magic bullet: it offers a whole bundle of perceived performance characteristics to those "shooting" with it. This is because the perceived objectiveness of risk analysis – as explained in the chapter's epigraph – can connect both to hopes of rational societal risk management

(Section 3.1) and to actors' attempts of rationalizing their own and others' relative positions in the policy domain (institutional risk management and governance by risk; Sections 3.2 and 3.3). Risk can be viewed both as a manageable event and as a decision-making heuristic (Paul, 2017b, p. 61; cf. Bora, 2007), thus offering a highly versatile analytical entry point for policymakers who need to engage with *both* problem-solving and polity policies.

This chapter elaborates the book's analytical framework further by (1) detailing the *specific merits* that administrators associate with risk analysis – most drawing on the ability of risk analysis to differentiate phenomena and therewith administrative action – and (2) categorizing these in terms of instrumental problem-solving, legitimacy-seeking, or power-seeking. It also discusses how variable appeals of risk analysis would translate into specific empirical applications. In so doing, the chapter develops sets of qualitative indicators[2] for each of the three ideal-typical considerations for the book's empirical analysis: (1) the administrative goals attached to risk analysis; (2) its empirical applications; and (3) its technical and organizational design (summaries at end of each section and in Table 3.1).

My operationalization of the ILP framework for risk analysis relies on an integrated review of otherwise widely scattered and highly interdisciplinary social sciences work across the fields of risk regulation, organizational sociology, risk governance and governmentality studies, and the sociology and history of quantification.[3] For those interested in risk analysis and quantification as part of their scholarly or practical activities, this chapter can be read as a free-standing text that

- offers the first integration and systematization of the fragmented and interdisciplinary literature on the role of risk analysis in public policy-making; and
- engages more substantially with the inherent logic of a distinct analytical tool and its variable interpretation in policymakers' sense-making processes (see Chapter 2).

3.1 Toward indicators for instrumental adoptions of risk analysis

Many regulation scholars draw on similar rational choice assumptions as do scholars of policy (tool) change (see Chapter 2) and explain the appeal of risk analysis in public administrations from an instrumentalist perspective. This draws on an information-theoretical interpretation of risk as a manageable event which can be regulated based on scientific analysis of probabilities and damage potential (Paul, 2017b, pp. 61–64). Rational choice accounts propose that "this simple mathematical formula – multiply the likelihood of an event by the magnitude of damages it would cause – should guide policymakers in deciding which problems merit policy priority" (Stone, 2012, p. 132). While critiqued for being ontologically and epistemologically flawed and normatively problematic in democratic societies (e.g., Stone, 2012, pp. 129–153; Douglas and Wildavsky, 1983; Shrader-Frechette, 1990; van Asselt and Renn, 2011; Haines, 2013), instrumental accounts of risk analysis in the literature describe potentially relevant rational problem-solving orientations among administrative actors. In particular, the search for cost-effective problem-solving, especially under conditions of uncertainty, renders risk analysis attractive because it can differentiate scenarios in the complex regulatory landscape systematically, thus creating evidence for priority setting in decision-making. Overall, from an instrumental perspective, risk analysis' ability to differentiate policy problems and interventions makes it a chief tool for rational societal risk management.

3.1.1 The efficiency and effectiveness goals of instrumental risk analysis

Three ontological positions inspire the claim of regulation scholars that risk analysis is and *ought* to be adopted because it enables more cost-effective risk management: (1) a belief in the dominance of functional problem-solving in public policy-making; (2) a view of risk problems as displaying irreducible uncertainty; and (3) a normative preference of (some) risk-taking over full risk aversion. It is important to spell these out because they are likely to shape policymakers' justifications for adopting risk-analytical frameworks for decision-making.

- First, hopes of gaining efficiency and effectiveness through risk analysis result from conceptualizing public administrators and regulators as instrumentally oriented actors who predominantly focus on solving societal risk problems. Instrumental views of risk analysis are common in parts of the literature on risk and regulation (Paul, 2017b), especially where risk regulation counts as a political strategy "designed to solve a problem, a goal-oriented practice for the purpose of reducing a tightly-defined and specific harm" (Haines, 2011, p. 10). I detail later how such instrumentality claims around risk analysis unfold.
- Second, regulatory decision-making in a complex world is said to face irreducible uncertainties (Renn, 2008; Majone, 2010; Rothstein, Borraz and Huber, 2011). Risk regulators have no exact way of telling, for instance, just how carcinogenic a new substance is in specific organisms and how many actual (rather than statistical) workers will develop cancers from being exposed to the substance in the production process. Majone (2010, p. 97f), for example, describes the "trans-scientific" features of most animal testing used to extrapolate dose-response relationships and castigates such experiments as being notoriously flawed pieces of guesswork. Similarly, administrators cannot predict for certain how well different companies will comply with existing work safety regulation and whether accidents or diseases will follow from firms' variable compliance behavior. Even when public administrators are oriented to cost-effective problem-solving, uncertainty may jeopardize the success of policy interventions, both ontologically and epistemologically (see a radical view on this: Chandler, 2014).
- Third, related to the previous claim, scholars increasingly doubt whether regulatory attempts at reducing societal risks to zero are even desirable. Some argue

that "absolute safety cannot be a sensible regulatory goal" (Majone, 2010, p. 94) and that "well-designed policies should not eliminate the diversity of risks and strive for a no-risk society" (Viscusi, 1983, p. 167). According to this view, uncertainty implies that absolute safety can never be achieved in the first place and that – more importantly – any attempt of eliminating risk would not only be doomed to fail but also require a disproportionate use of public resources as well as stringent regulations for businesses. Such a view is in line with promotions of self-aware risk-taking on behalf of governments and society as a liberating and entrepreneurial process, which can boost innovation and economic growth (Bernstein, 1996; Sunstein, 2009). This premise of necessary risk tolerance also shifts the focus of instrumentality itself. Rather than concerning actual outcomes, that is, the successful prevention of risks, an administration's instrumental choice of risk analysis would tend to focus on the cost-effectiveness of risk-related decisions.

3.1.2 The use of risk analysis as differentiation and priority-setting mechanism

How exactly can risk analysis, from an information-theoretical perspective on risk, help decision makers achieve cost-effectiveness goals? Majone's (2010) notion of "procedural rationality" helps develop this point further. When faced with uncertainty-riddled risk decisions, Majone argues, differentiating scenarios through risk analysis on the severity and likelihood of adverse events infuses rational systematicity into decision rules – based on the best available knowledge – even if outcomes themselves remain unpredictable. Majone proposes the design of a common and sufficiently detailed probabilistic formula for risk decisions – distinguishing between high-risk scenarios for urgent intervention, medium-risk for targeted risk reduction strategies, and low-risk scenarios can go without public intervention. Risk levels are thus directly linked to the urgency of the intervention, implying a risk-based logic of priority setting during decision-making.

Furthermore, several effectiveness gains are associated with systematic risk-based differentiation. To apply the same risk formula across regulatory issues, Majone argues, among others (Viscusi, 1983, 1995; Wiener, 2010), will make risk-related decision-making more consistent by avoiding over- and under-regulation, excessive compliance costs, or the unequal treatment of regulatees (cf. the wider discussion of the British "smart state" and "risk state" in Moran, 2003). In addition, independent and scientific risk analysis is believed to counter (allegedly undesirable) political biases and help de-politicize decision-making in a way that is beneficial to the society at large (cf. Sunstein, 2002). Risk-based forms of regulation and enforcement thus "become technical matters of calculation, policy-oriented scientific discourses that transcend political contests" (Tombs and Whyte, 2013, p. 67). While attempts to disguise the political nature of risk analysis have been criticized (e.g., Shrader-Frechette, 1990; Stone, 2012), such de-politicization may well be desirable for administrators from a problem-solving viewpoint. In a similar vein, risk-based differentiation can help forge common problem perceptions and paths of action among a diverse set of actors with potentially divergent political agendas and interests. For example, common risk analysis can help newly established regulatory authorities, especially those drawn together from different regulatory bodies, to create a collective identity and view on regulatory priorities (Black, 2010).

Concentrating on the worst cases, probabilistically speaking, is also deemed preferable from an efficiency perspective. For example, the British Hampton Review, a document propagating the wide application of risk analysis and risk-based decision-making in the public sector, argues that the approach helped reducing inspections by a third – thus saving many tax pounds – without compromising on effectiveness (Hampton, 2005; but see: Tombs and Whyte, 2013). It is argued that reduced inspection and enforcement loads and the related efficiency gains can go hand in hand with more effective regulation, precisely because high impact issues (e.g., explosions or asbestos in workplaces) and frequent non-compliers (i.e., employers whose behavior increases the likelihood of bad things happening) can be specifically targeted while resources can be saved on low-risk issues. According to the British Better Regulation Commission, a risk-based strategy for planning interventions can also help identify risks that are more efficiently dealt with by firms, private individuals, civil society, or lower levels of government rather than by central or state efforts and spending (Black, 2010). Similar efficiency-seeking motivations drove Kip Viscusi's (1983, p. 81) early warning that governments involved in risk regulation "should not adopt any policy whose cost exceeds its benefits". A close link between risk regulation and the use of CBA has been established both in the US (under Ronald Reagan's administration in 1981) and in the UK (streamlined via the Health and Safety Executive since the 1980s). As we report elsewhere (Rothstein et al., 2019), the UK successfully countered allegations by the EU Commission over its qualification of an EU Directive's absolute work safety goals with a risk-cost trade-off argument at the European Court of Justice. The Health and Safety Executive (HSE) (1989, p. 17) insisted that it is "impossible to eliminate all [workplace] risks" and, therefore, better to ensure that the cost, time, and effort required to reduce risk is not grossly disproportionate to the benefit gained.

The strategy of risk-based differentiation for efficiency and effectiveness gains is not limited to the UK or the US, though forerunners of risk-based strategies (cf. Chapter 4) and keen promoters of such approaches at the international level (e.g., on the entrepreneurial role of the British Health and Safety Executive: Rothstein et al., 2019). For example, when the Netherlands saw mergers of inspectorates in the 2000s, cross-sectoral risk analysis counted as a means for efficient priority-setting across previously divided domains in the new super inspectorates (Paul et al., 2017). Equally, according to internal calculations in the German state labor inspectorates, the number of inspectors decreased by almost a third from 4,103 inspectors in 2004 to 3,029 in 2010 (excel sheet informally shared with the author). Similar pressures on staff and budgets apply in labor inspectorates across the globe, as the International Labor Organisation (ILO) minutes:

> *Tight resources, increased public expectation, increasing workloads and some fundamental questioning of principles and ways of working . . . have led to . . . initiatives being undertaken within inspectorates under the general areas of increasing efficiency and maximizing the impact of work.*
>
> *(International Labour Organization, 2011, p. 14f)*

Accordingly, a recent report by an OECD inspections expert appreciates risk analysis' capacity to differentiate phenomena and related interventions:

> *All inspectorates have to be selective – the only question is whether to be selective "by default" (trying to check everything and in fact failing, thus noticing things at random) or "on purpose" – analysing where are the highest probabilities of serious harm, and concentrating on these. There is very strong consensus that random inspections . . . are poor options – the latter one being . . . excessively costly for the state and businesses. Risk-focused inspections are the way to go.*
>
> *(Blanc, 2014, p. 72)*

The focus on risk analysis as a tool for societal risk management comes with specific technical and organizational requirements from the perspective of its promoters, including the creation of independent risk assessment units that are organizationally separate from risk management (to avoid political bias), the development of a single and comprehensive template for risk analysis with a sufficiently specific risk formula (to differentiate in a manner that enables priority setting), and the development of clear guidelines for risk analysis and priority setting for enforcement units (OECD, 2010; cf. a similar discussion of indicators for RIA: Radaelli, 2010).

3.1.3 Indicators for actors' instrumental orientations toward risk analysis

Overall, an instrumental perspective – in the ideal-typical sense – would tend to see risk analysis as "an economically rational decision-making instrument for managing the uncertainties that are inherent in any regulatory intervention" (Rothstein, Borraz and Huber, 2011, p. 188). Administrators would cherish its perceived potential to optimize the use of public resources – based on the systematic differentiation of risk levels and a related priority setting – when a focus on fully achieving regulatory safety goals is deemed both unrealistic and/or (economically) undesirable (Rothstein, Borraz and Huber, 2013, p. 217). Beyond such views on cost-effectiveness, however, instrumental turns to risk analysis are – less often – also associated with collective problem-solving and the formation of shared models for priority setting among diverse actors.

Eventually, an ideal-typical instrumental turn to risk analysis will be shaped by actors' *goals* of

- efficiency and effectiveness gains
- mainstreaming societal acceptance that risks cannot and ought not be reduced to zero
- avoidance of (political) bias in assessment and management of risks
- shaping collective agreement about regulatory priorities

In *empirical applications*, instrumental risk analysis will fulfil the following roles:

- development of differentiated risk scenarios
- priority setting in intervention planning and spending

The *technical/organizational design* of an instrumentally minded risk analysis will involve:

- creation of specifically designated risk analysis units and/or independent advisory councils within departments
- design of a single, detailed template for risk analysis, including harmonized formula for the assessment of impact and likelihood of adverse events
- detailed guidance on design and use of risk analysis for enforcement units (e.g., development of "how-to guides", training programs, and common software solutions)

3.2 Toward indicators for legitimacy-seeking adoptions of risk analysis

The reign of instrumental problem-solving as the dominant appeal of risk analysis has been doubted since the publication of Mary Douglas and Aaron Wildavsky's *Risk and Culture* (1983). Their work lays down the foundation to understand the inevitable cultural biases in the definition and management of risks by comparing pre-modern and modern "pollution beliefs" and the attempt at regulating them.[4] Douglas and Wildavsky highlight the continuous relevance of the categories of blame and liability in the management of events that a society perceives as adverse and harmful. Much of the debate about legitimacy-seeking orientations to risk analysis gravitates around such processes of "laying blame at someone's door" (Douglas and Wildavsky, 1983, p. 38) and, more precisely, administrations' attempts of managing and minimizing the risk of being blamed. To elaborate how risk analysis addresses actors' considerations of "institutional self-interest" and the stability and legitimacy of an organization (Peters, 2002, p. 557f), this section introduces the notion of *institutional risk management* in which public administrations use risk analysis to define "the parameters of blame" (Black, 2005, p. 520), thus signaling the "limits of governance" and their own accountability for failure (Rothstein, Borraz and Huber, 2013). With this perspective, we also leave the information-theoretical perspective on risk behind and enter the terrain of a decision-theoretical concept; since risk-related decision-making can fail and such failures attributed to regulators, "the latter are likely to welcome rationalization to legitimate their decision-making" (Paul, 2017b, p. 68, cf. pp. 66–69).

3.2.1 The goal of institutional risk management

Several scholars have challenged the actuarial concept of risk analysis and promoted a legitimacy-oriented reading instead. Regulation scholar Haines (2011; 2013), for example, distinguishes between actuarial, sociocultural, and political risk concepts, arguing that risk analyses of the sociocultural and political kind adhere to legitimacy-seeking than problem-solving; the former does so with a view to what seems acceptable in terms of social norms, while the latter considers "the legitimacy of those who claim some form of authority over the collective" (Haines, 2013, p. 40). Stone's (2012, pp. 129–153) discussion of security as a policy objective equally problematizes instrumental accounts of risk analysis. While "in the scientific ideal, analysts recognize that perfect security is unachievable" (p. 133) and apply actuarial risk analysis to plan cost-effective interventions that can reduce harm, there is also a powerful "political ideal" of security according to which "politicians prevent bad things from happening by making good policy" (p. 132). Furthermore, Black argues that due to the methodological limits and normative biases of risk analysis, it would be unwise to expect instrumentalism to explain risk analysis' triumphal procession into many domains of public decision-making. Rather, she suggests, our analyses should focus on administrators' legitimacy-related motivations "to have a risk-based framework has increasingly become a badge of legitimacy for a regulator" (Black, 2010, p. 332; cf. also Baldwin and Black, 2016).

These claims resonate with a growing number of regulation and organizational sociology scholars, who conceptualize risk analysis as a strategy to defend organizations' mandate, activities, and decision-making processes against the expectations of those who are able to lay blame at their door (Black, 2010). Risk analysis becomes a way of managing accountability relationships in the public realm. Rather than merely targeting rational problem-solving with respect to specific "societal risks" and related uncertainty (as assumed in most instrumentalist accounts), risk analysis can help manage "institutional risks"– that is, legitimacy risks hinging on perceptions of organizational performance and accountability (Rothstein, Huber and Gaskell, 2006, pp. 99–103). This is especially relevant in contexts wherein regulators and administrators are held accountable for outcomes over which they have limited control.

Whatever the reasons for lack of control over outcomes,[5] the important point to take away from this debate is that perceived failures to meet risk-regulatory objectives "create institutional risks that can threaten the legitimacy of governance organisations" (Rothstein, Borraz and Huber, 2013, p. 217). This means that the potential failure to achieve societal risk management goals such as safe working conditions or safe food will be reflected upon ex-ante in executive decision-making. Organizations see in risk analysis "an attractive concept for rationalising the practical limits of what regulation can achieve and rendering given degrees of regulatory failure acceptable" (Rothstein, Huber and Gaskell, 2006, p. 99f). Failure is not only anticipated ex-ante but defined as acceptable[6] for certain types and levels of risk. Unlike in Majone's account of rational procedural rules for decisions, however, a risk-analytical innovation in pursuit of institutional risk management will not primarily focus on efficiency and effectiveness goals (even though to talk about these goals in public may be a badge of legitimacy in its own right, of course). Rather, it appeals to administrative actors for its perceived ability to manage expectations about what an administration *should* achieve vis-à-vis risks and uncertainty and, ultimately, to preserve the legitimacy of public administration bodies in the eyes of relevant beholders when accidents and disasters strike or when harmful non-compliance goes undiscovered. It is in this sense that risk analysis can be perceived as a tool for stabilizing existing regulatory mandates, which is in line with my ideal and typical view of legitimacy-seeking discussed in Chapter 2.

3.2.2 The use of risk analysis for defining the "parameters of blame"

How exactly does risk analysis facilitate institutional risk management in empirical applications? The wider social sciences literature on risk identifies two ways in which risk-based legitimacy-seeking can take place: (1) risk-based differentiation simultaneously constitutes and limits the regulatory role of the public administration and thereby defines the terms on which it should, and should not, be blamed for adverse outcomes; this differentiation strategy seems attractive to legitimacy-seeking actors because (2) trust in quantification techniques is generally high in political decision-making. Risk assessments create a strong backbone for claiming legitimacy irrespective of their scientific rigor. I detail the first point in this section and the second point in the next.

Many scholars of risk regulation have argued that *the differentiating logic of risk analysis* enables administrative bodies (or any organization) to define and refine the terms on which they or others should be blamed for adverse outcomes. Such differentiation is possible as most risk analyses in the administrative realm simplify the more complex actuarial calculations by transforming them into three-tiered schematic visualizations. The so-called risk carrot (see Figure 3.1), sometimes also called the traffic-light model, is popular; it differentiates between a high-risk level wherein risks are unacceptable, a medium-risk level wherein risks are tolerable but should normally be reduced, and a low-risk level wherein adverse outcomes are acceptable. This differentiation enables administrators to identify, and publicly announce, areas of priority intervention (red), areas where risks will be reduced further if this seems apt, given the cost and effort required to do so (amber), and areas where further risk reduction is not a governmental priority (green) (cf. discussion of models of risk acceptability and tolerability in Bouder, Slavin and Löfstedt, 2007).

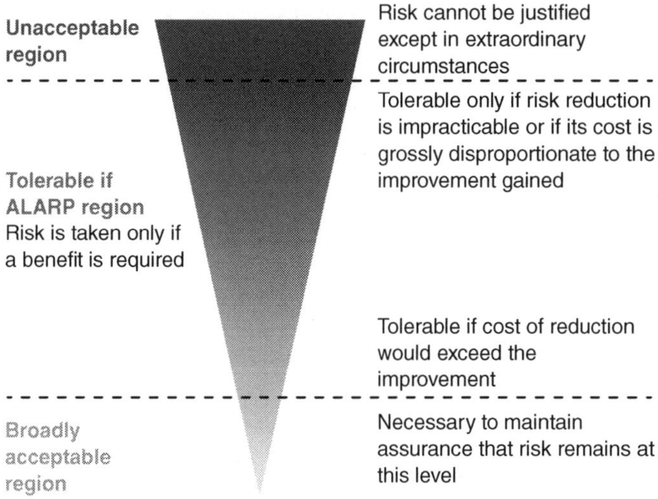

FIGURE 3.1 The risk carrot

Source: TÜV Rheinland and Risktec (2018, p. 8; cf. Health and Safety Executive, 2001, p. 42)

While informing instrumental uses of risk analysis as cost-effectiveness tests, as discussed earlier, the ex-ante rationalization of risk interventions also helps legitimize administrative actions. It infers, often very explicitly so in accompanying policy discourse, that administrators should not be blamed for bad things occurring ex-post in the green and parts of the amber regions of the risk carrot. This usually works without administrators necessarily having to invoke the scientific evidence for the differentiation of risk levels in the first place (see next section). As Black (2010, p. 336f) notes, "regulators use their risk-based systems in an attempt to define the terms on which they should be made accountable, and in effect to define the parameters of blame", they try to ensure that "they should not be expected to prevent every negative occurrence . . . and . . . that they should not be blamed for all those that occur".

This goes beyond mere mandate defense and can involve the pro-active carving out of a regulatory mandate in two ways. First, and more generally, risk analysis helps administrative bodies define their own responsibilities as risk-based differentiation facilitates the "ex-ante rationalisation of the limits of what governance interventions can, and *should*, seek to achieve" (Rothstein, Borraz and Huber, 2013, p. 217 highlight added by author). By stating upfront the risks they can and cannot control and want to and do not want to tackle, administrative bodies seek to (1) arm themselves against potentially de-legitimizing the blame for not avoiding bad things from happening later on, but also (2) to actively carve out the legitimate contours of their interventions. An example is the British HSE, which has been at the forefront of defining the "parameters of blame" by use of risk analysis (Demeritt et al., 2015). When under pressure to cut costs during waves of deregulation and austerity programs, the HSE used its long-established risk tolerability framework not only to become even more cost-effective in the instrumental sense; the regulator also saw in it a means for clearly identifying – and communicating toward politicians and the public – the extended limits of its own regulatory scope in a climate of scarcity (Paul et al., 2017).

3.2.3 "Trust in numbers" and the appropriateness of broad-brush risk analysis

The perceived legitimacy-enhancing capacities of risk analysis are founded on wider set of claims about "trust in numbers" (Porter, 1995). These suggest that the design of risk analysis does not even have to be rigorous to fulfil goals of institutional risk management. I will detail this logic briefly, as it matters greatly for the empirical identification of legitimacy-seeking in analytical tool change. Porter describes quantification in administrative decision-making – risk-based or otherwise – as a strategy of overcoming a lack of ascribed expertise to do the job. Where authority cannot, or can no longer be claimed based on professional training, expertise, and judgment alone, quantification becomes an important "technology of trust" (p. 15):

> *A decision made by the numbers (or by explicit rules of some other sort) has at least the appearance of being fair and impersonal. Scientific objectivity . . . provides an answer to a moral demand for impartiality and fairness. Quantification is a way of making decisions without seeming to decide. Objectivity lends authority to officials who have very little of their own.*
>
> *(Porter, 1995, p. 8)*

Numbers appeal, according to Porter, because "[t]hey provide legitimacy for administrative actions, in large parts because they provide standards against which people judge themselves" and their performance (p. 45). Drawing on the work of Jasanoff, Porter highlights that a culture of adversarial litigation in the US has created a climate of mistrust toward the administration in which numerical justification could blossom particularly well (Porter, 1995, pp. 194–199). Legitimation by numbers appeals in contexts where there is a widespread mistrust of an administrative body or regulator and where the accountability pressure on their mandate is particularly high. Boswell (2018) develops a similar argument about how measurement – by signaling rigor, commitment and the willingness to be held accountable against numbers – can generate political trust in a public administration (but she also explores the problems of discursive lock-ins to constant performance measurement for the British case).

Porter's vivid example is the introduction of CBA in the early 19th century by the US Army Corps of Engineers – a body responsible for planning and executing drainage, levee, and canal projects (also see Chapter 4). Unlike usually suggested by instrumental accounts today, the initial adoption of CBA was not at all related to hopes of efficiency gains but was "an attempt to create a basis for mutual accommodation in a context of suspicion and disagreement" (p. 148). In an environment "of political pressure and administrative conflict . . . cost-benefit methods were introduced to promote procedural regularity and to give public evidence of fairness in the selection of water projects" (p. 149). In this reading, the Corps turned to quantification because they could not rely on a great deal of externally ascribed authority in an administrative climate of "utter disunity and savage infighting" (ibid.). CBA became a strategy of convincing Congress, the Courts, and potential opponents in competing departments that the Corps' funding decisions on water projects were reasonable, fair, and politically unbiased. It became a tool for legitimating the Corps as a public actor.

While Porter uses the example of CBA, analogous claims have emerged for risk analysis, too. Actuarial assessment offers a way of quantifying phenomena and generating seemingly objective options for otherwise contested decision-making. Indeed, the well-charted methodological and practical limits to rigorous problem-oriented risk analysis (Black, 2010) *do not* impede its widespread application in "justify[ing] governmental regulation" (ibid.: p. 314). Hutter (2005) argues that risk analysis can legitimize administrative action not because of its rigor but because it is commonly accepted as an appropriate, business-like way of justifying choices: "their apparent objectivity and transparency could be used to explain the allocation of resources, in a way which was well tested and trusted by the business community" (p. 2f). These readings resonate with the arguments of institutional isomorphism, especially mimicry, rehearsed in Chapter 2 (DiMaggio and Powell, 1983).

Central to Porter, Black, and Hutter's analyses is the observation that the actual scientific rigor of CBA or risk analysis does not matter much for the fulfilment of their legitimizing promises. Indeed, Porter (1995, p. 158) describes a strong "implicit faith" among political decision makers in the Corps' CBA reports and the political independence of the Corps. Anecdotes about parliamentary hearings – where Congress may well have inquired the numbers and "asked many factual questions" about CBA, "but it rarely mattered what the answer was" (Porter, 1995, p. 157) – indicate that the authority of the Corps' decisions hinged on a generic trust in numerical assessment. Numbers were perceived as a more objective foundation for decisions than mere professional judgment (a similar argument is developed for the case of performance targets in the UK public administration by Boswell, 2018). However, parliamentary or judicial reviews did not usually provoke any detailed engagement with the assumptions and methodological decisions that underpinned any one CBA.

In summary, "trust in numbers" amounts to a rather unquestioned faith in the legitimacy of numerically founded decisions. The design of a risk analysis template and its ability to solve risk problems will thus be secondary to its rhetorical/symbolic ability to convince critiques of a fair and rational decision-making process. In terms of policy design, where administrators are mainly worried about the legitimacy of their mandates rather than the alleged problem-solving functions of risk analysis, there will be less reason to invest in the depth, uniformity, and scientific rigor of their risk-analysis template.

3.2.4 Indicators for actors' legitimacy-seeking orientations toward risk analysis

Overall, legitimacy-seeking orientations toward risk analysis pursue institutional risk management goals. Risk-based differentiation will be used to define the limits of one's own accountability and "blameability" vis-à-vis others. As cost-effectiveness is not the chief goal here, the need to design a detailed, uniform, and scientifically rigorous model for risk analysis is lower than in problem-solving contexts.

Legitimacy-seeking turns to risk analysis will feature the following goals:

- institutional risk management
- limiting potential to be blamed for adverse outcomes or shifting blame to others

In *empirical applications*, legitimacy-oriented risk analysis fulfils the following roles:

- differentiation of risk scenarios to signal fair, objective, and effective problem-solving to others
- risk-related signaling of one's limits of accountability for adverse outcomes

The *technical/organizational design* of legitimacy-oriented risk analysis will involve the following:

- no strong focus on scientific rigor and independence
- broad and/or alternative risk analysis templates with room for discretion (including for the assessment of likelihood and impact of adverse events)
- relatively broad guidance on design and use of risk analysis, leaving room for discretion.

3.3 Toward indicators for power-seeking adoptions of risk analysis

To discuss administrations' power-seeking orientations toward risk analysis triggers the wider question of how "tools of quantification advance the capacities of public administrations . . . in terms of being able to monitor and steer?" (Mennicken and Lodge, 2015, p. 8). This section turns to the critical social sciences literature on quantification which highlights how power can be wielded by statistical reasoning, accounting, and analytical models. In these debates, risk analysis often features as an enabler of governance and population control in the Foucauldian sense. By expanding the view of the "population" to be controlled from regulatees to actors within the public administration, my reading tweaks the usual argument toward a more explicit political science focus on polity policies: I suggest that central level administrative actors appreciate risk analysis as a way to pursue harmonized and consistent decision-making across the administration. This is either because a common risk analysis template can increase their control over other actors' pre-disposition in decision-making coercively and/or because they can use the outcomes of their own actuarial assessments to create incentives for other actors to voluntarily align their enforcement strategies.

3.3.1 Goals of governmental monitoring and steering

Almost as long as Foucault's governmentality framework exists, risk analysis (alongside other quantification methods) has been analyzed, explicitly or in a more loosely inspired manner, as an attempt for "governing by numbers" (Rose, 1991). At their most basic, governmentality approaches assume that statistics and other numerical simplification strategies are a key governance technology, – in Foucauldian terminology – which enables states to ensure governability in the first place. As Nikolas Rose's (1991, p. 675) highlights:

> *The organisation of political life in the form of the modern state has been intrinsically linked to the composition of networks of numbers connecting those exercising political power with the persons, processes and problems that they seek to govern.*

Such a link between quantified knowledge of a population and a state's ambition to govern it unfolds its influence, scholars argue, because quantification transforms "complex processes [in]to simple numerical indicators and rankings for purposes of management and control" (Shore and Wright, 2015, p. 22). This is precisely what Scott (though not a declared Foucauldian himself), in *Seeing Like a State* (1998, p. 22ff), describes as a process of rendering "legible", hence governable, the social world by transforming social facts from "raw" to "cooked", from complex qualitative relationships to simplified numerical representations. Scott's examples include the invention of "normal trees" in Prussian forestry science as a standard for commercially usable trees and also the invention of the metric system and cadastral maps for administrative information gathering and population control (e.g., mainly in the form of tax collection). His argument is that without these forms of numerical simplification and standardization, administrative control is weak – especially on central levels of government – if not altogether impossible. He shows, for example, how the goal of effectively taxing property relies upon the representation of messy lots of land in neat cadastral (metrical) maps. In short, "no effective central monitoring. . . [was] possible without standard, fixed units of measurement" (Scott, 1998, p. 30).

The association of the sciences of numerical calculation with population control agendas is not coincidental. Scholars have stressed the strong link – historical and contemporary – between the rise of quantification techniques on the one hand and administrative goals on the other. Some even suggest that

> *there can be no well-ordered political machinery or enlightened administration . . . without a knowledge of the state of the population, and the numbering of persons, goods, activities, births, crimes, deaths and much else provides the material on which administrative calculation can operate.*
>
> (Rose, 1991, p. 676)

Indeed, Desroisières' social history of statistics in *The Politics of Large Numbers* (2002), using examples from England, France, Germany, and the US, teaches us that statistics has risen since the 17th century at various places as the *combination* of developing quantification methods in the natural sciences and specific administrative practices. Statistics serves specific administrative (rather than scientific) needs and goals. The author discusses, for instance, the development of "political arithmetic" in 17th-century England – the intellectual parent of modern day statistics – which was motivated by a desire to know the population "on average" so as to act upon this calculated and calculable population judicially and administratively (Desrosières, 2002, p. 23). For example, to collect taxes or to identify and manage criminals or the mentally ill.[7]

Foucauldian scholars have expanded the general idea of external administrative control to discuss how quantification entices technologies of self-control precisely by aligning peoples' ideas of what constitutes normal and proper behavior with numerical averages and standards. In addition to stressing the facilitation of administrative control by numerical mapping, most historians and sociologists interested in quantification emphasize the constructive potential of numerical simplification (cf. Desrosières, 2002, p. 3). Miller and Rose (1990) argue, for example, that " 'intellectual technologies' . . . render aspects of existence amenable to inscription and calculation", making them governable in the first place (Miller and Rose, 1990, p. 3). In their review of critical accounting studies, for example, Mennicken and Miller (2012) stress that accounting and other quantification techniques can create wholly new subjectivities that enable new forms and modalities of governance. Accounting models constitute organizations as "competing, market-oriented entities" as organizations internalize the notions of competition and being accountable in efficiency-related ways, implied in accounting models, and use them to re-align their daily actions (ibid., p. 12). Therefore, quantification serves to put responsibility on individuals for regulatory outcomes and performance (on the de-solidarizing effects of this, see Mau, 2017). In this interpretation, risk analysis, comparative risk matrices, and risk carrots turn regulatees into analytical objects whose performance in terms of risk can be anticipated, compared (high, medium, low), and acted upon with differential regulation and enforcement decisions by the administration.

Overall, Foucault-inspired readings of quantification suggest that administrations use numerical calculation to make "legible", and hence more governable, populations and policy domains that are otherwise hard to control. This includes an external control dimension, where the administration uses models and standards to design and enforce policy and an internal dimension where those regulated by state policies internalize the normalizing logics of averages, standards, or the distinction of "low"- vs. "high"-risk levels and control their behavior, so that it falls into categories of average, standard, or low risk.

The dominant Foucauldian reading of quantification as *gouvernmentale* technology of self-control is fruitful not only in the sense discussed so far but also in the understanding of how risk analysis can substantiate actors' control ambitions. In the next section, I propose a twist in the above reading of the power-seeking appeal of risk analysis. Rather than being limited to governing populations in the sense of responsibilizing regulatees, actuarial quantification is also a tool for administrative actors to coerce onto, or entice among, the autonomous actors within administrative settings shared frameworks for decision-making.

3.3.2 Uses of risk analysis as (soft) coercion

First, given the lack of control of any one actor – including central government – over all enforcement decisions (and not just for the interdependent actors in the multi-level settings which this book focuses on from Chapter 4 onward), risk analysis, and risk-based interventions have been associated with administration's desire to increase "internal management controls over supervisors or inspectors" (Black, 2010, p. 331). This is because the risk-analytical differentiation "provides top-down reformers with an objective framework for standardizing how far government should go to prevent possible harm" (Demeritt et al., 2017, p. 4).

British regulators, for example, have come to appreciate risk-based regulation frameworks as "consistent guidance on priority setting [. . .] [and a means] for coordinating and rationalizing inspections of local authorities" (Hampton, 2005, p. 75). A comparative study on risk-based work safety inspections in four European countries indicates that both the British and French applications of risk analysis were chiefly concerned with rendering local enforcement decisions more consistent not only for reasons of efficient problem-solving but also to curb the discretion of front-line inspectors (Paul et al., 2017). Discussing RIA, Claudio Radaelli (2010, p. 170) stated that "the major implication of the adoption of cost-benefit analysis is not efficiency, but increased control of the agencies".

This implies that like the internalization of actuarial assessment models and their normative underpinnings by regulatees, highlighted in post-structuralist work, risk analysis can pursue the goal of streamlining enforcement decisions via centrally imposed notions of acceptable and unacceptable risks, adverse effects, and administrative failures. In the spirit of behavioral policy-making, actors' hope that common assessment will trigger common priority setting. Governments' wish to design "mostly soft forms of paternalism or, in other words, non-mandatory behaviour change" (Oliver, 2017, p. 1; cf. Straßheim and Beck, 2019a) thus includes analytical tools as instruments that can "pre-dispose" (Balla, 1998) autonomous actors' use of their bureaucratic discretion in enforcement. For example, experiments with local planning authorities have shown that the color coding of maps for flooding or wildfire risks affects authorities' likelihood to comply with risk regulation (Cheong et al., 2016; Seipel and Lim, 2017). Such behavioral information helps central governments manipulate visual clues on maps in a manner that "predisposes" local policymakers to perceive risk levels without political bias (e.g., where an area targeted for economic development is shown in dark red on a map) and engage in more effective risk management. This application of risk analysis would require central level design and top-down coercion of a rather detailed common risk analysis template onto other actors. In addition, detailed guidance for the use of risk analysis in enforcement decisions would accompany such a harmonization.

Second, however, numerical models, which provide common procedural templates for enforcement, can also entice more indirect harmonization of executive decisions among autonomous actors. In addition to mimetic emulation among independent administrative actors, among independent administrative actors, there are instances where central administrative bodies actively foster (though are unable to impose) the streamlining of executive decisions through forms of soft coercion which do not impose risk analysis on other actors but use the results of risk analysis to create risk-based incentive structures.

I develop this argument further based on Desrosières' (2002, chapters 1 and 6) discussion of the historical development of *Statistik* in 17th-century Germany, already featuring in the book's introduction. The German word "*Statistik*" had little to do with our contemporary understanding of the term. With the word "*Staat*" or state at its etymological core, *Statistik* or *Staatenkunde* (the sciences of states) had two main goals: (1) the holistic identification of sub-states on the German territory and (2) the facilitation of comparisons of states' individual features (such as climate, population, economic development, customs, or laws). Cross tables, which included qualitative information alongside numerical values, were used for this purpose. Only partly relying on quantification initially, the "systematic cataloguing" (p. 20) of state-related information pursued the purpose of "identifying the states" (p. 19), comparing and acting upon them centrally *without* centralizing authorities per se. In a highly fragmented administrative setting, these first (limited) attempts at quantification were not so much related to the vertical control of the bureaucracy – there was no lever for such control at a time when Germany was split up into over 300 individual states. Rather, comparative analytics were perceived as a chief requirement for the creation of a common though differential "we", which could advance horizontal economic and political coordination (a precursor of the German constitutional norm of "legal-administrative unity", which developed shortly after the invention of Statistik, as discussed in Chapter 4).

Actors can expand the scope of soft coercion mechanisms when they couple analytical models with existing (or new) incentive structures. To stick with the multi-colored wildfire maps, the red (high-risk) zones qualify for access to Federal or EU support for funding prevention measures, while the other zones do not. This informally rearranges policy-making responsibilities between the center and subnational actors with the former gaining influence over high-risk phenomena that it has itself defined as such. My own work on risk analysis in the EU border controls also indicates that the EU Commission[8] uses actuarial quantification models strategically in funding decisions vis-à-vis member states to harmonize national enforcement in a domain marked by a weak supranational mandate (Paul, 2017a). While analytical harmonization on its own may remain weak and rely on "naming and shaming" dynamics at best (though the OMC debate highlights the power of such communicative techniques), its coupling with financial incentives can institutionalize analysis-based priority setting for decision makers across the multi-level setting in even more substantial ways, potentially fostering harmonization of executive decision-making along the lines favored by the center without changing the de jure structure of the polity. Risk analysis could also serve as a rhetorical weapon where reporting duties on the outcome of risk analysis and its strategic use in priority setting exist toward higher administrative levels through benchmarking exercises and comparative performance measurements. Non-coercive and yet centrally induced harmonization processes have, for example, been observed in the context of the OECD's rankings of educational performance with the famous PISA studies (Grek, 2009; Martens and Jakobi, 2010; Martens and Niemann, 2013).

Depending on the policy domain under scrutiny, dynamics of centrally stimulated harmonization may originate both from the EU – where relevant quantification impulses come from Brussels – and a national government's attempts to influence enforcement decisions of other autonomous actors within the administration. As Rose (1991, p. 667) highlights, the European view of the relation between numbers and politics has been heavily influenced by the German *Staatenkunde* and the deliberate attempt to survey and control the individual states. As measurement techniques "have jumped scale", – they are no longer confined to the nation state and its administrative capacity-building but are increasingly used by transnational and supranational actors such as the OECD, World Bank, and the EU (Shore and Wright, 2015, p. 23; cf. Martens and Jakobi, 2010) – the very nation states that invented statistics to control their populations and autonomous actors in the administrative setting are now experiencing what numbers and analytics have "done to them".

In this context, Lascoumes and Le Galès (2007, p. 17) argue that any one (analytical) tool's appearance as technocratic or instrumental to problem-solving may in fact be a deliberate strategy for actors to hide power-seeking rationales: "the proliferation of instruments [is] a way of dissipating the political questions" about fought-over policy goals or the distribution of power within a domain. Such dynamics, others agree, may not be easily discerned at first glance because the "structural promises are not part of the functional set-up of instruments, and are usually not publicly proclaimed" (Voß and Simons, 2014, p. 739). This concurs with critical research on the rise of evidence-based policy-making and related de-politicization effects (Straßheim and Kettunen, 2014; Straßheim, 2017; more generally: Stone, 2012, 2020). Ostensibly technocratic policy tools and analytical approaches for problem-solving may hence play a major part in administrators' attempt to depoliticize and disguise their power political efforts. My research on risk analysis in European border control highlighted, for example, that the EU Commission's ambition to harmonize and steer nationally sovereign enforcement practices crucially hinges on the technical guise of risk analysis. It is *because* risk analysis seems innocent and technocratic to member states that they have accepted and followed the Commission's recommendations for improvements, otherwise a political hot potato (Paul, 2017a).

3.3.3 Indicators for actors' power-seeking orientations toward risk analysis

In summary, power-seeking adoptions of risk analysis pursue central level actors' goal of steering decisions among autonomous administrative bodies, including cases where there is no formal executive prerogative to do so. While Chapter 4 will detail these arguments for the different contextual conditions of strong regulatory agencies vs. settings with a diffusion of executive powers, let us summarize the abstract features of risk analysis as a form of governmental control. Risk analysis templates serve either (1) to predispose other actors' decision-making coercively around a centrally developed common analytical model for risk, or (2) to softly incentivize autonomous administrative actors to align their decisions with a common risk analysis model as it determines access to central level funding or serves as the analytical basis for reporting duties and benchmarking mechanisms.

Power-seeking turns to risk analysis, ideal-typically, will feature *goals* of the following:

- increasing an actor's control in a policy domain vis-à-vis other actors
- central level actors' desire to harmonize decision-making where they cannot control it

In *empirical applications*, a power-seeking orientation toward risk analysis will be as follows:

- impose a common risk analysis template on other actors (e.g., through executive orders)
- use common risk analysis model in central funding or benchmarking frameworks

The *technical/organizational design* of risk analysis in the context of power-seeking will involve the following:

- risk analysis templates developed and/or promoted by the central level (Federal government or EU)
- detailed prescription of risk analysis methods and especially their use in decision-making (coercion) and/or
- coupling of risk analysis to incentive structures (soft coercion)

3.4 Conclusion

By offering a detailed and integrated review of scattered literature, this chapter carved out the ideal-typical instrumental, legitimacy-seeking, and power-seeking appeals of risk analysis, and the ways in which these foci will likely shape its application. By operationalizing the ILP framework, the chapter hence bridged the gap between a general conceptualization of analytical tools as oscillating between problem-solving and polity policies, in Chapter 2, and the comparative empirical analysis of risk-analytical policy-making to follow. An interdisciplinary review of studies in risk regulation, organizational sociology, risk governance and governmentality, as well as the sociology and history of quantification – sieved through my ILP framework – revealed the following interpretive patterns around the specific credentials of risk analysis:

- *Instrumental* orientations toward risk analysis draw on the perceived ability of risk-based differentiation to increase the efficiency and cost-effectiveness of problem-solving. Since risk analysis differentiates risk levels based on the likelihood and impact of adverse outcomes, it renders different events and phenomena in a regulatory domain (or across them) comparable. This allows regulators to develop rational approaches to societal risk management by setting clear priorities for intervention and funding. The instrumental adoption pattern relies on thorough and detailed scientific risk-analysis template.
- *Legitimacy-seeking* orientations toward risk analysis build on attempts at institutional risk management of the administration, including the potential of being blamed for adverse outcomes of societal risk management. A broad-brush differentiation of risk levels helps actors define ex-ante and defend ex-post the "parameters of blame"; in other words, different risk levels and their visualization in maps help actors substantiate the core as well as the limits of their accountability for failure.
- *Power-seeking* orientations in the adoption of risk analysis perceive actuarial calculation as a way to centrally monitor and steer enforcement decisions of autonomous actors. Common risk analysis templates can be adopted either (1) coercively, where administrations impose a risk-analytical model on local enforcers to curb their bureaucratic discretion; or (2) through processes of soft harmonization, where a centrally designed and/or promoted risk analysis model is used by some (usually central or supranational) actors to set incentives for autonomous other actors, through funding criteria, benchmarking mechanisms, or reporting structures, to align their decision-making around a common understanding of risk.

Each section culminated in the development of a set of indicators (overview in Table 3.1) to aid the empirical identification of instrumental, legitimacy-seeking, and power-seeking orientations toward risk analysis. These include indicators that focus on (1) policy goals (e.g., increasing efficiency or avoiding blame); (2) the

TABLE 3.1 Qualitative indicators for mapping ideal-typical orientations toward risk analysis

	Instrumental problem-solving	*Legitimacy-seeking*	*Power-seeking*
Goal	Efficiency and effectiveness gains; increase societal acceptance that risks cannot reduced to zero; avoidance of (political) bias in risk assessment and management; collective agreement about policy priorities	Institutional risk management; limiting potential to be blamed for adverse outcomes; blame-shifting to others	Increasing one's control in a policy domain vis-à-vis others; central level actors' desire to harmonize decision-making where they cannot control it
Empirical application	Differentiation of risk scenarios attached to search for optimal (cost-effective) policy paths; risk analysis used to define priorities and negligible cases for spending public resources	Differentiation of risk scenarios directly linked to definitions of limits of accountability for adverse outcomes; use of common analytical model to signal fair, objective, and effective problem-solving	Common risk analysis template imposed on other actors (e.g., through executive orders); use of common risk analysis model as an incentive in funding streams or as part of benchmarking frameworks
Technical and organizational design	Creation of specifically designated risk analysis units and/or advisory councils within departments single; detailed template for risk analysis, including specific risk formula; detailed guidance on design and use of risk analysis for enforcement units (e.g., development of "how-to-guides", training programs and common software solutions)	No strong focus on scientific rigor and independence; broad and/or several risk analysis templates with room for discretion; relatively broad guidance on design and use of risk analysis	Risk analysis templates developed and/or promoted by central level (Federal government or EU); detailed prescription of risk analysis methods and their use in decision-making (coercion) and/or coupling of risk analysis to financial or other incentives (soft coercion)

Source: Author's compilation

empirical applications of risk analysis (e.g., used to prioritize spending or to incentivize decentral alignment of enforcement decisions); as well as (3) technical and organizational indicators (e.g., creating a new risk analysis unit or the design of single analytical template with detailed "how-to guides").

My comparative study does not treat indicators in a numerical manner; they do not have to accumulate to a certain sum, per se. However, as each of them offers hints for assessing the relative weight (qualitatively speaking) of instrumental and legitimacy-seeking and power-seeking orientations among (specific) administrative actors, I consider evidence for each one of the ideal-typical appeals among (a specific group of) actors the most conclusive when empirical indicators of different kinds surface in support of it. From the interpretive perspective on analytical tools (Chapter 2), empirical derogations from, or mixes of, ideal types offer reason to reflect carefully upon the complex interaction of several perceptions and respective institutionalizations of an analytical tool in a policy sector.

Overall, the chapter highlighted that risk analysis comes with a set of distinct performative features; in-built calculative and representational abilities in which actors can vest different hopes. Risk analysis can differentiate and thereby create focus and target, highlight redundancies, bring together, join perspectives, and discipline autonomous actors. Its ability to differentiate scenarios by a calculation of likelihood and impact of harm turns risk analysis into a magic bullet, from the viewpoint of policymakers, which can satisfy demands of societal risk management, institutional risk management, but also control ambitions through the governance by risk. How the underlying credentials of risk analysis play out in actors' meaning-making and actual adoption processes is a matter of context. Whether actors perceive them as useful for cutting inspection resources by a third, to come to a common understanding of which policy to favor, or even to expand resources and central state intervention in high risk areas, is shaped by their interpretations of both policy problems and the decision-making contexts in which they are situated. Contextualization of the book's typology of analytical tools, and my specific expectations about the credentials of risk analysis, is the purpose of the next chapter.

Notes

1 (Stone, 2012, p. 135)
2 Indicator development is inspired by Radaelli's work (2010, pp. 182–186) on RIA. He developed a list of indicators for assessing different types of RIA adoptions across countries, including "rational policymaking" (my "I" category), "symbolic politics" (my "L" category), and political control' (my "P" category). I adapt and expand his list, firstly because his definition of symbolic politics and political control is narrower than my understanding of polity policies (cf. Chapter 2), and secondly because risk analysis has different internal logics and technical abilities than RIA.
3 Quantification entails the provision of information "in the form of a numerical representation" (Mennicken and Lodge, 2015, p. 6).
4 Be it the Hima cattle-herders' reproduction control to maintain the preferred cattle-human ratio or our modern environmental regulations to preserve clean air and water.

5 One reason for this limited control may be that uncertainties and complexities involved in risk regulation make accountability for regulatory outcomes difficult, leading Majone (2010) to suggest that regulators should be assessed as to their procedural rationality instead. Other reasons may be more political in nature and relate to the ways in which limited – and increasingly tighter – resources but also the fragmentation of governmental authorities in multi-level polities disable effective state intervention. Lastly, there are of course more general state-philosophical debates about the possibility of governmental steering and intentional societal change (cf. a summary of related arguments in: Paul and Mölders, 2017). This book's interpretivist focus on administrators' motivations and justifications for using risk analysis in decision-making does not require detailed analysis of the limits of control per se but an understanding of how administrative actors' perceptions of limited control shape their institutional risk management strategies and render risk analysis appealing for legitimatory reasons.

6 Although not the focus of my analysis, it is noteworthy that this observation of failure acceptability relates to a larger discussion in the philosophy of sciences about "failure as an ontological necessity", as David Chandler (2016, p. 391) put it. This entails the argument that, in a world marked by complexity and uncertainty, failure to fully control social and socio-ecological systems alongside regulatory goals is not only inevitable but also necessary and desirable for reflexive learning and institutional transformation (e.g., Room, 2011, 2016; Davoudi, 2012; Chandler, 2014, 2016).

7 Several post-structuralist analyses stress how contemporary uses of actuarial risk analyses within administrations map and construct governable populations through the signalling effects of the label "high risk" (e.g., on young offenders: Gray, 2005; on migration: Neal, 2009; on pregnant women: Mansfield, 2012; on counter-terrorism: Mythen, Walklate and Khan, 2013; on the mentally-ill: Szmukler and Rose, 2013).

8 This argument also connects to the wider literature in European integration studies on "regulation by information" (Majone, 1997) and the rise of benchmarking processes, for example in the OMC (cf. Introduction).

4

ANALYTICAL TOOLS IN CONTEXT

Why (risk) analysis appeals in multi-level administrations

> *We need to "understand instruments not only in the abstract, but also in the contexts of the particular political, social and economic situations within which they will be put in operation".*[1]

The previous two chapters argued that existing controversies about analytical tools' appeal across public administrations can be addressed if we avoid bias on the "dependent variable". Through a review, critique, and interpretivist synthesis of the so far unrelated accounts, Chapter 2 proposed a multifaceted – and I suggest more accurate – concept of analytical tools. My unified typology of instrumental problem-solving, legitimacy-seeking, and power-seeking (ILP typology) not only charts ideal-typical variety in actors' meaning-making about why analytical tools seem useful but also engages head-on with the theoretical expectation that policy-makers' rationalization of such tools will involve polity policies *alongside* problem-solving. This view was elaborated for risk analysis in Chapter 3, which charted the versatile logics of actuarial analysis both as a means for supposedly rational societal risk management *and* as a promising decision heuristic in institutional risk management and governance by numbers. However, this important conceptual groundwork and systematization only addresses half the controversies portrayed in the book's introduction. To further our understanding of the attractiveness of analytical tools across diversely structured and oriented public administrations; to capture actors' *strategically selective sense-making* of problem-solving and decision-making structures in different contexts (Section 1.3), we also need to avoid bias on the "independent variable".

Many attempts to explain the rise of analytical tools across countries display a tendency to essentialize the British and US experience – a forerunner of analytical reform processes in Europe – at the expense of other forms of public administration. Certainly, fragmented administrations in Europe have indeed adopted analytical tools more scarcely, slowly, and patchily than the forerunners. For example, there is no equivalent to the generic UK requirement to do risk-based enforcement in Germany, Austria, Belgium, or Spain. However, such a comparative deficit judgment offers little explanation for why multi-level administrations adopt analytical tools, when they do, because it implicitly assumes that these tools can only emerge under institutional conditions that favored their appreciative interpretation in the forerunner cases. In this book's interpretivist account, the adoption of an analytical tool is not understood as a predetermined process in which policymakers neutrally cherish a tool's in-built "abstract" credentials for problem-solving, legitimacy-seeking, and power-seeking. Rather, the extent to which these three concerns matter in the appreciative interpretation of a tool's likely performance is shaped by, but also against, specific contextual factors (cf. Section 1.3).

To provide the basis to examine how actors' meaning-making about analytical tools interacts with the "contexts of the particular political, social and economic situations within which they will be put in operation" (Peters, 2005, p. 354), this chapter proceeds as follows. It reviews insights on why analytical tools appeal in the "benchmark cases" in Anglo-American contexts (Section 4.1) and discusses the limits of transferring these insights to other empirical contexts (Section 4.2). The chapter then introduces key structural features of German federalism (and it being situated in EU multi-level governance): the dual requirement (1) to coordinate policies between interdependent actors (Section 4.3) and (2) to negotiate the balance between legal-administrative unity and autonomous subnational decision making (Section 4.4). Along these lines, the chapter carves out context-specific expectations about how and why analytical tools appeal in terms of instrumental problem-solving (Section 4.3), and legitimacy-seeking and power-seeking (Section 4.4) in this setting. Toward the end of the chapter, Table 4.1 summarizes expectations about both the benchmark cases and the German multi-level administration for our analysis.

4.1 Benchmark cases: the appeal of analytical tools in the UK and the US

Much of the writing on analytical tools covers cases where they emerged early on and in comprehensive ways. As a study on impact assessment argues, choosing the UK as a case study seems self-evident when the country has – next to the EU and the US –"the most developed" system of RIA in place, compared to the much narrower scope in other European countries (Dunlop et al., 2012, p. 29). Naturally, assumptions of research pioneers about what drives the adoption of analytical models in these forerunner countries have inspired the field of research. Although context-specific and inductively produced, those assumptions might erroneously slip into new empirical applications. In this section, I briefly review the main assumptions about what drives the prototypical "benchmark" cases for analytical tools, using examples from CBA, RIA, and risk analysis. Then, I prompt their wider contextualization. The aim is not so much to offer a complete portrait of the US and the UK cases as it is to give readers a flavor of their pioneering turns to analytical tools. Through this knowledge, we identify implicit benchmark or "blueprint" assumptions in comparative work on analytical tools. This allows us to treat the divergent contextual conditions in multi-level administrations with coordinated forms of decision-making not as obstacles but as constitutive of distinct appreciations of analytical tools.

4.1.1 Instrumental problem-solving and cost-effectiveness in public interest cultures

The key selling point of analytical tools in the Anglo-American political and academic debate emerged from within the NPM agenda. While scholars rightly pointed out the chameleon-like characteristics of reforms travelling under the NPM banner (Pollitt, van Thiel and Homburg, 2007a, p. 1), their strict interpretation in the "core marketizer" countries Britain and the US has been embedded in more deeply entrenched norms about what public administration should do and how. While NPM reformers on the European Continent – piggybacked on a Napoleonic Rechtsstaat *tradition* – interpret "the state" and its administrative arm as a positive and integrative societal force that acts on behalf of the citizen and requires maintenance (Jann, Röber and Wollmann, 2006; Kuhlmann, 2010), the Anglo-American public interest approach depicts the state bureaucracy as "a necessary evil", which requires restraining (Pollitt and Bouckaert, 2011, p. 62).

An instrumental focus on cost-effectiveness is widespread for analytical tools in the core marketizer cases of NPM. For example, CBA proponents in the US of the 1980s hoped that "poor priority setting, excessively costly tools, and inattention to the unfortunate side-effects of regulation" could be avoided (Sunstein, 2000, p. 1660). As for RIA, scholars describe a "rational-synoptic model", – at least for the US forerunner and OECD blueprint – according to which the economic analysis of a planned piece of regulation can help identify the most cost-effective alternatives among the ones probed (Radaelli, 2005, p. 931). In the UK and the OECD framework on risk and regulatory governance, risk analysis counts as "an essential means of directing regulatory resources where they can have the maximum impact on outcomes" (Hampton, 2005; OECD, 2010).

Turning to risk analysis, scholars assumed that the in-built ability to differentiate the phenomena to be regulated (for more details, see Chapter 3) is particularly attractive where commitment to (or coercion to adopt) NPM and austerity measures are high. Hutter (2005) argues that the strongly market-oriented NPM reforms in the UK since the 1980s have increased "pressure" on public agencies and regulators "to prove their efficiency and efficacy" (p. 11) and thus created a climate that was highly "conductive to the emergence and development of risk-based approaches" in the UK (p. 1). The UK now counts as a jurisdiction that "has fully embraced" risk analysis as a decision aid for regulatory enforcement, at least since the 2000s (Black and Baldwin, 2010, p. 181). While some regulatory agencies, including Health and Safety Executive and the Financial Services Authority, had already adopted risk analysis as their guide for cost-effective enforcement strategies before, the 2005 Hampton Review suggests "that all regulatory agencies should adopt a risk-based approach to enforcement" (Black and Baldwin, 2010, p. 182). Its suggestion that "risk assessment to concentrate resources on the areas that need them most" (Hampton, 2005, p. 7) gained statutory force in 2008 through the "Regulators' Compliance Code" (Department for Business, Enterprise and Regulatory Reform [BERR], 2007). A 2013 National Local Authority Enforcement Code even "banned" local authorities from "unnecessary health and safety inspections" of low-risk premises such as offices and shops (Department for Work and Pensions [DWP], 2013). When large-scale budget cuts put many public bodies and local authorities at peril in Britain from 2010 onward, under the Cameron government's austerity regime, the ability to differentiate systematically – based on risk figures – where to spend the little remaining resources was welcome (Paul et al., 2017). Risk analysis – with its ability to differentiate phenomena and related interventions – arguably enabled British decision makers to cope with an increasingly difficult environment for public interventions under austerity conditions and optimize their societal risk management (cf. Black, 2010).

A few scholars have also discussed analytical tools in the British context as being capable of "stamp[ing] a new identity on a sometimes-disparate collection of regulators brought together as one" (Hutter, 2005, p. 13). Hutter does this for the case of risk analysis, arguing that its instrumental credentials foster a cross-fertilization of knowledge and regulatory approaches. Black continues this venue in highlighting how the former British Financial Services Authority (FSA) – abolished in 2013 – used risk analysis not only to justify its regulatory program in instrumental and legitimacy terms but also to create a common identity as a "rational" regulator in the first place (Black, 2010). These accounts point to the role of common analysis in processes of (collective) identity formation as a pre-requisite for rational problem-solving.

Beyond enforcement, the 1974 British Health and Safety at Work Act also prioritized standard setting, in a manner that enabled risk-based rationalization later on, promoted by an analytically committed central regulatory agency, the HSE (Demeritt et al., 2015). Notions of "regulatory crises", which involved "alleged over-regulation, legalism, inflexibility and an alleged absence of attention being paid to the costs of regulation" (Hutter, 2005, p. 1) have become part and parcel of deregulatory NPM agendas in the UK. Harvard regulation scholar Kip Viscusi also focused on "cost-effective" legislation in his critique of inflexible work-safety standard setting on carcinogens in the US as "abstract[ing] from almost all of the variations in the costs and benefits of regulating different substances" (Viscusi, 1983, p. 117). Using risk analysis to differentiate and target regulatory interventions in a more fine-grained manner, he claimed, would enable a more cost-effective allocation of scarce regulatory recourses and avoid "regulatory burden" on industry (for a wider review of the perceived merits of risk analysis, from a cost-effectiveness perspective, see Majone, 2010 and my detailed review in Chapter 3).

Arguably, the regulatory burden argument features in wider classifications of policy tools – though rather implicitly and without theorization of the specific context in which this argument "works". The idea of "sticks, carrots, and sermons" distinguishes tools alongside their degree of coerciveness and directness of intervention (Salamon, 2002; Vedung, 2011; overview in: Acciai and Capano, 2020). Of these accounts, Salamon's is perhaps the most explicit in theorizing how (ideological) context shapes tool adoption. He rehearses a widely cited story on "the new governance" of how command and control type interventions through hierarchy have increasingly given way to forms of governance based on market and network interactions (e.g., Jessop, 2016; Mayntz and Scharpf, 1995; Rhodes, 1996, 2000; Moran, 2000, 2003). In this context, he argues, we can observe a shift from direct to more "indirect tools of action": as governments (need to) avoid being seen as coercive, they prefer tools that help in "expanding public action without expanding the size of the government bureaucracy" (Salamon, 2002, p. 602). Such a view concurs with the NPM ideology insofar it demonstrates administrations' wish to reduce hierarchical interventions and direct state provision, substituting these with non-coercive and indirect forms of governance. It would suggest that analytical tools such as risk analysis are precisely en vogue, in settings with a strong buy-in to NPM reforms, because they are not coercive (of themselves), rather indirect in changing behavior, and operate technically and invisibly in the "analycentric 'backroom" of policy-making (Turnpenny et al., 2015, p. 14).

Finally, it is also no coincidence that the literature on analytical tools often focuses on regulatory policy-making and enforcement. A classic in policy studies, Lowi's policy types (1972) associated regulatory policies with the least ideological conflicts and the strongest role for expertise, while distributive and redistributive policies follow the logic of interest group and partisan politics, respectively. The assumption is that "optimal" decisions are easier to identify and establish in de-politicized and technocratically governed policy domains. Although very much focused on US-American policy-making and not concerned with analytical tools per se, Lowi's typology implies that instrumental problem-solving through analytical models might feature most in regulatory policy domains and/or political systems prone to use regulation such as the US, the UK, or the EU.

These accounts, overall, depict pre-decision policy analysis as a highly instrumental tool to help regulatory agencies allocate scarce resources in a cost-effective way and avoid regulatory burden and "red tape" in the industry. They can thereby rationalize their regulatory decisions about which behaviors to permit and where to concentrate their inspection activities on to spot non-compliance.

4.1.2 Polity policies in contexts of concentrated executive power

The executive structures of forerunners such as the UK and the US have arguably been favorable in introducing analytical tools. As Rothstein, Borraz and Huber (2013, p. 206) note, the emergence of risk-analytical ideas "is shaped by the institutional contours of contemporary cultures of blame and accountability. Where demands for accountability and laying blame are heightened, risk acts as a way of reframing or redefining the limits of the possible". Building on the role of cultures of mistrust (cf. Porter, 1995, more on this point later), it seems likely that the legitimacy-related appeal of risk analysis is higher in contexts where accountability demands and the threat of blame on the administration are high and concentrated (Demeritt et al., 2017). Let us consider our benchmark cases from that vantage point.

In the US, the dominance of strong, independent regulatory agencies in policy-making and enforcement has not only unified executive decisions in spheres where the Federal level leads on policies. It has also created a climate for actors to start rationalizing principal-agent relationships through the lens of analytical tools. In policy-making settings that rely on agencification, the control and oversight over delegated decision-making and the risk of agencies becoming too detached from majoritarian decision-making (or indeed exposed to unchecked dynamics of "capture") is a particular concern (e.g., Majone, 1997; Gilardi, 2002; Maggetti, 2009; Groenleer, 2014; Guidi, 2014). While principals – usually central government or individual ministries – delegate executive control and give agencies relative autonomy over policy-making, usually with the goal to achieve expert-led and politically "untainted" decisions, the delegation remains perilous for both sides. Agents thus need to show they deliver in the above sense and justify the trust vested in their expert decision-making. Principals in turn need to oversee the agencies to ensure they fulfil their delegated mandates. Several UK observers argue that NPM reforms have even amplified the requirement for agencies and public authorities to address blame and failure (Rothstein, Borraz and Huber, 2013, p. 220f.; cf. Boswell, 2018). In such contexts, agencies perceive CBA and similar tools as useful to justify their actions as objective, cost-effective, and impartial, hence stabilizing their powerful mandates for decision-making. Governmental principals, by contrast, are bought into such forms of analysis-based justification and realize the potential to harness analytical tools for their own agency control (or power-seeking) purposes.

Take RIA, for example; it first emerged in the institutional context of the US where almost all policy domains see governance through independent regulatory agencies with strong executive powers irrespective of federalism. These developed RIA due to a perceived need to justify their independent actions vis-à-vis their principals in the political system – Congress, the White House, but also the Courts – in terms of cost effectiveness (Radaelli, 2005, p. 931f). Closer to present times, the UK National Audit Office reported in 2005 that "in some regulatory processes, when political pressure to reach one specific decision is high, RIA is used in a post-decisional mode to justify a political choice" (Radaelli, 2005, p. 934). Similarly, historical accounts of how CBA first emerged highlight legitimacy-seeking as a core orientation among public administration actors. While the US Army Corps of Engineers, an expert body planning water and drainage projects since the 19th century, used a very rough form of CBA for their internal priority setting, they felt pressured to promote their decision-making via Congress based on the rational CBA when trust in their "objective" procedures over water projects had decreased among Congressmen (Porter, 1995, pp. 148–189). It was only *after* the Corps of Engineers introduced CBA from a legitimacy-seeking perspective into justifications of policy-making that economists elaborated the analytical tool further, thus giving it a highly formulaic appeal for instrumental problem-solving (ibid., cf. Sunstein, 2000).

Such diffusion of CBA was also successful through its morphing into a *polity policy* interpretation and one that also hinges on the agency model of executive policy-making. From the central government's perspective, CBA was also a tool for the political principal to increase "control of the agencies" (Radaelli, 2010, p. 170; cf. Baldwin and Veljanovski, 1984; Posner, 2001). Then the US President Ronald Reagan's move in 1981 to make CBA a legally prescribed method for *all* regulatory decision making (the famous Executive Order 12291) was justified both instrumentally in terms of cost effectiveness and with Presidential agency control purposes in mind (Posner, 2001). Similarly, RIA in the US has been described as a "centralised review of rulemaking . . . used to increase the grip of the President on regulatory agendas" (Radaelli, 2010, p. 166). In contexts where agencies enjoy far-reaching powers over regulatory standards and enforcement, analysis-based "naming and shaming" sticks' like CBA or RIA are, it seems, a welcome disciplining tool for political executives (ibid., p. 167).

My argument that the first pop-up of analytical tools must be situated in settings of strong executive power also works for the UK. Sure, regulatory agencies are less prominent here than in the US (but more important than in Continental Europe), emerged later on, and were not always the first to adopt new analytical tools (they were for risk analysis, as in the case of the Health and Safety Executive highlights). In the case of RIA, Cabinet Office viewed it as a tool for shaping and cohering the policy portfolios of individual Government Departments alongside a wider ideational orientation toward "better regulation" (Radaelli, 2010). This works arguably because Britain's Prime Minister-dominated executive – and its embedding in a strong fusion-of-powers system, where parliamentary majorities give the PM rather unlimited executive powers – forges equally straightforward lines of accountability and oversight as does the classic agency model of public policy-making. The risk-based regulation literature assumes that such strong and direct accountability pressures, next to the NPM-driven cost effectiveness, have been vital for the rise of risk analysis in the UK (Rothstein, Borraz and Huber, 2013; Demeritt et al., 2017; cf. summary in: Paul and Huber, 2015). As Demeritt and colleagues argue, "risk-based decision rules also have disciplinary and defensive attractions [. . .], which are particularly strong where devolved implementation creates principal-agent accountability concerns". They use the example of central risk-based flood risk management which was developed to "constrain local government discretion in permitting floodplain developments that then require centrally funded flood defenses" (Demeritt et al., 2017, p. 24). This example also indicates that such accountability concerns include relationships between Whitehall and the devolved nations' local authorities. Indeed, British regulators appreciate risk analysis as "consistent guidance on priority-setting [. . .] [and a means] for coordinating and rationalizing inspections of local authorities" (Hampton, 2005, p. 75). As risk analysis offers "an organisational objective around which regulators can orientate their activities", it can structure choices across different government departments and levels (Black, 2010, p. 324). A similar expectation surfaces in Radaelli's work on RIA wherein he expects central governments in decentralized states to use RIA as a method for developing and enforcing joint strategies in order to control "policy impact and outcome" from the center (Radaelli, 2010, p. 172).

Indeed, Hampton-like interpretations suggest a classic "control of the bureaucracy" argument (Dunsire, 1978) where risk analysis can pre-dispose discretionary decision-making of autonomous actors in strict principal-agent relationships. In unitary and/or relatively centralized executive regimes, it seems that central level actors interpret and cherish analytical tools for their perceived ability to direct dispersed local bureaucrats toward delivering centrally determined policies, thus addressing typical principal-agent accountability concerns. Of course, organizational theory tells us that the interaction of instrumental problem-solving orientations with actors' perceived need to manage principal-agent accountability concerns might well create "symbolic policies": "If organisations produce rituals of 'rational' analysis to increase their legitimacy in the environment, rational policy appraisal techniques will be de-coupled from the reality of decision making" (Weick, 1976 in Radaelli, 2010, p. 171). A recent study of the UK's "net migration target" confirms that the use of analytical tools – even among the forerunners of rational problem-oriented analysis – can become a routinized form of performance measurement, self-imposed in legitimacy-seeking endeavors, without much bearing for policy-related problem-solving (Boswell, 2015, 2018). Moreover, once they initiate routine analysis, governments can be locked in to continue this form of self-observation (on a similar argument for the "spiraling" logics of risk analysis within organizations, see: Rothstein, Huber and Gaskell, 2006 and Chapter 3).

Overall, work on the rise of CBA, RIA, and risk analysis in the British and the US contexts dominantly treats the countries' public interest culture and their relative concentration of executive powers – either through agencification (also in Federal settings) and/or in strong fusion-of-power systems – as favorable conditions. They portray how analytical tools in these contexts have emerged from a *mutually supportive interaction* of the following:

- a public interest culture that promotes an ideational focus on cost-effective policy-making (instrumental problem-solving) *with*
- a concentration of executive powers and heightened principal-agent accountability concerns, creating high pressure for agencies to justify executive decisions vis-à-vis their principals in the central government (legitimacy-seeking) and the principal's wish to control executive decisions of these autonomous actors (power-seeking)

4.2 Or different planets? The limits of essentialized Anglo-American explanations

What about contexts in which, first, the NPM ideologies matter less and, second, executive power is more diffused and features less direct forms of accountability? For the first point, indeed, much of the work on NPM reforms highlights that unlike the forerunners of new forms of governing and organizing public administration (Australia, New Zealand, and the UK and the US), countries in Continental Europe have maintained existing institutions and hierarchical decision-making through incremental reforms (Radaelli, 2005; Pollitt, van Thiel and Homburg, 2007b; Kuhlmann, 2010; Pollitt and Bouckaert, 2011; Atkinson, 2015). The German version of NPM might have promised efficiency and effectiveness gains in the delivery of public services, too, but it "forwent discussion of outsourcing and privatization" (Kuhlmann, 2010, p. 851). In Neo-Weberian reform countries, the classic ideal of a powerful and capable public administration has remained more or less intact, even if state authorities also needed to engage in cost-effective problem-solving. It is, therefore, likely that the more modest NPM reforms in Continental Europe offer less reason for administrations to adopt analytical tools with a view on cost-effective problem-solving.

Second, the Anglo-American literature on analytical tools is rather skeptical as to their adoption in more fragmented settings with more diffuse decision-making structures. Demeritt and colleagues highlight, for example, that only "contexts in which management responsibilities are concentrated will promote the use of risk analysis [. . . because this] creates both budgetary and accountability pressures that make risk instruments appealing for prioritisation and rationalising how far to go in pursuit of policy goals" (Demeritt et al., 2017, p. 6). Instead, contexts wherein neither a high degree of agencification (in the cases of the US and partly the UK) nor a strong executive (as the UK's fusion-of-power and Cabinet government) concentrates on decision-making powers, risk analysis seems less utile to solve accountability problems. Scholars of risk-based forms of policy-making thus suggest that in Germany, "horizontal and vertical fragmentation of policy responsibilities and accountabilities" – next to corporatism and a *Rechtsstaatskultur* within the public administration – create a "set of institutional factors [which] impede the extent to which it [risk analysis] has become an organizing principle of governance" (Rothstein, Borraz and Huber, 2013, p. 227).

In addition, and perhaps paradoxically, the system of "dispersed government powers [. . .] and negotiated policies" in Germany is coupled with low administrative discretion in a *Rechtsstaatskultur*, where "only plainly circumscribed functions" are delegated to administrative agents – whether Federal agencies or Länder-overseen local authorities – and these are "restricted to applying the law" (Döhler, 2002, p. 117). As Döhler argues, agency autonomy – and the related accountability pressures – are simply not a concern in such settings. This ostensibly lowers the appeal of analytical tools further as their role in actors' struggles over legitimacy and power seems less important. Observers of RIA agree that any "shift to a performance and economics-oriented regulatory management perspective [. . .] should be more difficult" in administrations with a *Rechtsstaatskultur* such as in Germany – where rule-based decision-making is the norm – than in the NPM-oriented public interest cultures in the Anglo-American world (Radaelli, 2010, p. 174).

Overall, this brief summary of comparative work on analytical tools emphasizes that scholars tend to treat the *absence* of the institutional conditions as favorable for the adoption of analytical tools in the UK and the US cases as grounds for expecting a low likelihood of such tools to appeal elsewhere. However, such symmetric reasoning around an essentialized vision of benchmark cases implies a bias on the independent variable. It misrecognizes how different institutional settings may trigger different problem perceptions among actors – both in terms of policy problems and decision-making structures – and thus shape vastly different interpretations of the instrumental, legitimacy- and power-related merits of analytical tools among actors. It is in this sense that the book follows Peter's advice, discussed in the epigraph of this chapter, that we need to "understand instruments not only in the abstract, but also in the contexts of the particular political, social and economic situations within which they will be put in operation" (Peters, 2005, p. 354; cf. Linder and Peters, 1989; Peters, 2002). Actors' selective appreciations of an analytical tool depend on how its assumed performative credentials speak to actors' strategic desire to shape the conditions for their own actions within the constraints of a specific institutional context (cf. Section 1.3 for my conceptualization of context). I turn to these institutional conditions and constraints next to develop more context-specific arguments about how these might shape actors' instrumental, legitimacy- and power-related orientations toward risk analysis.

4.3 Analytical tools and coordinated problem-solving in Germany's multi-level administration

This section reappraises insights on German federalism to discuss its likely role in furnishing instrumental orientations. The fragmentation of decision-making structures and the related difficulties in agreeing upon shared policy goals have been discussed as key obstacles for the emergence of instrumentally leaning common analytical frameworks (Radaelli, 2010; Rothstein, Borraz and Huber, 2013; Demeritt et al., 2017). When shared understanding about the problems at hand are impaired by fragmented structures of authority, the use of analysis in problem-solving seems futile from the outset. Or does it?

This section discusses the problem of coordinated problem-solving in multi-level administrations. It is based on the literature on German federalism which highlights that while policy coordination may often take voluntary forms, it builds on soft pressures to cooperate, including the normative guideline of legal-administrative unity across jurisdictions. In addition, in several policy domains, the enactment of executive federalism through an apolitical expert civil service – which may well be committed to problem-solving – ensures a focus on rational consensus-seeking in policy coordination. These conditions jointly inform my reappraisal of analytical tools' attractions in fragmented decision-making settings as highly appreciated instruments for rationalizing collective problem-solving.

4.3.1 Coordinated and cooperative problem-solving

Lamentations of German federalism and its perceived inability to produce more than the least-common-denominator policies, let alone far-reaching policy reform, are well-known. The case is invariably associated with the idea of "semi-sovereign statehood" (Katzenstein, 1987) and the so-called "joint decision trap" (Scharpf, 1988). Paradoxically, the very same institutional conditions said to hamper more than incremental policy (and structural) reform in Germany in these accounts can also be interpreted as constitutive for actors' orientations toward *collective* problem-solving. I chart these accounts briefly[2] to highlight a strongly institutionalized inclination for actors within Germany's (and the EU) multi-level administration to engage in coordinated problem-solving all the way down to implementation.

In his classic on Germany's semi-sovereign state, Katzenstein describes a tamed polity with several checks and balances, decision-making arenas, and a constant requirement of coordination and consensus seeking. In particular, "the decentralisation of the state contributes to the political predisposition for incremental policy change" (Katzenstein, 1987, p. 15). This is because, first, German Länder enjoy a great amount of executive powers not only in policy domains where they hold exclusive legislative power (as typical of the US competitive or dual federalism) but are also tasked – in a majority of policy domains – with the autonomous implementation of Federal law. Second, this phenomenon of *executive federalism* is amplified by the German administrative system which Katzenstein described as "the hallmark of decentralization" (ibid., p. 19). Importantly, institutional fragmentation in this setting must not be equated with policy fragmentation. Unlike in the US version of competitive federalism where there can be a vast array of different policy approaches across the states, the German system is marked by a "tightly integrated policy network" (ibid., p. 35), which informs an orientation toward collective decision-making even in policy domains without central level coordination powers. One important node[3] in this network, according to Katzenstein, has been the model of *cooperative* federalism, described in depth below.

Scharpf's "joint-decision trap" (cf. Scharpf, 1988) has prominently detailed the idea of a "tamed polity". His vantage point for a critique of systemic reform blockades in Germany's federal system ("trap") was the diagnosis of *constitutional requirements* for intergovernmental coordination between actors. Scharpf thus speaks of "joint decision" in policy domains where there is a coercion to coordinate decisions[4] between the Federal level and states and where actors, therefore, cannot exit negotiations (Benz, Detemple and Heinz, 2016, p. 55). The constitutionally defined "joint tasks" (*Gemeinschaftsaufgaben*) are illustrative: they include the development of economic structures and the development of agrarian structures and coastal protection,[5] where planning, implementation, and funding of policies is shared between Bund and Länder. It is in these domains that the actors in the multi-level setting can take veto positions and block policy reform for all (Kropp, 2010, p. 12).

It would be overly lacking, however, to view German federalism as one where the veto player structures block policy-making[6] for at least three reasons. First, there is a historically derived constitutional norm of "gleichwertige Lebensbedingungen" (equal living conditions), which binds actors of different levels to seek agreement in joint decision-making situations, but also in less formalized forms of cooperation (see the second point later). The constitutional norm springs off the much older programmatic idea of *Rechtseinheit* (legal-administrative unity), dating back to the foundation of the German Empire in Bismarckian times (Lehmbruch, 2002, pp. 71–74). *Rechtseinheit* counts as a compromise between the unitarian orientation of the German bourgeoisie at the time – following the French Republican ideal – and the self-reproduction desires of already existing (highly effective) subnational powers (Lehmbruch, 2002, p. 73; cf. Ziblatt, 2008): the latter kept much of their autonomy but were now bound to use their legislative and (more importantly) executive powers for a Federal common good. Importantly, the co-evolving norms of the German welfare state imprinted onto the ideal of legal-administrative unity a distinctly solidaristic orientation among German Länder (*Bundestreue*). This informs distinctive forms of redistribution between economically stronger and weaker states as well as a normative guideline of avoiding location competition or even "beggar thy neighbor" type of behaviors (Kropp, 2010, p. 17f). This normative orientation is certainly one of the reasons why Benz, Detemple and Heinz (2016) note, in a recent comparative study on multi-level decision-making in Germany, that intergovernmental gridlock occurs much less often than the country's formal state structure alone might suggest.

Second, there are forms of voluntary cooperation – both vertical and horizontal – with a potential for harmonizing policy approaches and little risk of blockade. Indeed, recent reappraisals of Germany's federalism during the new Corona virus pandemic stress the surprisingly swift intergovernmental coordination for lock-down measures and (less so) first relaxations (Behnke, 2020; Rothstein et al., 2021). These forms of "cooperative federalism", existing since Bismarckian times (Lehmbruch, 2002), are distinct from coerced negotiations because actors' decisions are less interdependent, structurally speaking (Kropp, 2010, p. 12f). Scholars of German federalism depict pressure to cooperate also in policy domains where Länder have a relatively autonomous executive and (more rarely) legislative role. Embedded in the more general norm of equal living conditions and solidaristic behavior, described earlier, Germany's fragmented jurisdictions tend to have a comparatively strong awareness for avoiding typical collective action problems, unlike in the US's competitive federalism: negative or positive externalities of individual actions, the inability to address border-crossing problems in any one jurisdiction, and free-riding with respect to collective goods (Kropp, 2010, pp. 13, 21). The existence of 330 voluntary Bund-Länder and around 140

Länder cooperation fora, back in 1989 (ibid., p. 126), highlights both the strong currency of cooperative forms of problem-solving across Germany's fragmented jurisdictions and its relative dominance over (internationally much more cited) joint decision settings.

Some have argued that the weight of cooperative forms of decision-making has increased with Europeanization not only in the already tightly coordinated case of Germany but also in federations with a more competitive orientation between states, such as Belgium and Spain (Börzel, 2002, p. 381). The EU is the context in which the notion of "multi-level governance" first appeared in the early 1990s to describe "a system of continuous negotiation among nested governments at several territorial tiers – supranational, national, regional and local" (Hooghe and Marks, 2003, p. 234, citing the authors' earlier work). While such forms of negotiation in mutually embedded governance levels is not new to European federal states, as Börzel (2002) argues, the insertion into EU decision-making structures has created new forms of interdependence: the Federal level depends on states for policy implementation and the development of common positions for negotiations in Brussels; states rely on the Federal level to have their interests represented at EU level. The "concordance pressure of Europeanisation [has informed] the development of cooperative structures" and made them more stringent where they already existed (ibid., p. 381).

Third, executive harmonization also draws on a hierarchically structured and rational bureaucracy in which a traditionally un-political civil service (cf. Döhler, 2002; Pollitt and Bouckaert, 2011) seeks to implement law uniformly across the country. Rather than being coerced by central guidelines or control of the bureaucracy type interventions, common policy implementation strategies often develop in horizontal interactions among Länder (and even municipal) civil servants. Once adopted by the local spearheads of executive federalism, such strategies can spread widely across hierarchical government structures within each independent state through coercive forms of isomorphism. To achieve legal-administrative unity, indeed, lower rank civil servants, rather than politically motivated ministers, populate many of the aforementioned cooperation fora and engage in problem- and consensus-oriented discussions over enforcement (cf. Kropp, 2010, p. 127). Indeed, the relative dominance of executive federalism in several policy domains – both in the sense of autonomous executive powers of the Länder and a strong lead of Federal and Länder executives in vertical and horizontal cooperation processes – has been arguably accompanied by a "problem- and consensus-oriented style of negotiation", in which party lines or ideological positions[7] matter less (Kropp, 2010, p. 127). The role of a technical and apolitical civil service in fleshing out the balance between executive federalism and legal-administrative unity is also captured in the policy styles literature. Indeed, Germany's "rationalist consensus" orientation (cf. Richardson, 1982; Howlett and Tosun, 2018, p. 7) captures not only a distinct mode of expertise-driven corporatist negotiation (cf. Paul and Huber, 2015) but also efforts *within* the multi-level administration to let evidence engender multi-level consensus seeking about policy problems and solutions across jurisdictions. This goes beyond control of the bureaucracy type arguments discussed for the

Anglo-American benchmark cases in that it focuses on voluntary harmonization processes among autonomous actors.

4.3.2 *Analysis-based policy coordination in Germany's multi-level administration*

The combination of strong norms of legal-administrative unity and federal solidarity, intergovernmental cooperation, and a problem- and consensus-oriented civil service requires reappraisal of analytical tools' attractions in Germany's multi-level administration. Actors in coordination-heavy multi-level settings may perceive analytical tools as unifying frameworks for collective problem-solving. Such an instrumental view is likely to emerge where collective action is formally required (joint decision), incentivized by constitutional solidarity norms, and/or normatively embraced by the actors involved (most other forms of interactions in German federalism). Eventually, analytical tools can emerge as a distinct form of rational problem-solving in contexts wherein the coupling of (1) a cross-jurisdictional common good orientation (here: equal living conditions and legal-administrative unity) with (2) more or less institutionalized forms of cooperation works as an intervening variable between the seemingly contrary poles of collective problem-solving and a fragmented state structure. Indeed, the existence of an apolitical expert civil service, which is committed to legal-administrative unity in its enactment of executive federalism, suggests that respective policy domains might see substantial instrumental interpretations of analytical tools as useful for multi-level policy coordination. Chapter 3 already pointed toward the *enabling* functions of risk analysis in such an institutional context.

For the wider argument, let us recall Majone's proposition that evidence and related processes of argumentation and persuasion *enable* decision-making in "an increasingly complex and interdependent world" (Majone, 1989, p. 269). Rather than being obsessed with optimal policy solutions in the sense of cost-effective decisions, actors in multi-level settings with interdependent forms of decision-making may interpret analytical tools as useful for structuring dialogue with others about suitable policy goals and paths. This rehearses the claim that before they can coordinate policies, actors need to engage in knowledge-based argument about the causes of a policy problem and the effects specific solutions might wield (Heinelt, 2016). From this perspective, the guideline for "rationality" of collective action is not necessarily related to finding cost-effective policy options, though it can be. Rather, rationalization is about enabling autonomous actors to coordinate problem perceptions and courses of action. Analytical tools can rationalize, in that way, because they offer a shared lingua franca through which potentially disparate problem perceptions can be filtered (e.g., risk analysis as a way of differentiating problems into degrees of severity and likelihood). They also appeal because, as scholars of risk-based regulation show, their ascribed ability to avoid assessment bias can inform processes of collective strategy and identity formation (Hutter, 2005; Black, 2010). Forms of shared knowledge provision can thus facilitate policy coordination among disparate actors by creating the very "precondition of collective action" (Voß and Freeman, 2016, p. 1).

Contrary to what the literature on analytical tools claims, Heinelt suggests – convincingly so, in my opinion – that multi-level settings with tightly coordinated forms of decision-making are even more likely to develop shared problem definitions and causal assumptions "about how world and society work than those marked by pluralist competition" (Heinelt, 2016, p. 44). This is because they habitually engage in collective meaning-making as part of their institutionalized forms of policy coordination; for example, in the regular meetings of inspectorate chiefs in a Länder working group on work safety enforcement (cf. Chapter 7). As research on RIA confirms, with a wider set of stakeholders in mind, "in consociational democracies like Denmark . . . RIA is eminently a tool used by socio-economic and governmental elites to define the content of policy" (Radaelli, 2005, p. 933). My own study on corporatist negotiations of thresholds for carcinogenic substances at workplaces in Germany highlights that fragmentation of decision-making powers – in this case, between the state, social partners, and a set of para-public regulatory bodies – does not hamper the emergence of analytical tools (Paul and Huber, 2015). Rather, the use of risk analysis created trust and a sense of impartiality among autonomous actors and was thus vital for forging a shared understanding about work safety risks, their relative acceptability, and suitable regulatory solutions.

Importantly, analysis-based forms of seeking consensus might well be limited to some forms of policies. In extension of Lowi's (1972) argument on regulatory policies and their likelihood of being embedded in evidence-based policy-making in the agency model (cf. Section 4.1), we might also expect the dominance of a "rationalist consensus" orientation in Germany's multi-level administration to be higher in non-redistributive policy domains. Scholars of federalism observed that the conflict structure of a policy problem shapes the likely success of policy coordination in multi-level settings (Scharpf, 1985, 1988). While multi-level coordination of regulatory standards and levels of provision can be reached with shared standard-setting and incentive structures, distribution and redistribution require discriminating decisions which (affected) actors will find harder to accept (Benz, Detemple and Heinz, 2016, p. 25). We can hence expect analytical tools to arise mainly in contexts of regulatory policy-making and enforcement and will discuss three such cases in depth later on.

4.4 Analytical tools and polity policies in Germany's multi-level administration

My critical governance perspective conceptualizes public policy governance as the mutual co-constitution of *policy substance* with *positional struggles* in a policy domain (Section 1.3). Scholars of multi-level policy-making in Europe have also argued that any attempt of coordinating for problem-solving purposes always *also* involves actors' distinct perspective on the legitimacy of and the allocation of power in the domain, potentially leading to conflict over these questions

(Benz, 2009; Heinelt and Knodt, 2011). By detailing the contours of such positional struggles in Germany's multi-level administration (Section 4.4.1) and pointing out differences to the Anglo-American concern with principal-agent accountability and autonomy we can develop context-sensitive expectations about legitimacy-seeking (Section 4.4.2) and power-seeking (Section 4.4.3) appeals of analytical tools.

4.4.1 The constant (re-)negotiation of unity and autonomy between center and subnational actors

The historical account of German federalism discussed earlier already pointed to a constitutive tension between unitarization demands and the wishes of subnational territorial entities to retain their autonomous decision-making powers. Lehmbruch's (2000, p. 94) evaluation of Germany's public administration after World War II suggests, for example, that "contemporary German federalism is . . . characterised by a strange combination of decentralization of autonomous bureaucracies with substantive harmonisation of policies and highly developed procedural uniformity". Mapping these countervailing pressures helps identify the institutional conditions under which actors in Germany's multi-level setting act upon their own and others' relative position when they engage with policy-making. Thus, I argue, it is in this context of constant (re-)negotiation of the balance between unity and central steering on the one hand and subnational autonomy on the other that the legitimacy and power-related appeals of analytical tools in the German public administration must be understood.

Lehmbruch highlights that the German ideal of legal-administrative unity – informed by the border-crossing development of capitalism and the welfare state – led to *both* "outright legislative centralisation. . . [and] co-operative harmonization" between state administrations (ibid., p. 92). He describes the model of concurrent legislation (*konkurrierende Gesetzgebung*), the diffusion of the hegemonic policy templates from Prussia across the Reich and horizontal coordination between Länder executives as the main drivers of unitarization (Lehmbruch, 2002, p. 81). The first of these concerns a form of co-legislation, still widely used today and much relevant for our three cases, in which Länder are free to take legislative action in so far the Federal level does not use its law-making prerogative in the domain. The degree of unitarization in a policy domain thus often depends on the extent to which the Federal level has used this prerogative. Indeed, some argue that the Federal level has increasingly accumulated central legislative powers in areas where there was a "contrast between the welfare state postulate and the variable performance of Länder" in their very own areas of legislative responsibility (Kropp, 2010, p. 18). In other words, as discrepancies in socio-economic policies and outcomes conflict with the norms of equal living conditions and legal-administrative unity, such a discrepancy has repeatedly given the Federal level an "authorization to intervene" in Länder affairs[8] (ibid.). This type of harmonization works via coercive forms of isomorphism.

The second and third drivers of unitarization, described by Lehmbruch (2002), involve mimetic forms of horizontal policy diffusion. As for voluntary coordination, the power of the Federal level to use its prerogative in concurrent legislation has been a Damocles' sword from the perspective of autonomy wary Länder. As Kropp argues, Länder have engaged in horizontal forms of self-coordination – already in the 19th century – to explicitly counter "possible demands for relocating . . . Länder responsibilities to the central state" (Kropp, 2010, p. 130). We observe a conflation of a collective problem-solving orientation with legitimacy-seeking rationales here: by showing that they can overcome the structural weaknesses of federalism and engage in coordinated problem-solving (instrumental orientation), Länder can demonstrate the legitimacy of the existing decision-making structures and thus obviate potential calls for centralization.

Lehmbruch's example of "hegemonic" policy templates from Prussia may be historical, but legitimacy-seeking subcentral actors still rationalize their policy coordination efforts as appropriate by drawing on the templates of Länder level or municipal "reform laboratories" (Pollitt and Bouckaert, 2011, p. 282). Indeed, research on German NPM reforms highlights that the modernization of public administration in Germany has to be understood "in terms of a bottom-up revolution", with reform templates being trialed at the local and at best Länder level and then spreading to other jurisdictions via horizontal coordination (Pollitt and Bouckaert, 2011, p. 282, quoting Klages and Löffler, 1996, p. 134).

In addition to the inner-German institutional debate, the cursory review of literatures on European integration, the OMC, and international bureaucracies in the book's introduction suggested – already with a focus on why analytical tools appeal – that the dynamic co-evolution of unitarization pressures and the defense of subnational mandates for autonomous decision-making is heightened in multi-level settings. With the EU having gained regulatory powers in several policy domains, Bund and Länder are embedded in an even more complex structure of "nested governments" for coordinating policy solutions as well as negotiating their own positions of legitimacy and power vis-à-vis other actors (Hooghe and Marks, 2001; cf. more generally: Heinelt and Knodt, 2011).

4.4.2 Analysis-based legitimacy-seeking in Germany's multi-level administration

Multi-level settings imply a constant need for actors at lower levels of governance to not only justify their substantial policy actions *individually* – and potentially for similar reasons to agencies in the UK and US setting – but also to demonstrate their *collective* ability to coordinate policies without central state intervention (and thus countering potential centralization claims). This requirement has at least four implications for how actors perceive and use analytical tools as legitimacy boosters.

First, and from an individual perspective, a legitimacy-seeking perspective is likely to emerge for any public administration body experiencing critique of their decisions. Critical voices multiply where public authorities are confronted with severe institutional risks (Rothstein, Huber and Gaskell, 2006, in more detail in Chapter 3) due to increased budgetary pressures and fiscal squeezes, a heightened problem load (e.g., after a focusing event), policy-related uncertainty, perceived regulatory failure, and scandals (Hutter, 2005), but also the increasing complexity of policy problems (Thomann, Trein and Maggetti, 2019). In this context, risk analysis' ability to demarcate the limits of one's own accountability and "blameability" vis-à-vis others (Chapter 3) is certainly appealing. It is not clear how fragmented decision-making structures play out though. In principle, instincts of organizational self-defense should increase in multi-level settings where competition over fragmented mandates for policy-making is high and the involvement of different levels of decision-making (subnational, national, and EU) as well as non-state actors reduces the scope for administrations (or any one agency) to govern unilaterally. In this context, Radaelli observes a defensive dynamic among the EU Commission which uses RIA to "defend its proposals vis-à-vis a plethora of aggressive stakeholders" with the help of seemingly rigorous ex-ante evaluation (Radaelli, 2010, p. 175). Yet, others have suggested that while the high concentration of executive powers in agency models creates particular accountability pressures to which both principals and agents respond with comprehensive analysis-based decision making, the diffusion of executive powers in multi-level settings lowers such accountability pressures for any one single actor and, with it, the appeal of analytical tools as legitimacy boosters (Demeritt et al., 2017). This suggests that individual executive bodies at the subnational level may well use analytical models to legitimize their mandate in local accountability relations, but the diffusion of such models across the country seems less likely.

However, second, actors in multi-level settings have strong *additional* – and indeed rather *different* – reasons to engage with analytical tools in their legitimacy-seeking strategies when compared to regulatory agencies. The *level* of accountability pressure is not the sole determinant of the legitimacy-oriented appeal of actuarial analyses. Instead, different decision-making settings also come with different *forms* of accountability and legitimacy pressures, hence different contexts for institutional risk management. For the case of risk analysis, the common interpretation of risk analysis as blame management (Chapter 3) must be slightly expanded to acknowledge institutional variety in executive decision-making.[9] Indeed, when leaving concentrated executive structures behind and entering contexts of more spread-out forms of executive decision-making in multi-level settings, risk analysis may become a distinct strategy of blame management in which actors seek to *allocate* "blamability"[10] across actors and levels of governance. Risk-based differentiation enables authorities in multi-level settings to carve out the limits of their own mandate and accountability for failure *vis-à-vis other administrative levels*. In the EU context, for example, where the empirical meaning of subsidiarity requires constant confirmation, the reference to various risk levels gives authorities a useful shorthand for negotiating how responsibilities for high, medium, and low types of risk are best distributed across levels. An example of such a dynamic system occurs in European border control where the EU Commission uses risk analysis to shift back blame for any ineffective management of medium and low border risks to member states and regions (while also taking on a powerful role as a high-risk regulator) (Paul, 2017a).

Third, these reflections lead to the role of risk analysis in *collective* instances of self-defense where several state-level authorities experience similar individual legitimacy pressure. For example, after a scandal with cross-border implications, they may consider it wise to respond to them collectively. In this context, analytical tools offer not just a way for any one subcentral actor to signal their "being modern" and not even just a way to signal them being as modern as others in the sense of mimetic isomorphism; they can also show their effort in being modern in a *coordinated* way. Risk analysis seems particularly fruitful, in this context, as its differentiation techniques can signal a modus of rational consensus-seeking about policy priorities; a key selling point in Germany's federalist setting where the structural tensions between unity and centralization vs. subnational autonomy has long incentivized states to coordinate their actions. Risk analysis, building on its ability to differentiate conditions for blame and to incur trust in numbers, can thus be a tool for the collective counteraction of both failures in societal risk management *and* (related) unitarization demands. Importantly, from the perspective of sociological neo-institutionalism, such processes of horizontal emulation rely on the existence of both a locally trialed and ostensibly successful analytical template and coordination fora through which they can spread, bottom-up, as blueprints for coordinated policy-making. As Porter (1995, p. 5) suggests, "once put in place, they [numerical templates for analysis] permit reasoning to become more uniform, and in this sense more rigorous".

The expectation of the dynamics of self-defense through coordinated emulation of analytical blueprints that count as rational and "modern" concurs with findings on German public administration reform. Several authors have discussed constant micro-level adaptations at the level of tools as essential prerequisites for the bureaucracy's (infamous) macro-level stability (Ellwein, 2001; Seibel, 2001). Seibel (2001, p. 87), in particular, has highlighted that the "adaptability" and "problem-solving capacities" of the German system lie precisely in the potential of cooperative federalism to induce adaptive changes to the ways policies come about from below. For example, while usually associated with a "sporadic potential to shape" policy-making, enforcement bodies have "re-constituted themselves procedurally" through "important innovations" to decision-making processes (Döhler, 2006, p. 219, translation by author). Executive federalism may survive as an institutional set up because the demonstration of an ability to incrementally adapt procedures for coordinated decision-making legitimizes the decentral organization of policy implementation as an appropriate institutional choice. The coordinated emulation of new analytical methods, as a means of coordinating executive decision-making across Länder boundaries, then seems crucial not only for collective problem-solving (Section 4.3) but also for justifying the perseverance of executive federalism[11] itself.

Finally, the instrument constituency literature (see Chapter 2) suggests that the joint commitment to a tool also strengthens subcentral actors' commitment to one another (Voß and Simons, 2014; Béland and Howlett, 2016; Voß, 2016; Simons and Voß, 2017) and allows them to take on "collective actor qualities" (Simons and Voß, 2017, p. 12). Whatever initial promises actors associated with risk analysis or its fellow tools, this can prompt a distinctly *endogenous* and self-reinforcing process of collective identity formation (= constituencies) around and through its joint promotion. Actors' joint effort in keeping it "alive both as a model and as an implemented practice" (Béland and Howlett, 2016, p. 397) may become a cause of its own that keeps "attract[ing] and generat[ing] agency" (Simons and Voß, 2017, p. 9) or even lead to the creation of "constituency-internal institutions and organisations" (ibid., p. 12). This means that the existence of an instrument constituency, with a vision of collective actorness, is likely to strengthen the cause for analytical tools across the levels and ranks of executive federalism. This is even more so since instrument constituencies cut across formal decision-making structures and unite actors from across most diverse organizations (government departments, international organizations, NGOs, interest groups and social movements, scientific associations, the media, etc.).

4.4.3 *Analysis-based power-seeking in Germany's multi-level administration*

I argued that administrative actors and policymakers may adopt analytical tools where they promise to facilitate actors' power-seeking strategies and, in particular, their wish to expand their mandate for, and influence over, collectively binding decision-making (Section 2.5). Chapter 3 specified this focus for risk analysis: it speaks to actors' desire for harmonized and consistent policy enforcement across the administration and is developed into (soft) coercive strategies for streamlining decision-making around the notion of risk.

Attempts to increase control over the bureaucracy through coercive and softly coercive mechanisms will matter in multi-level settings, too. Vertical control – from the top of government (the EU or the Federal government) down to local authorities – is always an issue in public administrations because the enforcement of policies decided upon at higher levels of government typically relies on executive discretion "on the ground" – by local inspectors or public service officers. The earlier discussion of the Anglo-American benchmark highlights that the strict accountability relationships in agency models make analytical tools attractive as instruments to bind agencies' autonomous decisions, from the perspective of a political principal. As actors can turn risk analysis into visualizable cues on how to differentiate policy problems and solutions to softly steer others' decision-making, its appeal as a tool of meta-governance rises in multi-level settings too. As discussed in the Introduction, the EU Commission has chiefly relied on the promotion of analytical tools – often by Regulations or Directives – to induce soft policy-harmonization processes, including the requirement for member states to do risk analysis in several policy domains. Less often, the EU also couples member states' access to its funding schemes to the outcomes of prescribed risk analysis, as is the case in border control

(Paul, 2017a). By changing the conditions for action for member states, such meta-governance can induce risk-based forms of policy harmonization. Whether analytical tools will emerge through coercion or soft coercion in a multi-level administration will vary with the EU's and the national government's power *and* appetite to shape subcentral policy execution in a domain. They are easier at hand in policy domains where central level actors – be it an EU Directorate General or Federal Ministry – possess the formal power to coerce analytical models onto lower levels, or where they oversee specific monies and can tie eligibility criteria to an analytical model in their meta-governance of a domain.

I propose a second interpretation of power-seeking through analysis, as more closely related to deliberate power-distributional strategies, in settings with strong executive autonomy of subnational actors. As policy reforms in multi-level polities have been associated with the always concurrent consideration of the distribution of competencies and resources between authorities of different levels (Behnke, 2015, pp. 9, 12; more generally: Benz, 2009; Heinelt and Knodt, 2011), an influence-related logic of analytical tools will be of special relevance here. In a context of strong executive federalism with much subnational autonomy to make and implement policies on the ground, central level actors, in particular, will perceive analytical tools as potential game-changers in the polity and adopt them with a view of tilting the formal or informal allocation of decision-making powers in their favor. This claim fits well with previous arguments on the politics of instrumentation and instrument constituencies that tools can not only have "unintended structuring effects" (Lascoumes and Le Galès, 2007, p. 10f) but be "a site of power politics in which expectations towards structural positions are negotiated" (Voß and Simons, 2014, p. 739).

The constant re-negotiation of unity and autonomy between the center and subnational actors in German federalism, as discussed earlier, means that central level coercive powers themselves are in a flux. While the legitimacy-seeking perspective highlighted the subnational counteraction of unitarization demands, power-seeking suggests that new coercive powers at the center could also be justified through common analysis. As detailed earlier, discrepancies between the norms of equal living conditions and highly uneven socio-economic outcomes in Germany has repeatedly given the Federal level an authorization to intervene in Länder affairs (Kropp, 2010). The EU or Federal level actors could interpret and strategically embed analytical tools in the existing decision-making structures in ways that enable them to meta-govern autonomous actors' actions or to even introduce new central level powers, formally or informally. The literature on the EU as an international bureaucracy, for example, highlights that soft coercion through benchmark exercises can develop a dynamic beyond the manipulation of local authorities' autonomous decision making (meta-governance). More generally, a wide discussion of the European integration of core state powers (Genschel and Jachtenfuchs, 2013) so far notes that the building of EU level administrative and executive powers "by stealth" has relied on the EU Commission's (including DGs and agencies) technical-analytical and coordinative capacities (e.g., Heidbreder,

2013, 2017; Trondal, 2013). Several studies illustrate how the EU Commission develops a sense of "strategic agency" around its organization of analysis-based benchmarking and performance measurement with the explicit goal of centralizing decision making, at least informally, through newly centralized procedures of analysis, central monitoring, and recommendations (e.g., Radaelli and Meuwese, 2010; Paul, 2017a; Jankauskas and Eckhard, 2019). These accounts point back to the older interpretations of analytical tools and methods, met in the book's introduction. Analogously to Desrosières' statistics in the fragmented German states in the past, analytical frameworks in multi-level administration today are likely "one of the mechanisms that sustain a state when its stability is problematical" (2002, p. 180) with central measuring and monitoring becoming the pretext for harmonization claims.

The specific de-politicization potential of risk analysis will aid centrally induced harmonization processes. Risk models can be expected to appeal to administrative actors as methods for harmonizing executive decisions across autonomous bureaucracies *precisely because* their calculative basis appears to be fair and neutral (cf. "trust in numbers" argument above) and risk-based harmonization attempts do therefore not openly challenge or overhaul other actors' authority. It is in this seemingly innocent capacity that any *de facto* harmonization around a risk-analytical model may seem more readily acceptable than attempts of *de jure* centralization or integration of policy-making and enforcement (cf. argument in Paul, 2017a). From my polity policies perspective, policy domains characterized by highly fragmented decision-making – a rather insurmountable obstacle for Rothstein and colleagues in their assessment of Germany's likelihood to adopt risk-based approaches (2013) – should hence be regarded as particularly likely targets for common risk-analytical frameworks.

4.5 Conclusion

This chapter laid the foundations for a contextualized analysis of analytical tools in the German multi-level setting – and beyond – in two ways. First, it reviewed insights about what drives British and US policymakers to adopt CBA and its cousins. These benchmark cases feature a strong public interest culture and relatively high dedication to the NPM agenda which jointly inform instrumental interpretations of analytical tools as cost-effective problem solving. This view interacts with a special focus on legitimacy-seeking and power-seeking that emerges from the context of concentrated executive power in the agency model (see Table 4.1).

Second, I showed that multi-level settings represent not so much deviant cases from this sometimes essentialized benchmark but "different planets" on which analytical tools flourish for different sets of interpretations of their I, L, and P merits. German federalism operates with distinct constitutional and structural conditions: a strong requirement for policy coordination between interdependent actors – also beyond the much cited spheres of formal joint decision making – and a need to constantly confirm or rework (if ever so incrementally) the balance between

TABLE 4.1 Analytical tools and their context-specific appeal in multi-level administrations

	Instrumentality	*Legitimacy-seeking*	*Power-seeking*
Logic of	Consequentiality	Appropriateness	Influence
Underlying goal	Wish to solve a policy problem	Wish to defend one's mandate against criticism	Wish to expand influence in a policy domain
The appeal of analytical tools in the "benchmark" cases			
Interpretation in benchmark cases	Cost-effective problem-solving	Justification of executive decisions	Control of executive decisions of independent agencies or subnational enforcement actors
Favorable contextual conditions	Public interest culture; "core marketizer" NPM agenda	Accountability pressure from principals/ central executive	Concern over agency performance and accountability
The appeal of analytical tools in the German multi-level administration			
Interpretation in German multi-level administration	Collective problem-solving across fragmented jurisdictions	Polity policies as individual and collective stabilization of subcentral autonomy	Polity policies as expansion of central level influence and meta-governance
Favorable contextual conditions	Legal-administrative unity and federal solidarity norms; perception of a policy problem as requiring collective action; practice of intergovernmental cooperation; problem- and consensus-oriented civil service open to expertise	Higher competition over executive mandates creates legitimacy pressure but also fragments accountability structures; constant need to counteract unitarization of executive decision-making; experience with horizontal coordination; availability of seemingly workable blueprints and/or existence of an instrument constituency	"Appetite" for central influence in multi-level setting; existence of coercive powers to introduce analytical tool; ability to tilt incentive structures for sub-central actors alongside analysis (meta-governance); use of normative ideal of legal-administrative unity (or in EU: common market) as pathway to intervening with sub-central decision making
Ideal-typical expectations	Adoption of a shared analytical tool with a view to overcome collective action problems; focus on developing shared understanding of causes of a policy problem and effects of likely solutions; more likely in contexts of regulatory policy-making and enforcement (exemption of re-distributive issues)	Adoption of a shared analytical tool with a view of countering individual or collective legitimacy pressures on subnational actors through horizontal coordination; diffusion through mimetic isomorphism; potential constituency-building around an analytical tool beyond actors of executive federalism	Adoption of a shared analytical tool with view of central level actors to gain influence over sub-central decision making; use of soft coercive powers to bind behavior of autonomous actors through common analysis; naming and shaming dynamics; creation of analysis-based incentive structures to harmonize subcentral decision-making

Source: Author's compilation

legal-administrative unity and autonomous subnational decision making. These conditions are likely to favor (I) an instrumental appreciation of analytical tools as enablers of collective problem-solving and keys to rational consensus-seeking between interdependent actors, (L) horizontal emulation of analytical tools to defend subnational decision making powers against unitarization demands, and (P) hard and soft coercion toward analytical tools imposed by central level actors, potentially paired with meta-governance attempts to change the conditions for governance for autonomous sub-central actors, but also efforts to tilt decision making structures toward the center formally or informally (see Table 4.1). Rather than inhibiting analytical innovation, – as often assumed in comparative studies of administrative reform and public policy – executive fragmentation must be re-conceptualized as a context which nourishes its very own efforts in collective problem-solving *and* a distinct form of polity policies in which analysis helps actors (re-)negotiate positions of legitimacy and power in the complex decision-making setting.

Insights from this chapter clearly demarcate the limits of the widespread methodological decision to compare *national* administrations with an empirical focus on the central state level (e.g., Demeritt et al., 2017; Radaelli, 2005; Pollitt, van Thiel and Homburg, 2007b; Pollitt and Bouckaert, 2011; Rothstein, Borraz and Huber, 2013). Methodological nationalism both elides the ability of analytical tools to emerge "bottom-up" through coordinated forms of emulation *and* underestimates the impact of supranational (rather than just national) "hard" or "soft" coercion in engendering analytical tool change. Indeed, just as Chapter 2 suggests I, L, and P orientations will interact, the present chapter highlights that I, L, and P orientation might cut across the EU, national, Länder, and municipal level of decision making in complex ways. For example, where national governments welcome analytical frameworks coming in via EU level coercion because they promise to expand their own administrative control in an otherwise decentralized domain, we might observe a reinforcing dynamic between both perspectives. Individual subnational actors might initially favor risk analysis for instrumental problem-solving at state level but then feed its template into Länder coordination processes which might twist from collective-problem-solving to collective legitimacy-seeking. I shift up (including the EU level) and down (including sub-national administrations) analytical attention from the national level to enable an adequate examination of why analytical tools appeal to decision makers in multi-level administrations.

My conceptual approach to context (Section 1.3) also suggests that the same nominal tool can display *highly variable adoption patterns* across countries over time and across policy sectors within the same jurisdiction. I expect the exact institutional conditions for multi-level decision-making – both with respect to problem-solving and to polity policies – to vary by policy domain (Section 1.4). One aim of the subsequent empirical analyses is to chart and explain potentially important *sectoral* specificities in actors' perceptions of the following:

- policy problems and related collective action problems to which risk analysis can be an answer

- individual and joint legitimacy pressures and the existence of templates and specific forms of emulation
- the allocation of decision-making powers in a sector, and administrative actors' struggles to re-negotiate that very allocation across the multiple levels of the fragmented administrative setting.

Chapters 5–7 take up this methodological cue, in line with the interpretivist and ideographic paradigm in comparative social sciences, by offering an in-depth qualitative and historical review of each policy domain (Sections 5.1, 6.1, and 7.1). This covers both historical origins and contemporary features of problem perceptions, collective action problems, the allocation and substance of administrative mandates in the multi-level setting, and potential struggles over legitimacy and executive powers. Case reviews draw on secondary literature and primary documents (e.g., legislation, executive orders, reports, and guidelines by federal coordination fora, state-level decrees and guidelines, statistical information on variable numbers of inspectors/controls, etc.), but also include background information from interviews. Provided with this contextual anchoring, the chapters then reconstruct the introduction of risk analysis in each domain (Sections 5.2, 6.2, and 7.2), drawing mainly on primary data from policy documents and laws (including the EU legislation, wherever relevant) and background details on the specific application of risk analysis from expert interviews. The respective sections identify patterns of adopting risk analysis based on the indicators developed in Chapter 3. The last section of each chapter (Sections 5.3, 6.3, and 7.3) explains the dominant adoption patterns through an interpretive analysis of policymakers' instrumental, legitimacy-seeking, and power-oriented justifications – and their combinations – for introducing and applying risk analysis in their respective domain.

Notes

1 (Peters, 2005, p. 354)
2 For wider reviews of German federalism, see the recent works of Benz, Detemple and Heinz (2016) and Kropp (2010).
3 The other two nodes are the multiple party system with a tendency to form coalition governments and parapublic institutions which regulate sectoral issues – including unemployment, work safety, or health care – independently from but on behalf of the central government (Katzenstein, 1987, p. 35ff).
4 Scharpf's joint-decision only concerns cases of constitutionally require policy interaction where actors have no exit option and stalemate can block problem-solving for all. Cooperative federalism, by contrast, involves more voluntary forms of interaction (Kropp, 2010).
5 These joint tasks exist since 1969 in the constitution, as did university development, which was abolished in 2006 (cf. Benz, Detemple and Heinz, 2016).
6 Indeed, as Benz, Detemple and Heinz note (2016, p. 20ff), Scharpf himself was explicit about his model applying to only one of the various forms of policy coordination in Germany's multi-level setting.
7 Of course, this executive dominance comes with a problematic lack of meaningful parliamentary scrutiny and involvement (Kropp, 2010). Unlike in the case of regulatory agencies, which also involves power shifts to the executive but creates direct lines of

accountability between the politically elected principals and the agencies, executive federalism in Germany creates rather diffuse forms of accountability and produces decisions in less transparent ways.

8 It is no coincidence, from the perspective of equal living conditions, that the two remaining Gemeinschaftsaufgaben with joint decision structures in the narrow Scharpfian sense cover the country's economic and agrarian structure – domains where location competition between Länder ought to be avoided.

9 In a study with Michael Huber, we also found that risk analysis can "operate to stabilize corporatist arrangements over time by nourishing their core ingredients: trust, consensus, and solidarity" (Paul and Huber, 2015, p. 27). We argue that in decision-making settings where external accountability pressures are low but where, instead, intense reciprocal accountability relations between negotiation partners require long-term trust and coordination abilities, risk analysis may appeal as much as in the British agency model, albeit for very different legitimacy-oriented reasons.

10 This is different from the notion of "blame-shifting" which has been described as an impulse for administrations' to split responsibilities for regulation and regulatory enforcement so as to be able to blame the respective other should one get "squeezed" in demands to account for outcomes of risk regulation (Hood and Rothstein, 2001; Hood, Rothstein and Baldwin, 2001).

11 More generally speaking, the notion of Germany as a Neo-Weberian state, which keeps its basic structural features – including executive federalism – in place by modernizing its standard operating procedures from within, captures this pattern of simultaneous stability and change well (Pollitt and Bouckaert, 2011). Much of the work on NPM reforms confirms a trend of stabilizing existing institutions through incremental reforms of administrative decision-making procedures (Pollitt, van Thiel and Homburg, 2007b; Kuhlmann, 2010; Pollitt and Bouckaert, 2011; Atkinson, 2015).

PART 2

Comparative analysis

Risk analysis across three policy domains in Germany

5

FORGING "ONE VOICE" ON THE COMMON MARKET

Risk analysis and the unitarization of food safety controls

> *I do want the same level of protection in Cologne and [the Frisian island of] Borkum to start with.*[1]

The first comparative case study is food safety enforcement[2] because it has the longest history of tight policy coordination across the multiple executive branches in Germany's public administration, it involves the strongest coercive role of both the EU and the national government, and has seen risk-based priority setting first, since 2004. I first delineate the historical evolution of a regulatory mandate for food safety inspections, its comparative strength, the strong focus on policy coordination, and the relatively strong role of the national (and later EU) level administration in the domain. I then describe how risk analysis was introduced in the domain, via the EU venue, and taken up in the German enforcement regime, using the indicators developed in Chapter 3. The last section explains the adoption pattern – an over-compliant and rather centrally steered embrace of the modest risk-analytical requirements of the EU – by situating policymakers' justifications within the ILP typology (cf. Chapter 2) and linking their interpretations to the institutional conditions of multi-level decision-making (cf. Chapter 4). Policymakers see a dire requirement to enforce food safety law consistently across the common food market in Europe for the sake of both consumers and food businesses – much in line with the historically derived normative goal of legal-administrative unity and equal living conditions. The strong desire for collective action in the multi-level setting makes risk analysis an effectiveness-oriented remedy for overcoming limits to coordinated controls in a context of high executive fragmentation. Whilst a collective problem-solving orientation seems to dominate the domain, it both relies on and reifies a historical decision on *polity policies*: to endow the central level government with a key regulatory role and strong coordination mandate over formally autonomous enforcement bodies. The dominant instrumental reading of risk analysis is flanked by less relevant but mutually reinforcing hopes of efficiency gains and a blame-shifting desire by inspectorates toward regulatees.

5.1 Food safety controls in Germany: early focus on problem-driven coordination

Until the late 19th century, the food safety administration on German territories resembled a "complex jigsaw of municipal and territorial provisions", which created a "highly fragmented, confusing bulk of norms" (Hierholzer, 2010, pp. 340 and 355, translations by author). Before the foundation of a unified German Empire in 1871, most states had their municipal police authorities conduct food safety inspections. The so-called medicinal police (*medicinische Policey*) – a distinct entity of the police force at the time – was in charge of enforcing medicinal codes (*Medizinalordnungen*), which combined the statutory duties of danger prevention with the provision of welfare (*Gefahrenabwehr* and *Daseinsvorsorge*) (e.g., on the Grand Duchy of Baden: Reusch, 1986; Hierholzer, 2010, p. 55). While similar regulatory constructions for policing food safety, characteristic of the absolutist police state at the time, existed across German states since the 18th century, control foci and frequencies varied considerably, and implementation lagged behind in many peripheral districts. For example, while the Prussian city of Cologne only saw 149 inspections in 1878, the much smaller city of Erlangen in Bavaria conducted 1,679 controls in the same year (Hierholzer, 2010, p. 67, table 2). Adding to the much variable municipal police inspections, guilds performed their own controls of bakeries, slaughterhouses, dairies or wine factories, but the relevance of these diminished with the establishment of freedom of trade in the mid-19th century (1862 in Baden) (Reusch, 1986, p. 40f).

5.1.1 Early pathway of evidence-based policy coordination

This extreme fragmentation of regulatory authorities and practices came under increasing pressure in the 19th century when a strong regulatory mandate, centralization and tight policy coordination across the multi-level setting came to be considered chief solutions to a perception of severe *collective* problem pressure. Swift industrial progress in the food industry, related market failures, and the simultaneous loss of relevance of guilds as self-regulatory forces informed a widely perceived necessity for centralizing food safety regulation and enforcement (Hierholzer, 2010). As food was produced with ever intensified divisions of labor, involving progressively elaborate chemical manipulations, and embedded in increasingly complex markets – much in contrast to the local and often self-sustaining forms of food supply preceding industrial food production – information asymmetries and consumer health in industrialized food systems came to be perceived as major policy problems which cut across the many German jurisdictions (cf., Reusch, 1986; Grüne, 1994; Hierholzer, 2010). Public outrage about adulterated food (e.g., red dye in wine, watered down milk, or sausages thickened with flour), food-borne illnesses and fatalities culminated in calls for tighter and more coordinated state regulation. Reform calls were backed by increasing media attention, the strong advocacy of parliamentarians of the Reichstag (e.g., August Reichensperger), Chancellor Otto von Bismarck, and the formation of a profession of food chemists who interpreted their role as expert advocates of the (ostensibly) notoriously betrayed and powerless consumers (Reusch, 1986; Hierholzer, 2010).

The perception of a severe policy problem and its causes – in this case, illness and deaths due to food market failures – created a climate of reform urgency during which the Imperial Government assumed a surprisingly "uncontested central role" as a regulator (Hierholzer, 2010, p. 79). Indeed, an early normative focus on "*reichseinheitliche Bestimmungen*" materialized in the food safety domain around that time (uniform provisions across the Empire, Reusch, 1986), predating the constitutionalization of legal-administrative unity and equal living conditions as a more general norm in German executive federalism (cf. Chapter 4). In 1876, the *Kaiserliches Gesundheitsamt* (Imperial Health Office) was founded to conduct nation-wide scientific assessments of food hygiene and food safety, partly replacing state and municipal level authorities or at least standardizing their methods (Grüne, 1994). By then already highly institutionalized and standardized profession of food chemists became a central player in the newly founded Imperial Health Office and the food safety regime. Food chemists were responsible for gathering academic knowledge on food, hygiene, and food-borne diseases, advised the government in health and hygiene policies, co-wrote legislation, and defined the methods and standards for the newly founded state inspectorates (Hierholzer, 2010, p. 159). Even before this official inauguration, they were the much-trusted expert consultants of lay police inspectorates in the states. This early involvement of, and trust in, scientific expertise created a path of evidence-based problem-solving in the domain which enabled a far-reaching coordination of subnational executive decision-making in which central coercion played a major (uncontested) role from the very beginning (cf. Hierholzer, 2010, p. 76f).

In 1879, another source for harmonization came with the first comprehensive Food Law (Hierholzer, 2010). The *Nahrungsmittelgesetz* aimed at "avoiding dishonest practices in industrial food production and to prevent health risks and thus improve the national food supply overall" (Sewekow, Schmidt-Faber and Frost, 2010, p. 314, translation by author). It gave inspectors across the *Reich* the same legal basis for interventions, defined sanctions and provided options for further decrees. The law marks an early example of what we would call concurrent legislation today: based on article 4 of the Imperial Constitution of 1871 "binding legal provisions for the medicinal police – including the control of food markets – were subject to Imperial legislation" which would immediately abrogate existing state law where it counteracted "reichseinheitliche Bestimmungen" (Reusch, 1986, p. 54f, translation by author).

Subsequent legislation mainly filled legal voids and sought to ensure relative consistency in enforcement by harmonization and de facto centralization further

(Reusch, 1986, p. 327ff). A Food Law amendment in 1927 entailed clearer definitions of legal terms such as "adulteration", provided clearer assessment criteria for food inspections, and gave more detailed standards for the chemical analysis[3] of food (Sewekow, Schmidt-Faber and Frost, 2010). The amendment did not only ask states to coordinate their activities voluntarily, but also established a right for the central state to coerce states to follow common guiding principles for decentral enforcement by help of executive orders (Reusch, 1986). This is an early example of how the central administration sought (and still seeks) to counter executive fragmentation in the German food safety domain – a tool not widely used in our other two cases. Indeed, the passing of one of the first executive orders in the domain in 1934 has presumably contributed to consistent enforcement and increased effectiveness of controls (Sewekow, Schmidt-Faber and Frost, 2010, p. 314). It introduced a still applicable rule that at least five food samples must be taken and analyzed per 1,000 inhabitants in routine food inspections. Smaller amendments apart, the Imperial regulatory regime remained largely intact in Western Germany[4] after the Second World War, until the Food and Consumer Products Law set common national food safety standards for the first time in 1974.

5.1.2 Contemporary intensification of policy coordination

The interaction of traditionally autonomous enforcement by *Länder* and municipalities, centrally organized scientific information-gathering, framework regulation by the central government, and central level efforts to ensure the consistency of enforcement through executive orders set the path for present day German food safety governance. The contemporary allocation of authorities in Germany's executive federalism looks remarkably similar to the historically established pattern.[5] The German Basic Law makes the health protection of consumers on food markets subject to concurrent legislation (art. 74/20), meaning that state laws apply so far as no Federal law regulates the same issue. Since a reform of federalism in 2006 states can deviate from national regulation in justified cases, yet they do not tend to do so in the food safety domain, arguably because regulation at the EU and national level usually leave enough discretion for the local execution of policies.

Länder usually fulfil their executive duties in specifically tasked ministerial resorts. State ministries or central *Landesämter* are responsible for coordinating inspections on their territory whilst municipal districts supervise the local enforcement bodies (*Lebensmittelüberwachungsämter*) in cities and councils. Overall, roughly 2,400 to 2,500 local inspectors were in charge of controlling about 1,217,000 premises in 2015 (BVL, 2017). On average, approximately 150 inspectors per state each conduct about 2.1 inspections per day (survey with leading food inspectors in each state), with Bavarian inspectors inspecting just over fifty percent more premises per day as their colleagues in Saxony, but at the same time also having a higher staff/premises ratio to afford lower numbers of controls per inspector. The overall share of controlled premises per year in 2015 was at 43.7 per cent. This is a comparatively high inspection ratio – especially compared to work safety where only about 2.5 per cent of premises get inspected per annum (see Chapter 7). It speaks of a relatively low tolerance of failure in achieving food safety goals in Germany (Ansell and Vogel, 2006; K. T. Paul, 2007).

Several interlinkages between and across governance levels in the domain serve to counteract the risk of executive fragmentation. Theoretically, there is scope for voluntary horizontal emulation processes for new policy tools in two relevant inter-state coordination fora: a Länder working group on consumer protection (LAV) and the standing conference of state ministers of consumer protection (VMK) regularly discuss issues of common interest and develop coordinated guidelines for enforcement. However, the domain also exhibits several coercive governance mechanisms which give the national administration the power to curb local discretion over enforcement decisions in food safety relatively directly:

- First, municipal *Überwachungsämter* (inspectorates) are subject to a chain of hierarchical ministerial control within states, both in terms of common policy guidelines (*Fachaufsicht*) and legal compliance (*Rechtsaufsicht*). Länder themselves are also subject to the legal supervision by Federal authorities (*Bundesaufsicht*) and can even be brought before the Constitutional Court if they do not fulfil their (otherwise autonomous) enforcement duties in line with legal provisions (art. 84/3 and 4 Basic Law). Hierarchical control can hence be expected to constrain the actual discretion of local enforcers in the sense of bureaucratic control (Section 4.4).
- Second, the Federal government can pass administrative decrees (*Allgemeine Verwaltungsvorschriften; AVV*) to coordinate Länder enforcement approaches but needs approval of the Länder chamber *Bundesrat* to do so. The goal of these negotiated and internally oriented enforcement rules is to coordinate decentral administrative decision-making where framework legislation grants a lot of discretion to decentral enforcers (Seibel, 2001, p. 89; on food safety specifically: Roth, 2012). Many AVVs serve to implement EU-level regulation consistently across German states. Decrees are a rather institutionalized form of *vertical policy coordination* as they bind local administrative practice directly (via coercion by joint Bund/Länder action) and relatively steadily over time (Benz, 2001). Two AVVs govern the food safety domain: the AVV RÜb on control guidelines and the AVV DÜb on data exchange between competent authorities (Roth, 2012). The former is of considerable relevance for the specification of risk analysis in German food safety inspections (see Section 5.2) and will form a major part of the analysis later.
- Third, the *Federal Office of Consumer Protection and Food Safety (BVL)* coordinates Länder activities in case of nation-wide crises. This means that there can be a temporary and often informal softening of the allocation of competencies within German executive federalism when the scale of a food crisis "goes national". In a similar manner, the *European Food and Veterinary Office* (FVO) conducts audits and inspections to monitor the effectiveness of surveillance systems in member states (as well as on third countries which import foodstuffs

and feed to the common market). The FVO can also recommend improvements where its reviewers see compliance deficiencies and set soft incentives for harmonization through benchmarking and reporting duties.

5.1.3 Policy coordination one level up: strong Europeanization after the BSE scandal

The more recent era of German food safety governance has seen history repeat itself one level up, in Brussels. Indeed, the historical administrative setting – with its fine-tuned balance between subcentral enforcement paired with strong coordination mechanisms and its focus on evidence-based problem-solving on a common market – has been lifted to the EU level. The *Federal Ministry of Food, Agriculture and Consumer Protection (BMELV)* notes that up to 90 per cent of food-related legislation comes out of Brussels nowadays (BMELV, 2013, p. 17), meaning that state enforcement practices within Germany are being largely shaped by directly binding EU regulation. Interviewees widely share the assessment that food safety is – and indeed ought to be! – a largely integrated policy domain (see Section 5.3). Academic observers have befittingly described food safety as a "prime example of multi-level governance in the sense of a substantial and growing influence of the EU level on national regulation" (Lodge and Wegrich, 2011, p. 91).

The EU's rise to a chief food safety regulator is founded on similar collective problem perceptions and ideas about suitable governance solutions as during the inauguration of the Imperial governance of food safety in the past. To protect consumers against harmful failures in increasingly de-bordered food markets in Europe, member states have conceded the creation of strong EU level regulatory institutions and embedded their autonomous activities in common standardized scientific information-gathering. The relatively early supranational interventions – especially when compared to our other two policy domains – were justified with the pronounced cross-national character of food markets from resource harvesting, production, and processing, to retail and consumption (Roth, 2009). A Council decision in 1975 was the first to highlight the right of consumers to have their health and life protected, to be properly informed, to have their economic interests protected and be compensated for losses and damage (Roth, 2009, p. 11). These guidelines have been transferred into primary EU law (article 169 of the Lisbon Treaty and article 153 of the TEU) and forged a mandate for subsequent expansion of supranational legislative, executive, and judicial activity in the food safety domain. As I will detail later, interviewees highlight the links between the common food market and far-reaching legislative integration and executive harmonization: they assume that fragmented jurisdictions are ineffective in addressing food risks because food travels freely across the borders of these jurisdictions (cf. Section 5.3). In other words, the perception that food safety is a collective problem on a common food market nourishes acceptance of tight policy coordination in the domain.

The most important regulatory landmark on member states is the EU's umbrella regulation 178/2002 on general principles of food safety (EU Council, 2002), transposed into German Federal law in 2005. Other innovations apart (Oosterveer, 2002; cf. Ansell and Vogel, 2006; K. T. Paul, 2007, 2012), the regulation constituted a paradigm shift for German enforcement decision in as much it highlights the "duty of care" of producers and food businesses.[6] It has shifted legal responsibilities for food safety explicitly to producers and left statutory inspectors with the task of controlling – rather than ensuring – compliance (Knipschild, 2003, p. 228f). This is a considerable break with the German *policey* tradition of enforcement when guaranteeing "impeccable food" was a duty of municipal medicinal policemen (e.g., Reusch, 1986 as quoted earlier). EU regulation might hence have changed the pre-disposition of state-level administrators from seeing themselves as being responsible for food safety to being in charge of controlling the compliance behavior of food businesses, all whilst accepting that the state cannot guarantee safe food (but see the divergent French interpretation of regulation 178/2002: Borraz et al., 2020). It might thus have lowered inspectorates' legitimacy pressure. The regulation also formed the European Food Safety Authority, EFSA, as a central and independent scientific expert authority, similarly to the Imperial Health Office at the time. Already since 1997, the responsible Directorate General – currently DG Sanco – can impact national enforcement directly through "infraction/infringement proceedings [and even] the imposition of immediate trade restrictions in case of a 'serious immediate risk'" (Lodge and Wegrich, 2011, p. 96). Through regular inspections of the control regimes in member states and food-importing third countries, the FVO assists the DG by identifying enforcement gaps and recommending best practices (Borraz et al., 2020). Where the risk of harm transcends national boundaries, the EU Commission now has executive powers over member states and their (often municipal) enforcement bodies. Most importantly for this book's analysis, a 2004 regulation on food safety inspections coerced member states to adopt risk analysis as a basis for priority-setting in enforcement (Council of the European Union, 2004). Before I detail this policy, its emergence requires contextualization in what was perhaps one of the largest EU-wide scandals in risk regulation.

The comprehensive EU-level regulation and institutionalization were sparked off by the infamous scandal around BSE first in the late 1990s – when British cattle suffered from the disease – and second in the early 2000s – when transmission to humans caused first Creutzfeldt-Jakob disease deaths and BSE was detected in German cattle. There is no need to review the extensive literature on BSE and European food safety regulation here (Vos, 2000; for good overviews, see Ansell and Vogel, 2006). For the purposes of this book, it suffices to acknowledge that the BSE crises have provoked far-reaching and sustained shifts in the institutional arrangement of food safety with an even more prominent role for central level – and in this case supranational – regulation (Steiner, 2006; K. T. Paul, 2007, 2012; Lodge, 2011). Several scholars have framed the BSE crisis as a "point of no return" with a need for "radical" policy and institutional shifts in the eyes of the public and policymakers in Europe (K. T. Paul, 2007). Most importantly, from this book's perspective, the perception of dire and lethal regulatory problems on a common food market provoked a far-reaching and relatively uncontested deepening of the already comparatively advanced coordination in the regulatory domain across the multi-level setting (K. T. Paul, 2012). As an EU official related to my colleague Mara Wesseling in an interview:

> *People forget that the BSE crisis was . . . a very real crisis . . . But at that time, you know, there were epidemiological studies suggesting that anything up to half a million people were going to die from Creutzfeldt-Jakob disease. So, there was a big political scandal over it, huge damage to the European beef industry, huge damage to the credibility of European control mechanisms, the safety of the food chain, huge political consequences.*
>
> *(FSY-EU)*

Political consequences were serious in Germany where the Minister of Agriculture and his colleague from the Department of Health had to resign over the BSE scandals. Blame on the wider public administration and inspectorates – or the organization of controls – was limited, however, when compared to other European countries affected by BSE outbreaks (Oosterveer, 2002; but Lodge, 2011). It was with respect to the regulatory role of the EU level and its interactions with national and subnational administrative levels that BSE left most considerable traces. High scandalization of market failure and its resulting in a life-threatening border-crossing risk gave the EU robust justification to strengthen its role as supranational market-correcting regulator on the single food market, making food safety arguably *the* most harmonized policy domain in the EU (Havinga, 2014). Most importantly, there was a turn from softer directive-based legislation to the use of regulations as main legislative tool. Interviewees interpret this as the EU's attempt to limit variability and diversion from common standards:

> *It was always difficult: one (member state) did not transpose (directives) correctly, or not on time . . . the other (member state) interpreted it differently, it was a constant seesaw. At some point the EU said: let's get serious, we simply pass regulations, and these are directly binding law in all member states.*
>
> *(FSY-10)*

In stark contrast to other policy domains, where the EU governs merely with Directives and little substantiated standards and enforcement principles (cf. Chapters 6 and 7), the EU framework for food safety sets out strict safety standards with Regulation 178/2002 and specifies in some detail how public administrations must organize regulatory inspections with Regulation 882/2004 and 625/2017 to uphold those standards (Borraz et al., 2020). We observe how a historical pattern of strong "bureaucratic centralization" in executive federalism (Lehmbruch, 2002, p. 78, quoting Treitsche, 1886, p. 144), present in Germany since Bismarckian times, has been capturing the whole EU since the early 2000s based on strong notions of collective problem pressure and ineffective fragmented enforcement policies.

5.2 How risk analysis emerged in German food safety inspections

Not surprisingly from the above reflections, Brussels initiated Germany's turn to risk analysis in the food safety domain to respond to the BSE crises and the related notion of an effectiveness crisis in enforcement. Brussel's Regulation 882/2004 (Council of the European Union, 2004) set out to rationalize food safety inspections across Europe around a common risk analysis model. However, coercive isomorphism is but one aspect of the adoption pattern. As the second half of this section details, German Länder agreed to coordinate their risk-analytical modeling of inspection priorities much beyond the EU requirements. Following historical antecedents, they use a joint executive order (Bundesrepublik Deutschland, 2008) and its detailed risk analysis model to quasi automate municipal inspection planning around a common model, by passing very detailed coordinated guidelines and transposing them into algorithms in IT solutions for administrative priority-setting.

5.2.1 The EU control regulation: coercion toward (broad-brush) risk-based inspections

Regulation 882/2004 – the so-called Control Regulation (Council of the European Union, 2004) requires "Member-states shall ensure that official controls are carried out regularly, on a risk basis and with appropriate frequency" (art. 3–1). With this, the EU has coerced member states to introduce risk-based inspection priority-setting to help ensure that inspections target those food businesses that most threaten consumer health. Formally, the EC requires that official food safety controls consider four parameters in calculating their risk-based inspection priorities. The first (1) relates to the inherent hazard posed by a food product or business activity and thus the consequences of any food safety violation, while the other three (2–4) relate to the probability of violation by regulatees (art. 3–1):

- identified risks associated with animals, feed or food, feed or food businesses, the use of feed or food or any process, material, substance, activity or operation that may influence feed or food safety, animal health or animal welfare,
- feed or food business operators' past record as regards compliance with feed or food law or with animal health and animal welfare rules,
- the reliability of any own checks, and
- any information that might indicate non-compliance.

This combination of parameters for risk analysis has been confirmed in a more recent version of the regulation (Council of the European Union, 2017, art. 9).

The EU's main rationale for introducing risk-based inspections has been, according to its own records, to increase the effectiveness and efficiency of enforcement in the scandal-struck domain by further harmonization and coordination of executive decision-making across member states and their subnational authorities. Brussels sees great merit in "a single legislative framework for the organisation of official controls" as harmonization has ostensibly "greatly improved the efficiency" of food safety enforcement all while safeguarding the regulatory goal "that food and feed are safe and wholesome" on the single market (Council of the European Union, 2017, pts 16, 3). A major goal, according to this document, was to increase both the effectiveness and efficiency of controls by rationalizing and simplifying the legislative framework (ibid.: pt. 19).

Whilst this rhetoric on policy goals suggests a neat fit with the expectations for instrumental turns to risk analysis, the cross-check with the indicators on the empirical application and technical/organizational design of risk analysis, as developed in Chapter 3 (cf. Table 3.2), indicates a low level of detail and reliance on voluntary specification of the framework for executive priority-setting. The EU refrains from postulating how exactly countries should measure those variables or combine them to calculate risk as some function of both consequence and probability. German interviewees have fittingly described EU food safety law as "an elastic band" that can be bended according to national goals and norms (FSY-8). Indeed, the FVO, which regularly audits member states' inspectorates and their compliance with the specific obligations of 882/2004 (now 625/2017) to organize official controls on a "risk-basis", welcomes member states' ability to adapt the risk-analytical approach to their food safety enforcement regimes (a recent comparative study speaks of "customization" in this context: Thomann, 2019; also see: Borraz et al., 2020):

> *You have to give member-states the flexibility to adapt their control systems to what they identify to be the biggest risks because, frankly, they're best equipped to do it . . . Basically you have to have confidence in the member-states that they have the ability and the local knowledge to identify how best to deploy their resources and how best to target risks.*
>
> *(FSY-EU)*

As a result, apart from mentioning broad factors which inspectors need to consider, there is neither a differentiation of risk scenarios nor a definition of priorities for enforcement. For EU-level institutions, therefore, it seems as if risk analysis is mainly a post-BSE legitimatory tool to signal to consumers and regulatees that ineffective enforcement is being targeted and that jurisdictional boundaries no longer stand in the way of effective control of the common food market. This is situated, however, in a longer trajectory of bureaucratic centralization in which the EU gained more influence over subnational and national executive decision-making in the domain which it justifies with the desire of effective collective problem-solving.

5.2.2 The quasi-automation of risk-based food safety controls in Germany

The EU's permissive approach to the operationalization of risk and determination of respective inspection strategies has led to a surprising variety of risk analysis templates across member states. Thomann's recent study (2019) indicates that food safety in the EU, despite its high degree of integration and formalization, is customized to the needs of member states. A comparative study of the implementation of the Control Regulation in England, France, Germany, and the Netherlands traces highly diverse – and contradictory – operationalizations of risk (Borraz et al., 2020). The relative breadth of the EU's risk-analytical requirements, evidence of member state divergence, but also the EU's lenient position toward organizational variety in enforcement suggest that, in principle, there is no strong coercion for Länder to coordinate their inspection planning beyond somehow taking risk factors into account.

Yet, inspection practices have become more consistent *within* Germany after the Control Regulation (my qualitative survey with chief inspectors in 14 of the 16 Länder). Länder now follow a jointly negotiated and regularly updated General Administrative Decree (*Allgemeine Verwaltungsvorschrift* Rahmenüberwachung – AVV RÜb) which specifies the EU's basic parameters for determining inspection frequencies (Bundesrepublik Deutschland, 2008). Interviewees are clear about the harmonization purpose of the decree: "The goal of such administrative decrees is to achieve uniform enforcement among the German administration" (FSY-06), in line with the historical focus on legal-administrative unity. While the EU's role is seen in having consecrated risk analysis as a (rough) modus operandi in enforcement, interviewees highlight the significant role of vertical policy coordination, and especially the AVV RÜb, in harmonizing food safety inspections within Germany (FSY-02). Indeed, the AVV goes into much detail in its specification of risk assessment methods in a 15-page long appendix. Most importantly, this provides a legally non-binding[7] but widely emulated risk assessment model (Tables 5.1 and 5.2), which has harmonized food safety inspections immensely irrespective of Germany's executive federalism.

The AVV risk assessment model includes a specification of the following:

- thirteen indicators (for specifying the four parameters described by the Control Regulation),
- an exemplary allocation of points per indicator across different risk categories, summing up to 200 points overall,
- a detailed description of indicators for determining how many points a business can score per subcategory during inspections, and
- nine different inspection frequencies depending on the number of points scored by an inspected business, ranging from daily for high-risk FBOs to once every three years for those with the lowest risk scores.

TABLE 5.1 Risk analysis model for determining food safety inspection targets and frequency

Factor	*Points*
Hazard	
Handling of product (six risk categories predetermined in a detailed product list)	0/20/40/60/80/100
Product risk (sizes, direct consumer contact, etc.)	0/10/20
Probability of compliance	
Legal compliance record of producer	0/1/2/3/5
Traceability/Documentation of product chains	0/2/3
Staff training system	0/2/4/6/7
Use of HACCP principles	0/3/6/9/12
Own sampling and controls	0/1/2/3/5
Temperature control and cooling	0/2/4/6/8
Architectural features (walls, surfaces, etc.)	0/1/2/3/5
Cleaning/disinfection systems	0/2/4/6/8
Staff hygiene (during illness, work suits, etc.)	0/3/5/8/11
Production process hygiene	0/4/7/10/13
Bug/pest monitoring and control	0/2/3
Total	0–200

Source: AVV RÜb (Bundesrepublik Deutschland, 2008)

TABLE 5.2 Frequency of inspections according to risk category of the food business operator

Risk class	*Risk score*	*Risk category of the FBO*						*Frequency of controls*
		1	2	3	4	5	6	
1	200–181	200-						Daily
2	180–161		180-					Weekly
3	160–141			160-				Monthly
4	140–121				140-			Quarterly
5	120–101					120-		Semi-annually
6	100–81	100					100-	Annually
7	80–61		80					Every 18 months
8	60–41			60				Biannually
9	40–0				40	20	0	Triennially

Source: AVV RÜb (Bundesrepublik Deutschland, 2008)

Whilst Länder transpose the AVV template with their own guidelines, this results in only residual cross-state variation of risk-analytical approaches.[8] Guidelines include even more detailed descriptions of indicators to ensure a consistent determination of numbers of points a food business operator scores per subcategory, including anchor examples from inspection practice (GeViN, 2007).[9] As one head of a local inspectorate relates for the case of North Rhine Westphalia: "the further grading was not done at Federal level [with the AVV RÜb], we detailed this, the Land

NRW specified this in a working group: defining the optimal, so to say, what do they [food business operators] need to do to achieve zero points" (FSY-02). States did not only use the AVV to coordinate approaches better among themselves at a state level; they also targeted more consistency within their respective state by binding local authorities as front-line enforcers of food safety legislation.

Going even further in their within-state harmonization push, most Länder also introduced a common software for inspection planning as part of their E-government strategies. Lower Saxony, for instance, uses a centralized IT system called GeViN (*Gemeinsames Verbraucherschutzinformationssystem* Niedersachsen = common consumer safety information system Lower Saxony). Most Länder have designed similar systems based on the IT solutions for consumer protection, mostly using software provided by BALVI (FSY-01, FSY-02, FSY-05, FSY-10, and survey data on 14 Länder). These IT systems contain algorithmic models which use inspectors' up-to-date risk assessment based on the AVV RÜb model to calculate inspection frequencies for each premise in the cadastre. The combination of the Federal risk analysis model with a common IT solution enables a hierarchically ordered quasi-automation of inspection planning in municipal inspectorates, thus harmonizing enforcement approaches within each Land.

Several interviewees detail the logic of algorithmic decision-making as a key shift in enforcement strategies since 2008:

> *We have a software which programs risk assessment. I only conduct the risk analysis which is predetermined by the guideline [of the respective Land] and I must specify the kind of food business operator beforehand. Everything is then controlled through the software. At some point a schedule for inspections is flagged on my screen, and I know: well, this or that premise needs inspection again.*
>
> *(FSY-02)*

> *Well, if you do this correctly, you reach some kind of points result. Let's say 142 [points] and you see, 142, this equals a monthly control frequency. And this is how the software generates automatic inspection schedules.*
>
> *(FSY-05)*

In summary, the harmonization of risk analysis within Germany reaches much beyond what the EU requires for inspection planning. Germany's national risk analysis template for food safety inspections provides a rather thorough and detailed guideline for Länder and municipal authorities, suggesting an instrumental adoption pattern (cf. Table 3.2 in Chapter 3). The AVV RÜb's appendix, which includes risk analysis methods, may be non-binding but has been enforced across the country in even more detailed Länder guidelines. The AVV provides a holistic model for assessing both product risks and the likelihood of a business to comply, a detailed list of indicators and lengthy description of scenarios to decide how many points firms score across the different categories, and a widely emulated model for determining inspection frequencies. Moreover, the computational use of a common risk analysis model to determine inspection frequencies via similar IT systems automates priority-setting in Länder inspection planning. This streamlines municipal decision-making within each state and may increase their control of the local bureaucracy (cf. Sections 4.1 and 4.4). Since Länder invariably draw on the common executive order and its risk analysis model in developing their coercive IT solutions, enforcement priority management across states is also unified to a point where state-level variation in food safety enforcement strategies – though constitutionally granted in Germany's executive federalism – becomes marginal.

5.3 Understanding over-compliance with risk analysis in German food safety controls

At first, the wide adoption of the detailed AVV model might not surprise given its joint negotiation in a Bund-Länder working party. Working within the usual constraints of federalism (particularly the Bundesrat veto power over the executive order and the resulting need to ensure Länder consent) lent itself to a lowest common denominator approach:

> *risks are different across the Länder. But we can of course get to a joint assessment, that probably a small firm with 3–5 staff members constitutes a bigger risk in general compared to a certified producer. And then one has to make a statement, does everybody agree on that point? And if we arrive at the conclusion that one is riskier than the other across many Länder, we can think about writing this down as a principle in the general administrative decree on inspections.*
>
> (FSY-02)

But why was such a compromise sought in the first place? Each Land would have been free to implement its own version of the EU's relatively broad risk assessment scheme or, at least – and as in the case of work safety – retain more room for local discretion by adopting a less detailed common model. In fact, even EU officials accept variation of risk-analytical approaches alongside the needs of member states' internal governance structures legitimate so long the regulatory goal of food safety is not hampered by institutional fragmentation (interview FSY-EU). So why did the German multi-level public administration, where inspection responsibilities are institutionally much fragmented and where such constitutionally guaranteed autonomy is usually much guarded by Länder, opt for a uniform, highly standardized and enormously detailed risk analysis template? Why did German Länder turn scandal-induced EU coercion toward a rather broadly defined risk-analytical model into a highly prescriptive model for administrative decision-making which, in combination with the widespread use of an algorithmic software tool, leaves local inspectors little say in their day-to-day priority-setting?

As this section will detail based on interview material, answers to these questions relate to the overriding and shared perception of *collective* problem pressure among policymakers. Just like in Bismarckian times, when a central level regulatory mandate was first created in food safety, a strong desire to avoid market failure connects diverse administrative levels and leads them to pursue more effective control of the common food market in Europe (and within Germany) through *coordinated* enforcement. In this context, risk analysis is perceived as a remedy for overcoming limits to effective and consistent enforcement in a context of executive fragmentation. In their coordinated problem-solving effort, state-level and local authorities accept central coordination of priority-setting through risk-analytical automation. Now, like then, the structural answer to the perceived problem of market failure is central coordination, and risk analysis helps substantiate this answer. Whilst instrumental justifications are almost mono-causally dominant in the domain and reinforce central level influence in the domain, they are further backed by instrumental hopes of efficiency gains and legitimacy-related desires of inspectors to shift blame for failure to the regulated firms.

5.3.1 Collective problem-solving on the common market through uniform inspection priorities

A first argumentative complex in which administrators justify Germany's over-compliant and unifying turn to risk analysis has it that the common food market can only be regulated – and controlled – with a tightly coordinated, evidence-based inspection approach. Policymakers within Germany perceive EU integration in the domain not so much as a threat to national, Länder, or municipal executive sovereignty but as an instrumental requirement for collective problem-solving to confront the risks of common market failure. They describe the role of risk analysis as one of facilitating an evidence-based coordination of inspection approaches which will render enforcement more consistent and thereby more effective (see illustration with anchor quotations from interviews in Box 5.1). The argumentative thread runs as follows.

First, the deep harmonization of food safety regulation in the EU in general – not solely with respect to risk-based enforcement – is discussed as a classic functional spill-over of the common market (Statements 1 and 2). The "common market competence" (FSY-03) drives regulatory integration, it is argued in a typical neo-functional fashion, because the freedom of movement for products and related food safety risks and market asymmetries can only be managed with uniform regulatory standards. Importantly, such harmonization does not only concern inter-state variation but also remaining variation within federal or devolved member states. Indeed, one interviewee highlights how the common market dynamic for food safety issues in Europe amplifies the necessity to coordinate approaches better *within* Germany's fragmented executive: "well, the common market also concerns Germany itself" (FSY-01). The coordination requirements for a federal polity seeking to effectively regulate a common food market represent an ever-rehearsed theme ever since the Imperial Health Office took on a harmonization agenda across German territories in the face of then scandalous market failures.

BOX 5.1: UNIFORM FOOD SAFETY REGULATION AS A NECESSITY ON THE COMMON FOOD MARKET

Statement 1: *"The driving force behind this integration [of food safety legislation and enforcement] is the single market principle. Meaning: you have a common market in Europe and that implies that products, . . . and also food, can circulate freely in Europe. That works only if you have harmonised rules".* (FSY-03)

Statement 2: *"The completion of the common market . . . came with a concession to the EU Commission that it shall harmonise food safety regulation to a large extent . . . to have comparable norms in international trade and to thus also signal reliability towards our trade partners".* (FSY-04)

Statement 3: *"This is our . . . this is not only a demand of the market, the EU demands it, too: to have consistent controls; third countries also demand it. And that means that we, as Länder, are also compelled to deploy ourselves in a uniform manner. And we thus establish uniform interpretations and implementation procedures".* (FSY-01)

Statement 4: *"Our companies benefit, too. They are the ones always demanding consistent rules and complaining . . . that they have to deal with twenty different authorities . . . We have a lot of companies in the food sector that produce for the European, if not global, market. And for them it is always beneficial to have consistent rules".* (FSY-03)

Statement 5: *"[thanks to harmonised regulation in the food safety domain] Europe can speak with one voice: These are our rules, you have to respect them from Finland down to Malta and from Slovakia to Ireland. Now, and that is an asset with which we can navigate international trade, much more than when acting from a position of scattered regionalist regulation"* (FSY-04).

Pursuing the argumentative thread further, but on a global scale and with a more interest-based explanation in mind, one interviewee highlights that the EU also requires harmonized rules for political reasons. The idea is that member states will be more successful in international trade negotiations and vis-à-vis globally acting firms if they are able to "speak with one voice" via the EU (Statement 5). Importantly, several interviewees insist on the decisive role of scientific evidence in this context. They argue, for example, that trade must operate at a "high level of protection . . . not on the basis of protectionist considerations but based on scientific data which lead me to regulate in a certain manner or to tighten specific rules" (FSY-04). The interpretation rehearses arguments in the literature on risk analysis which depict it as a tool to avoid political bias and produce fair and transparent regulatory decisions (cf. Majone, 2010). It also recalls the role of food chemists in forging common food safety standards in Imperial Germany and highlights the continuous salience of scientific advocacy for rational problem-solving ambitions in the domain, including as a weapon against the potentially protectionist endeavors of autonomous jurisdictions.

The request of forging "one voice" against the power and potential failure of global food markets seems to concern standard-setting mostly in the statements above. Second, however, this general framing of the regulatory requirements stemming from European food market integration also fuels an acceptance of tightly coordinated enforcement. Unlike in other policy domains where EU umbrella legislation comes with much-used leeway for member states (and subnational entities within Germany) to implement legislation – our flooding case being one such domain – there seems to be a widespread belief among Länder and municipal administrative actors in German food safety that the remaining scope for interpretation in enforcement needs to be restricted further within member states to ensure the efficiency and effectiveness of food safety rules. As I detail in the next two subsections, this is where detailed and coercive risk analysis enters the scene.

5.3.2 Risk analysis as a tool to ensure equal treatment in a fragmented enforcement landscape

Policymakers in German food safety invariably believe in the ability of a common risk analysis model to increase regulatees' acceptance of, and compliance with, food safety rules – to the benefit of consumers. Risk analysis – and especially the automation of enforcement decision through risk-algorithmic inspection planning – counts as a tool for formalizing professional judgment over enforcement priorities around a consistent assessment standard. In line with the rationalization dynamics claimed in the more instrumentally oriented branches of the risk regulation literature (Viscusi, 1983; Sunstein, 2002; Majone, 2010), they suggest that, by treating regulatees and consumers equally and fairly on the common market based on risk-related evidence the effectiveness of food safety regulation can be increased. Importantly, concerns over the de facto surrender of subcentral executive competences over priority setting in food safety enforcement are being sidelined by a rationality-driven buy-in to uniform risk analysis as an effectiveness booster.

Venture point for this argumentative thread is the now century-old ambition of ensuring equal living conditions, in this case, similar safety levels for consumers, and legal-administrative unity (Statement 6) across Germany. As one Länder inspection lead highlights: "Well, I *do* want the same level of protection in Cologne and [the Frisian island of] Borkum to start with" (FSY-01). Importantly, the underlying norm of legal-administrative unity does not just concern levels of consumer protection, but also inspectorates' relationship with regulatees (Statement 6; cf. Statement 4). Evidence suggests a modern continuation of a historically chosen path: the attempt to ensure "*reichseinheitliche Bestimmungen*" via strong centrally induced legislation and regulatory institutionalization under Bismarck (Section 5.1) finds its present day parallel in elaborate IT-based risk modeling which puts a common administrative decree and Länder executive guidelines into practice. The goal remains the same: to counter fragmentation of enforcement outputs (who is being inspected) and outcomes (how safe is food for consumers across the country) in executive federalism.

BOX 5.2: TOWARD UNIFORM AND FORMALIZED PRIORITY-SETTING IN FOOD SAFETY THROUGH RISK ANALYSIS

Statement 6: *"it [risk analysis] especially helps, I would say, the inspection side of things, because I want to ensure that everyone is being inspected consistently and fairly".* (FSY-10)

Statement 7: *"Well, it [risk analysis] is also a tool to ensure [at a state level] we have equal administrative decision-making and, well, in the end, we also implement [EU food safety legislation] requirements in similar ways, which is important . . . To steer 42 local food safety authorities so that they act similarly, which is almost impossible in practice".* (FSY-05)

Statement 8: *"That is the eternal discussion we have with Länder, to what extent is enforcement uniform across Germany, whether we, well, should have comparisons of performance, or to have quality management in the states. That is, well, as I said . . . the Bund tries to push Länder a little in that sense, but Länder also do not want us to interfere . . ."* (FSY-03)

Statement 9: *"We used this earlier, 'trust in the food business operator'. This was part of the risk assessment. From my perspective a clear subjective evaluation, which is not objective and hence contestable. To say 'I don't have trust [in a specific FBO]'; and they then say: 'they [the inspector] just don't like me'. And how should I then explain my assessment to a judge?"* (FSY-02)

Statement 10: *"Well, in earlier times we used our gut feeling. This is, of course, not be the right starting point. Instead, we now use our guideline 'risk assessment' [in our federal state] and this directs us. Depending on the points [a firm scores], I get an inspection frequency as a result. And this brings us away from gut feeling, so to speak".* (FSY-10)

Decision makers consider risk analysis essential in this context; they think it possible to equalize decision-making across disparate and formally autonomous authorities based on transparent comparative insights on risk levels. Interviewees believe that by ensuring a uniform (and by implication: fairer) assessment during inspections across political boundaries, by the help of common risk analysis, the effectiveness of food safety will further improve to the benefit of consumers. Nested within this overarching ambition of coordinated problem-solving and effectiveness gains is a rather classic control of the bureaucracy argument: the goal is "to steer 42 local food safety authorities [in one German state] so that they act similarly" (Statement 7). Harmonization impulses come from states directed toward local authorities (Statement 7) and from the Bund with Federal states as their target (Statement 8). Bund and Länder representatives utter hopes that risk analysis can help "steer" or predispose otherwise autonomous subcentral enforcement priorities in a similar direction, in line with what accounts about control of the bureaucracy (Dunsire, 1978; Balla, 1998) and more recent behavioral policy approaches suggest (Straßheim and Beck, 2019b).

The argumentative link between levels of detail and prescription of risk analysis in inspections, the perceived need to steer subnational decision-making, and the effectiveness of food safety relies on at least three assumptions plus a recent twist in the justification pattern.

- First, Länder level administrations seek to avoid the impression of protectionist bias (cf. Majone, 2010) when controlling firms whose headquarter is situated in another political constituency, be it another state within Germany or another EU member state (FSY-04). They believe that a risk-based objectivation, especially when based on a common model across constituencies, makes regulatees more likely to comply with norms as the expected scope for political assessment criteria – and potential regulatory negotiations of standards in practice – is reduced to a minimum. To some extent, this is an amalgamation of an instrumental belief in the transparency of risk evidence as effectiveness booster and a more legitimacy-oriented narrative according to which regulatees are also more likely to accept public intervention as legitimate where such intervention seems balanced and fair.
- Second, the development of comprehensive and harmonized risk analysis algorithms offers policymakers a way, they claim, to keep pace with digital innovation in the global food market. A masterplan on digital reform in Lower Saxony argues, for instance, that an elaboration of the GEViN IT system for harmonized inspection planning in the state is paramount for controlling digitally organized firms in the first place. More than that: the masterplan even proposes its future "development towards a central control database of the Länder" (Land Niedersachsen, 2018). Whilst such a centralization of inspection data is not on the official Federal agenda yet, the BVL in particular has repeatedly mooted criticism of the lack of uniformity and consistency across Länder as key hindrance to heightened food safety effectiveness. For the BVL, more harmonized enforcement is a logical step given the high level of legislative harmonization in the domain (cf. Abels and Kobusch, 2010). Rather than presenting this as an explicit power-seeking argument (of course, the potential of gaining regulatory competences might be tempting also for the BVL), however, Federal level officials justify their unification call as did the Imperial Health Office in the past: with the hope for increased effectiveness of food safety enforcement on a global and technologically rapidly developing market (cf. Statement 8). Power asymmetries and looming failure on a global and swiftly developing food market, with potentially devastating consequences as in the BSE case, justify the imposition of highly prescriptive common analytical models on subnational enforcement units – via states – in what equals an act of silent surrender of local enforcement autonomy.[10]

- Third, there is evidence of a bottom-up professionalization through common risk analysis models among local inspectorates which coincides with top-down unification demands by Bund and Länder. Normative isomorphism around risk analysis is fueled by a wish to objectify the infamous "gut feeling" in inspection planning (Statements 9 and 10). This concerns, in particular, the behavioral aspects of inspectors' evaluations which, unlike the long-formalized and explicitly evidence-based comparative assessments of product risks, can be easily castigated as relying on inspectors' subjective or even actively biased judgment. To avoid such bias may well be the instrumental goal of local authorities in problem-solving mode but has relevant implications from a power-seeking perspective, too. While local authorities reject any formal centralization of competencies, the widespread instrumental buy-in into risk-analytical automation among local officers supports the central level attempts to predispose enforcement decisions around the results of common risk analysis from below. It explains why contestation of the most recent unification of executive decision-making in the domain goes relatively uncontested.
- Lastly and extending the discussion around the amalgamation of coordinated problem-solving and polity policies in the adoption of analytical tools further, bias in professional judgment is considered problematic not just for reasons of fairness and equal treatment but also as a looming institutional risk where inspection decisions are being contested in court (Statement 9). In a typical Porterian manner (Section 3.2), the ability of risk analysis to objectify administrative decisions vis-à-vis regulatees, and by extension the courts, gains in significance with a recent shift to a fees-for-inspection regime in Europe (Council of the European Union, 2017): indeed, where companies are billed for inspection visits in line with the amended Control Regulation, the decision to inspect them in the first place espouses a more adversary character and requires, from the viewpoint of inspectors (FSY-01, FSY-03, and FSY-10), a legitimatory formalization of professional judgment based on numerical assessment (as argued for the case of the Army Corps of Engineers and their embrace of CBA: Porter, 1995). Interestingly, the increasing judicialization of the domain, via a still to-be-carved-out fees-based system of food safety enforcement, might catalyze a process in which the now predominant instrumental use of risk analysis in Germany might be tilted toward stronger forms of institutional risk management and legitimacy-seeking.

5.3.3 Welcome side effects of risk analysis: efficiency gains and blame shifting to regulatees

Although not central to their stories about risk analysis, policymakers describe efficiency gains and blame-shifting dynamics as relevant for their appraisal of risk analysis in enforcement. As expected, in context of tight budgets in local authorities, bureaucrats welcome risk-analytical prioritization for efficiency reasons: "Capacities are not as dense as to ensure comprehensive controls in any way . . . We cannot put an inspector next to every food product[11]" (FSY-03). Priority-setting based on risk analysis hence features as a smart enforcement strategy: "I have staff resources and financial resources. And I should deploy them in a manner that is justified" (FSY-10), meaning that a risk-analytical prioritization can help inspectors "use the rationalized resources to put a focus on my problem firms or issues, to improve them further" (FSY-04). From the perspective of several interviewees, such efficiency-seeking includes a risk-based consideration of firms' ability to operate effective self-controls, for example, by lowering the inspection load for accredited businesses with certified quality management schemes (FSY-02 and FSY-06). Such concerns, however, are of limited relevance overall when set against the all-dominating effectiveness hopes and the wish to ensure high levels of safety.

Blame-shifting also matters from the perspective of some interviewees. They highlight that risk analysis allows authorities to insist on the duty of care of food business operators, in line with a principle strengthened in EU law after the BSE crisis. As one interviewee highlights: "I tell them [businesses], folks, this is your responsibility! You have to design your control systems in line with the risks. If you don't, you'll get a problem" (FSY-01). Another one insists: "The food business operator is the responsible person. Not us. We can only use samples to check their risk management" (FSY-02). Risk analysis, in this context, helps inspectorates specify where non-compliance with businesses' own legal risk analysis and management duties is more likely and/or would have too large an impact for the state to ignore: "We control whether they do this [the quality management] correctly. This is the job of official controls" (FSY-10).

Importantly, arguments about efficiency and blame shifting, often portrayed as predominant in the scholarly debate of risk-based regulation (e.g., in the British blueprint: Hampton, 2005) are rather marginal in the German food safety domain. There is an overriding focus on how to best coordinate enforcement across formally autonomous jurisdictions stemming from the shared desire to enable collective problem-solving and counter the health-related risks of common food market failures. This interpretation explains why Länder and local authorities are ready to surrender much discretion over food safety inspections to a relatively detailed common risk analysis model, to the point of automating priority-setting through an algorithm.

Notes

1 Interview partner FSY 01.
2 To avoid repetition with Chapter 8, which will bring together comparative findings, Chapters 5–7 provide no individual conclusion.
3 This progressively detailed standard-setting process drew largely on work of food chemist associations since the late 19th century and their decisive interest in the advancement of scientifically founded statutory regulation of the food industry (Hierholzer, 2010).
4 This was very different in the German Democratic Republic where controls were centrally steered and a comparatively "transparent and generally accessible" law created a coherent statutory food safety regime (Sewekow, Schmidt-Faber and Frost, 2010, p. 315). As in most cases, Western German rules were transferred to the whole territory after German reunification.

5 Indeed, as commentators on German federalism rightly point out, the federal structure and related sharing of power is a historical guiding principle for the organisation of the state (Hesselberger, 1995, p. 164f). Both the unification in 1871 and the post-War creation of a Federal Republic opted for federal solutions not as second best options but consolidated well-established and well-performing executive practices (Ziblatt, 2008).

6 The responsibility of regulatees was further highlighted when administrations were provided with the possibility of collecting fees for planned food safety inspections (European Council, 2004).

7 The AVV itself is legally binding as executive order but its appendix illustrates an "exemplary model" for doing risk analysis which is not binding.

8 For example, the matrix in Brandenburg equally uses an overall score of 200 but allocates one point differently between two indicators (my own survey among 14 out of 16 Länder).

9 The AVV was published internally already in 2007 and some Länder, including Lower Saxony, were very quick to adapt risk-analytical priority-setting for their inspections.

10 A similar argumentative support of unification emerges for scenarios of nation-wide (or EU-wide) crises: in the interest of developing an effective and rapid cure against food market failures and health threats, the informal delegation of subcentral executive competences to the next higher level is widely accepted, as in the case of a task force dealing with a lethal *E. coli* outbreak in 2011 (FSY-03, FSY-04, and FSY-06).

11 While savings occur across public policy sectors, the pressure on food safety inspectorates – who still check 40 per cent of all firms on average per year – seems mild when compared to the existential cuts experienced in work safety (Chapter 7).

6

ADDRESSING TRANSREGIONAL RISKS

Risk analysis, policy coordination, and the re-allocation of flood prevention duties

It's idiotic to stop at Länder borders in flood prevention.[1]

I examine flood protection and prevention[2] next as a domain where German policymakers have streamlined risk analysis shortly after the food safety domain, since at least 2007. Like in the previous case, the analytical turn came in via the EU venue, but it did so less coercively with a broad-brush Directive. Like in food safety, German states – in interaction with the Federal level – decided to substantiate Brussels' vague imperative to do risk assessment and even developed risk-based eligibility rules for a new national prevention funds, propelled by a strong instrument constituency in the Rhine catchment which had long promoted risk analysis for instrumental reasons. Justifications for the rather substantiated emulation of risk analysis in flood prevention divert from the coercive pattern in food safety controls due to their embedding in a quite different – much less coordinated – setting of executive federalism. The particularly high degree of fragmentation and a weak public mandate in the domain has more recently invited criticism as to the inability of federal flood prevention to tackle dire collective action problems. In this context, risk analysis features as an instrumental facilitator of coordinated problem-solving across territorial boundaries. The convolution of a strong instrumentally oriented regional forerunner of risk-based cooperation – the Rhine catchment – with both EU and Federal level efforts to entice policy coordination helps explain the wide and substantial emulation of risk analysis in the domain. The case for risk-based policy coordination has, however, also found support by (1) state-level legitimacy-seeking, with Länder shifting blame for flood-related damages to private and municipal actors; (2) a Federal desire to increase central monitoring and steering in a domain where they lack regulatory power; but also (3) state-level power-shifting efforts, with Länder claiming a stronger national role in the identification and funding of high-risk prevention measures. As in the previous chapter, I start with a delineation of the institutional heritage and characteristics of the domain, continue with a depiction of how risk analysis entered the stage in flood prevention, and finish with an in-depth interpretive analysis of how policymakers justify the turn to risk analysis in the domain.

6.1 Flood prevention in Germany: extreme fragmentation without clear mandate

Germany has a long history of highly variable local flooding policies without much of a national program. This legacy of extreme regulatory fragmentation and unspecific mandates shapes the domain until present day, but it has come under increasing pressure since the 1990s in the context of larger border-crossing floods which created ever higher financial damage. An ever-stronger perception of collective action problems and related requirements for tighter policy coordination in the multi-level setting has set the scene for an especially appreciative interpretation of risk analysis in the domain (details in Section 6.3).

6.1.1 A legacy of highly fragmented mandates

In medieval Germany, municipal non-state actors traditionally oversaw land use planning, the related drainage works, and the prevention of inundation. An early legal code, the *Sachsenspiegel*, already mentioned the obligation of villages protected by a dike to manage the structure of and finance dike works in a self-administered way in the 13th century (Repgow, 1984). Some did so in loose interest associations, others in more institutionalized self-regulated mutual associations, the so-called *Deichverbände*[3] (Allemeyer, 2006), but protection standards remained uneven and several riparian communities were not regulated by any such association.

The exclusive responsibility of self-regulated local associations for managing flood protection waned over the centuries. As municipalities got more involved in the regulation of land use on their territory, they also assumed a greater role in flood prevention. In addition to dike associations, Länder and municipalities are now the most relevant actors in the domain. The constitutional power to regulate, enforce, and finance flood prevention and protection measures largely lays with the states (Bundesrechnungshof, 2016). The Federal level only operates its own hydraulic engineering works – mainly in the Elbe, Ems, and Jade estuaries – to protect major ports and ensure navigability on the Rhine, Danube, and other federally designated waterways of great economic relevance (ibid.). Whilst municipalities have no discrete legal obligation to provide flood protection (see later), their local water authorities and planning commissions need to approve planned activities (including flood defense structures) in line with state regulation. They also oversee existing flood protection infrastructures such as dikes, reservoirs, or retention areas. Individual state law defines the conditions for land use and flood prevention but remains broad enough for variable standards to emerge across and even within each state.

To increase horizontal coordination, a Länder working group on water issues has been established in 1956, but its conclusions and recommendations on issues of joint concern are non-binding. Only since 2005 does the Federal government and its Ministry of the Environment also have a seat at the table (now: *Bund/Länder-Arbeitsgemeinschaft Wasser, LAWA*) mainly because Berlin needed to be able to report back to Brussels on the increasingly Europeanized issues of water quality in a more coordinated manner (FLO-11, see later on the role of the EU). Scholarly observers relate the lack of strong national guidance to the longstanding German perception that flooding is a governance problem of usually local – at best regional – impact which requires local geographical, geological, hydrological, and biological knowledge[4] (Heintz, Hagemeier-Klose and Wagner, 2012). Lack of nation-wide intervention may also pay respect to municipalities' political unwillingness to concede their dominant influence over highly politicized and distributional questions of land use and protection from riparian flooding; existential issues for their community's development. As I will discuss in Section 6.1.3, the acceptance of fragmented decision-making changed with an accumulation of border-crossing flooding disasters which highlighted the need for policy coordination in the fragmented setting.

6.1.2 Lack of clear regulatory duties

The strong executive decentralization of flood prevention is amplified further by the lack of detailed national standard-setting. Unlike in food safety, in the past, the Federal Government could only pass umbrella legislation on issues of water use (*Wasserhaushaltsgesetz*), land use, and building activities (*übergeordnete Raumplanung und Baurecht*), making the domain's regulatory fragmentation particularly pronounced when compared to food safety. With the reform of German federalism in 2006, these legal domains were shifted to concurrent legislation, but the Federal level has not used its new powers to interfere with Länder legislation thus forth. Given the amount of open clauses and abstract prescriptions in national water laws, legal experts have described legislation as a toolbox which Länder and municipalities *can* make use of as they see fit but are not particularly bound by (Schneider, 2005).

In addition, Germany knows no positive right or "individual entitlement to flood protection" (LAWA, 1995, p. 1). Until present day, German statutory actors have few absolute duties to prevent or protect against flooding – unlike in other countries (Demeritt et al., 2017) or in other domains, including food safety – to any specific level (Hartmann and Albrecht, 2014): "The state's duty to protect against flooding does not automatically found a right to demand specific flood protection measures or to claim a [statutory] responsibility in case of damage" (FLO-11). Whilst interviewees associated food safety with the goal of offering similarly high levels of protection across the country (Chapter 5), in flood prevention "it is the personal responsibility of anyone who lives and works by or on the water to adapt his use . . . to objective flood risks" (LAWA, 1995, p. 2). The national or state government consequently has no legal obligation to compensate for damages; these are a private concern and require funding "through insurance or the accumulation of reserves" (LAWA, 2010a, p. 37).

As an effect of the coupling between extreme fragmentation of responsibilities and the lack of a clear regulatory mandate for the state, flood protection and prevention standards vary widely in Germany, but not according to any consistent principle (Bubeck et al., 2012; Demeritt et al., 2017). The only national standard was set by the 2005 Flood Protection Act, which prohibits development in unprotected areas prone to more than 1 per cent annual exceedance probability (AEP 0.01)[5] of flooding. But as municipal authorities can bypass restrictions with exceptional permits (Hamburg's famous Hafencity being a prime example on development in an inundation area), the land use standard had rather limited harmonization effects.

Funding patterns of local hydraulic works remain equally uneven. The constitutional principle of unity of task and funding in federal governance relationships – ensuring that the territorial governance level to regulate and execute policies also has to pay the bill and avoid *Mischfinanzierung* – has long prevented shared funding responsibilities in riparian flood defense (Bundesrechnungshof, 2016). Until recently, national money for prevention has only been available for coastal flood defense and local prevention measures with respect to agrarian landscapes via the "shared task" agrarian structure and coastal protection (GAK, "Gemeinschaftsaufgabe Agrarstruktur und Küstenschutz"– one of two remaining shared tasks typical of joint decision in the narrow Scharpfian sense, cf. Chapter 4). GAK funds are fed to 70 per cent by the Federal level and to 30 per cent by the Länder (Deutscher Bundestag, 2015). The harmonizing effects of these funds on prevention standards were limited, however, since the GAK does not entail a set of criteria for national priority-setting. For example, North-Rhine Westphalia co-funds municipal measures of *at least* AEP 0.01 and more capacity (FLO-02); Baden-Württemberg uses cost-benefit analysis to determine when to co-fund, meaning that both higher and lower levels of protection than against an AEP 0.01 flood can exist depending on a nuanced assessment of impact against prevention costs (FLO-05 and FLO-06); Schleswig-Holstein does not fund any measure "simply put, if one can still wade through the water in wellies", even where it is a statistical AEP 0.01 event (FLO-12); and in Mecklenburg-Vorpommern, dike extensions need to display a positive cost-benefit ratio (FLO-11).

6.1.3 Collective action problems and increased pressure for policy coordination

While experts cherish the fragmented governance of (land use and) flood prevention in Germany as flexible, they equally argue that lack of coordination decreases the efficiency and effectiveness of flood risk management (Heintz, Hagemeier-Klose and Wagner, 2012). A typical collective action issue, local flood protection measures tend to have a direct – potentially detrimental – effect on downstream neighbors. For example, opening a flood-prone dam to protect a local village upstream heightens the expected water gauge downstream. Similarly, prevention measures such as the creation of large retention areas or dams – usually involving heavy investment and/or infringement of property rights – tend not to benefit the local community but downstream neighbors most. In other words: flooding raises questions of negative and positive externalities and free-riding which scholars of federalism have identified as central for coordination requirements (Scharpf, 1985; cf. overviews in: Kropp, 2010; Benz, Detemple and Heinz, 2016).

The impression of insufficient coordination grew among policymakers with the accumulation of highly damaging[6] cross-regional flood events in the 1990s and 2000s. Major Rhine floods hit in 1993 and 1995, the Odra flooded in 1997, a devastating Elbe flood in 2002, repeated in 2006, and Danube floods in 2002, 2005, and again in 2009 and 2010 jointly with the Odra and other rivers in Eastern Europe. While the Rhine floods were still perceived as regional disasters, the 2002 Elbe flood entered the campaign trail for the General Elections, attracting enormous attention by national policymakers (Müller, 2010; Krieger, 2011). Pictures of chancellor and MP candidates filling sandbags and maintaining dikes swamped the TV screens. Beyond such political vote-seeking behavior, however, experts consider the Elbe flooding as a paradigm-changing disaster in German flood prevention, both with respect to regulatory goals and the acknowledgment of coordination requirements (cf. Unnerstall, 2010).

The 2005 legislation on "precautionary flood protection" was a direct response to the Elbe flooding. It departed from the previous reactive technical flood defense approach and promoted natural retention management and pro-active flood prevention. Länder were now tasked to develop flood protection plans (§ 31d) with a dual focus on technical protection and the (priority) recuperation of flood plains, though actual prevention levels remained a local prerogative. This mirrored a wider trend in Europe to move from flood control to a so-called spatial approach – what the Brits call "making space for water" (Defra, 2004) (cf. our review in Demeritt et al., 2017). After the Rhine floods in the 1990s, the Länder working group (LAWA, 1995, p. 8) already reminded Germans that "it is impossible to guarantee preventing major floods" and that the state was giving neither protection nor compensation promises. The 2005 Act now codified this individual responsibility for flood protection and damage compensation.

However, LAWA's 25 years old recommendation that "the state must respond by defining to what extent it can meet [public] expectations" of protection (LAWA, 1995, p. 2) has long been frustrated by the fragmented architecture of flooding policies in Germany. As long as executive duties remained highly fragmented and uncoordinated, indicating the exact limits of public responsibilities for flood prevention (and compensation) seemed impossible. The border-crossing flood events since the 1990s hence nourished an urgent sense that policymakers across autonomous jurisdictions ought to coordinate flood prevention standards and communicate the limits of public provision vis-à-vis the public in a more systematic and transparent manner. The Act (§32) thus has Länder coordinate their individual flood hazard assessments and protection plans and enthrones the Federal government as conflict mediator. In a similar vein, the EU Water Framework Directive in 2000 had already established, among other things, *river basin districts* as the chief governance entities (Council of the European Union, 2000). The directive demands coordinated water use plans and flood risk maps across regional and national borders but does not prescribe standards for flood prevention. Catchment-based coordination is not new in Germany: the earliest coordination group was the Rhine Commission, founded at the Congress of Vienna in 1815, which removed parts of the river's management from the sovereign decision-making of littoral nation-states.[7] Today, catchment-based organizations exist for the management of the Danube, Elbe, Mosel, and Odra. Yet, flood prevention philosophies vary considerably across catchments with some readily accepting regular flooding and others being more protection-oriented.[8]

6.1.4 The formation of an instrument constituency around risk analysis

Coordination impulses might stem from yet another source. The review has so far been silent on scientific advocacy for risk analysis in the domain, not least because flooding policies in Germany lack a unified professional actor group comparable to food chemists. Some argue that probabilistic standards and the reliance on risk analysis fit with the professional proclivities of engineers, who long dominated flood management (Disco, 2002). Yet, others have described high degrees of professional specialization and fragmentation of standards because of the many disciplines involved in flood prevention (e.g., geography, hydrology, meteorology, spatial planning, and statistics) (Klijn, Samuels and Os, 2008).

However, some observers describe how, since the 1990s, a relative "uneasiness" about scientific fragmentation has provoked the first inner-academic initiatives for bridging the gaps between different disciplinary and national approaches to flood risk measurement (ibid., p. 307). Risk analysis took on a unifying role in this context as scientists from across disciplines and regulators started uniting behind this tool. Since the early 1990s, we thus observe the formation of an instrument constituency (Sections 2.5 and 4.4.2) which grew stronger over time and has shaped the EU's turn to risk analysis in flooding policies. In particular, scientists were able to exploit grievances over the Rhine (and Meuse) floods in the 1990s to promote risk analysis, both in academic circles – to unite across disciplines – but also at their respective national governments and at EU level, as a tool which can render prevention efforts more (cost-)effective. On the side of regulators, the Rhine Commission had a piloting role in the empirical application of the academic consensus around risk analysis with its 1995 coordinated action plan on flooding. Part of the plan was to develop a common tool for measuring flood risks across the Rhine's political boundaries. The ICPR presented this tool in 2001 and publishes findings – which visualize flood risks along the catchment at high granularity – regularly with its influential "Rhine Atlas" (ICPR, 2015). Assessment is based on a nuanced mathematical formula of damage potential for different levels of inundation. In line with expectations in the literature on instrument constituency actors, the ICPR actively promotes its risk-analytical modeling tool as blueprint at EU level, within Germany in the LAWA, but also in the wider scientific community (Schmid-Breton et al., 2018).

The convolution of an academic consensus around risk analysis and its practical elaboration in the Rhine catchment evidently favored its adoption at the EU stage in the early 2000s. Arguably, from an instrument constituency perspective, scientists and Rhine catchment regulators successfully joint efforts in keeping risk analysis "alive both as a model and as an implemented practice" (Béland and Howlett, 2016, p. 397). From 2004, the FLOODsite project was funded as an EC research action, running for five years with the goal of developing "an integrated, European, methodology for the assessment and management of flood risk" (ibid., p. 308). Interviewees confirm that the Rhine model served as a blueprint here (FLO-EU, FLO-03, and FLO-04). Efforts to put the scientific consensus for harmonized flood risk measurement into regulatory practice culminated in the EU's 2007 Flood Risk Management Directive (Council of the European Union, 2007), which prescribes an actuarial assessment of flood events to member states (Section 6.2). The coming together of (1) recently unified scientific voice in favor of risk-based flood prevention, (2) its much elaborated empirical application in the Rhine catchment and promotional efforts by the ICPR, and (3) the recent buy-in to the Rhine model at EU level arguably increased the likelihood of substantial emulation of risk analysis; especially so in a context where an urgent sense of collective problem-solving requirements peeled actors' searching eyes toward successful blueprints for policy coordination. While the next section portrays how risk analysis emulated in Germany after the EU Directive impulse, Section 6.3 recontsructs and explains the emulation pattern across the ILP typology based on interview material.

6.2 How risk analysis emerged in German flood prevention

Similar to food safety controls, albeit in a less coercive manner, EU legislation initiated a Germany-wide turn to risk analysis in flood prevention. Some river catchments – notably the Rhine and Mosel cooperations – had already used risk-based information-gathering and prevention standards before (and as I discuss later, these actors saw the EU's efforts as a chance to promote their favored analytical instrument as one for more collective problem-solving across Germany and the EU). Yet, the extreme fragmentation of administrative duties in the domain coupled with the lack of a strong regulatory mandate have inhibited a wider diffusion of risk-analytical models as the basis for flood-related public decision-making (Krieger, 2013; Demeritt et al., 2017).

In 2007, Brussels introduced a common risk analysis model, in relatively broad terms, and set a reporting structure for member states' six-annual flood risk maps and flood risk management plans. Like in the food safety case, Germany transposed risk-analytical requirements keenly, with LAWA guidelines operating at a high level of methodical and application-oriented detail. In addition to non-binding horizontal coordination, the 2014 National Flood Protection Program emulates the Rhine catchment's risk model to differentiate eligibility criteria for funding and thus sets up – for the first time – a soft coercion mechanism for more harmonized and cost-effective prevention planning across autonomous state-level and municipal administrations.

6.2.1 The EU Flood Risk Management Directive: impulse for coordinated flood risk mapping

The EU decided to harmonize flood risk assessments in the early 2000s in reaction to the devasting border-crossing flood events at the time. An instrumental perspective initiated this step: better coordination and science-based standardization of measurement techniques along shared rivers and coasts would help reduce flooding-related damages (interview expert at DG Environment). The Flood Risk Management Directive pursues these goals (Council of the European Union, 2007) through establishing a common understanding of risk, coordinated assessment and planning requirements, and regular reporting duties for member states.

The directive prescribes an actuarial definition of flood risks as the product of probability and impact: "the combination of the probability of a flood event and of the potential adverse consequences for human health, the environment, cultural heritage and economic activity associated with a flood event" (ibid., article 2.1). On the basis of this risk concept, national authorities are to identify "those areas for which they conclude that potential significant flood risks exist or might be considered likely to occur". This identification is based on a two-step risk analysis:

A *probability* assessment for

- "floods with a low probability, or extreme event scenarios;
- floods with a medium probability (likely return period ≥100 years);
- floods with a high probability, where appropriate";

and an *impact* assessment which cross-tabulates factors such as affected number of inhabitants and economic values across the three likelihood categorizations.

Both the actuarial risk terminology and the procedure for risk-based information-gathering have been new to many member states at the time, including most sub-national administrations within Germany but also, for example, in France (Paul, Bouder and Wesseling, 2016). Yet, the EU leaves the definition of the low and high probability events open to member states and does not touch upon standard-setting or enforcement questions – a regulatory flexibility that is amplified by the less straightforward legislative impact of a directive vis-à-vis a regulation. In addition, the Directive does not detail prevention standards or enforcement approaches. Member states are formally free to conduct risk analysis in line with EU requirements without using its results to discriminate their prevention or compensation policies (unlike in food safety where controls must be risk-based!). EU officials therefore express clear limits to the Flood Directive's harmonization potential:

> *What I can say is that for both, for the defining what is a significant historical or future flood and for assessing the severity of the impact of past and future floods, there has not been, you know, one methodology for mapping. But there have been many and this goes back to the previous question whether there can be harmonisation in Europe. I mean, every member state literally has a different approach. . . . So a framework [for risk analysis] is created, some milestones are there. . . . But we are not saying to member states 'you have to reduce risk by ten per cent the probably of something.' This is left to the member states.*
>
> *(interview FLO-EU)*

Indeed, neither is the methodology for flood risk mapping very detailed (the same is true for the initial identification of areas at significant risk of flooding for which flood risk mapping must then be conducted) nor do the resulting flood risk management plans come with any justiciable goals. Compared to the EU regulation of food safety controls, therefore, its rather generic outfit lowers the potential of the Floods Directive to induce unified risk-based decision-making within the fragmented German public administration.

However, and maybe more importantly from a polity policies perspective, the directive also sets milestones for a centrally coordinated reporting mechanism, to be revised every six years. A first step asked member states to report areas "at significant risk of flooding" to the EU in an accumulated manner – a challenge for federal Germany. For these areas, it then demanded the drafting of so-called "flood hazard maps" (probability) and "flood risk maps" (probability times impact) by 2013 (first revised in 2019). Next, "flood risk management plans" (FRMPs), which are based on the differential risk information, needed to follow by 2015 (to be revised in 2021). A national competent authority had to report on all of these steps (Council of the European Union, 2007). Regular revisions, every six years, ensure that progress is checked against the objectives that member states set out in their FRMPs. EU bureaucrats hope – quite typically for soft governance mechanisms in the EU – the Directive can steer member states' aspirations and rationalize prevention standards through repeated cycles of flood risk mapping and prevention planning and related reporting duties:

> *We want to . . . see progress. . . . [W]e will try to arrive at some conclusions and recommendations and good practices, which we will try to incorporate into the next cycle of implementation of the Floods Directive. . . . I mean this is an aspiration for the floods directive.*
>
> *(FLO-EU)*

So how has this impulse for soft coercion been taken up within Germany?

6.2.2 Between patchy and keen transposition, local autonomy and national coordination

The transposition of the Flood Risk Management Directive in Germany showcases a struggle between subnational executive autonomy and (newly inaugurated) central coordination typical for cooperative federalism (see Chapter 4). The analysis in Section 6.3 indicates that risk analysis plays a crucial role in establishing a new consensus about how to address these tensions in the domain, but let me describe the transposition dynamics in more depth first.

As flooding policy is a Länder and communal matter, with Berlin delegating the planning and financing of flooding policies to the 16 Länder, the more than 400 municipalities, and self-regulated dike associations, transposition was first and foremost a subnational governance effort that produced patchy results. Transposition practices varied depending on local authorities' and water basin districts' variable legacies in flood risk mapping. They range from half-hearted business-as-usual approaches to keen and sciences-based transposition. For example, while the municipal district of Cologne spent ten million Euros and staffed three additional full-time civil servants to coordinate the risk mapping, there is evidence of rather symbolic transposition elsewhere where authorities "built on a lot of old things" (FLO-08). One interviewee reports that their municipal district had produced a list of risky water bodies – not founded on any actuarial assessment – before the EU Directive kicked in and decided to simply add those areas classified as risky to the list for the EU, without further updates or methodological reconsideration (FLO-13). In addition to such business-as-usual strategies, lack of staff and resources, for example in some Eastern states ("there is one full-time civil servant and a part-time assistant to deal with issues of flooding for the whole state"!), explain the half-hearted transposition of the Floods Directive in some places (FLO-07).

By contrast, experts from states in the Rhine catchment argue that long-standing cooperation in the ICPR has informed mutual actuarial definitions of flood risks long before the Directive and lead to the establishment of differentiated risk reduction goals since at least the late 1990s (FLO-03, FLO-04, FLO-05, and FLO-06), meaning that the transposition of the Directive was smooth and substantial. More recently, in 2018, the ICPR's pre-existing risk-analytical effort even resulted in a geo-information-system modeling software tool called FloRiAn (flood risk analysis). The tool simulates the effects of planned prevention measures and calculates their relative effectiveness ex-ante. An ICPR expert describes how the software automates risk assessment and the planning of new measures in line with the reporting cycle of the EU Floods Directive: "with this tool, we want to evaluate measures every six years . . . the cycle for the flood risk management plans, to see what they actually brought. Not only in monetary terms . . . x Euros in terms of avoiding damages. But also x people are better protected or x industrial sites less affected" (FLO-03).

This account of fragmented transposition based on variable desire and ability to embrace the Directive's actuarial risk concept in a thorough assessment exercise needs to be clarified with a view on coordination pressures and potential emulation dynamics. Most importantly, the need to establish a national competent authority – a new subdivision of the Ministry of the Environment – to report progress on the several steps of the Floods Directive's risk assessment and planning to Brussels forced the German national and state governments to come together, discuss their methodologies, and forge a joint analytical position to report back to Brussels. This was not necessarily a smooth process: like for actuarial risk concepts, some states lacked experience with coordinated prevention efforts altogether (this diagnosis concurs with statements by FLO-03, FLO 05, FLO-06, FLO-07, and FLO-12). Cooperation is long-standing for some (Western-European) catchments, including for the Rhine, Mosel, or Saar, and has enabled an evidence-based and harmonized enforcement of the EU directive beyond political-territorial boundaries. As discussed earlier, efforts to model risk-based prevention planning *across* the multi-national Rhine catchment are highly elaborate. By contrast, actors in other river basin districts were coerced to "come together" for the first time in the new Millennium (FLO-EU). In this uneven context for transposition, the Rhine-based forerunners had an advantage in promoting their template for risk analysis as blueprint for coordination *within* Germany, especially so as their promotional efforts are embedded in a wider instrument constituency around risk analysis with scientists in the domain and the EU Commission (see Section 6.3).

To enable national level reporting across disparate catchments and municipal bodies, the LAWA worked out a joint transposition strategy as well as two specific guidelines on how to develop flood hazard/risk maps and flood risk management plans (LAWA, 2008, 2010a, 2010b):

- The strategy paper remains rather vague about risk analysis methodologies but highlights the need to develop common criteria for identifying areas at significant risk of flooding for the flood risk mapping, a guideline for risk mapping itself, and a template for the FRMPs (LAWA, 2008).
- The recommendations for risk mapping (LAWA, 2010a) dispose quite a high level of detail in several regards: the document details models, information and existing data bases a map needs to be built on; the variables which need factoring in (e.g., subsections on how to assess hydrology, topography, or hydraulics in a common model); and strategies for visualization and category-building on the maps (e.g., standard color codes for different water depths or different velocities of run-off, the same calculation methods and similar pictograms for different types of adverse impact). LAWA's guideline (2010a, pp. 22 and 24) show examples of the detailed methodological and visual standardization attempt.
- The guideline on FRMPs (LAWA, 2010b), just as the EU Directive, does not prescribe any specific measures. Yet, it establishes a standard catalogue and categorization system for flood-related policy-planning and reporting to the EU. The guideline summarizes the broad EU-level categorization of measures, presents a template to translate EU categories into existing LAWA fields

> of action, then details this template in a 28-pages long detailed catalogue of types of measures (including a qualitative description of their effectiveness in different scenarios and guidance on how to plan and implement them), and finishes with a 15-pages long appendix with a detailed template for categorizing measures in a consistent way for reporting to the EU.

The high level of detail and thorough identification of key variables in risk analysis, existing assessment methods, databases, catalogues of measures by the LAWA may speak of an instrumental turn to risk analysis in German flood prevention at the Bund-Länder cooperation level (cf. indicators in Table 3.2). However, as is typical of horizontal and vertical coordination in Germany's cooperative federalism (Chapter 4), LAWA decisions are non-binding. A state representative thus evaluates the harmonization impulse of such guidelines rather skeptically: "Well, you return to your state with a nice LAWA decision and want to implement it and then you get stuck sometimes with the legal and financial conditions . . . and then I am sometimes forced to do things differently than [what we] negotiated in the LAWA" (FLO-11).

6.2.3 Beyond mere assessment: risk-based funding in the National Flood Protection Program

An important elaboration of the Floods Directive beyond mere analytical harmonization concerns the *National Flood Protection Program* in 2014. Remember that Länder and municipalities' only access to Federal money for flood defense and prevention used to be via the "shared task" agrarian structure and coastal protection (GAK). After another round of devastating floods across central and Eastern Europe in spring 2013, affecting large parts of Germany, too, German states and the Federal government decided to accelerate investment in protection and prevention infrastructures by involving the Federal level more prominently in funding (Bundesministerium für Umwelt, Naturschutz und nukleare Sicherheit, 2019). Since 2014, a specific sub-department within the Ministry of the Environment is responsible for coordinating measures and developing the program further (Bundesrechnungshof, 2016). States can submit proposals of measures to the funding stream but only a selected number of "priority" measures with "transregional" effects for the lowering of water gauges during floods will be co-funded (to 60 per cent) from the national pot. As the Ministry reports, the national program aims to "contribute to the accelerated implementation of priority, transregional measures of preventative flood protection" (Bundesministerium für Umwelt, Naturschutz und nukleare Sicherheit, 2019). These include the creation of retention areas/dike relocation, steerable polders, and the improvement of existing protection infrastructure. The required budget until the 2030s is over 5.4 billion Euros to implement 102 selected projects across the five nationally relevant water basin districts (LAWA, 2014, p. 6).

The new funding stream constitutes a genuine track change in Germany's multilevel flooding policies: it partially shifts funding responsibilities, and not least the decision over which flood prevention project to support and according to which criteria, from Länder to a Bund-Länder consortium (LAWA). This gives the central level a bigger say in the execution of flooding policies and increases incentives for risk-based vertical coordination of prevention priorities. Pre-existing GAK funding, by contrast, operated more on a case-by-case basis without an overall view on funding priorities or transregional coherence of measures (Buschhüter et al., 2018).

The selection criteria for measures to be funded via the national program explicitly use the flood risk maps manufactured in response to the EU's legal requirements. There is evidence of a central level promotion of common risk-analytical priority-setting in national funding decisions (cf. indicators in Table 3.2) which might well unfold a nudging effect through financial incentive setting. LAWA decided to prioritize measures which address the "common good" at national level, meaning that they come with expected prevention benefits for a significant share of residential areas, industrial/commercial sites, and inhabitants. The basis for calculating such shares ought to be, LAWA suggests, the very flood risk maps local authorities designed in line with the Floods Directive (LAWA, 2014, p. 6). The prominent use of risk maps in defining access to new streams of funding can be interpreted as an instance of self-inflicted meta-governance onto states wielded by their own vertical coordination forum. As funding is much sought after, the scheme may well mainstream a common risk-analytical approach and counter executive fragmentation in flood prevention beyond what states originally had in mind.

Overall, the analysis in this section exposes a rather keen transposition of the EU Floods Directive in Germany, going much beyond what the EU requires and involving, notably, strong coordination efforts among otherwise independent Länder authorities. This is explicit in the non-binding, yet detailed, LAWA transposition guidelines which are flanked by the following:

- far-reaching scientific elaboration of computational flood risk analysis in some fore-runner states (Rhine catchment area) which automates priority-setting in flood risk management at least partially,
- the continuing promotional efforts of these fore-runners in establishing their model as blueprint for German-wide policy coordination, and
- the use of flood risk maps as a scientific foundation for establishing funding priorities in a new national flood protection scheme which creates financial incentives for subnational decision makers to engage more substantially with risk-based prevention planning.

6.3 Explaining the keen transposition of the EU's flood risk analysis requirements

What explains the keen adoption pattern of risk analysis in German flooding policies? To whom and why has risk analysis appealed as an analytical tool for governing the flooding domain beyond the – modest – requirements of the EU Directive? How do different support logics for the case of risk analysis interact? Answers to these questions, based on actors' meaning making around risk analysis in interviews, fall into four argumentative complexes as follows:

- risk analysis helps states reject claims on public budgets for prevention and compensation, reinforce the legally codified limits of accountability for failure, and specify that accountability lies with municipalities and private actors (orientation toward legitimatory blame-shifting);
- risk analysis facilitates collective problem-solving, from the perspective of decision makers, by enabling transparent comparisons of the relative cost-effectiveness of measures across political boundaries (orientation toward instrumental policy coordination);
- the dual risk analysis and coordination requirement endowed central level government with a more powerful role in policy coordination while at the same time enabling "pioneering" actors to promote their own policy as a benchmark for all (power-seeking orientation through the formation of strategic constituency around an analytical model); and
- risk analysis also enables the multi-level setting to overcome collective action problems through more central involvement in implementation – via the identification of national priorities for funding flood prevention projects – but without forcing Länder to formally renounce their executive prerogatives (power-shifting orientation).

6.3.1 The limits of public protection duties: risk-based blame shifting

Part of the documentary and interview material depicts blame relocation for adverse outcomes as key justification for turning to risk analysis. In line with arguments around institutional risk management (Rothstein, Huber and Gaskell, 2006) and the power to define the parameters of blame by risk-based differentiation (Black, 2010) (Section 3.2), German states try to redirect accountability for flood protection and funding to municipalities and private owners.

This is no new development; rather, risk analysis offers a welcome occasion to reinforce and justify historically derived (but practically somewhat nebulous) accountability structures and defend them against local and private budgetary demands. As outlined earlier, there is no legal duty for German states to provide flood protection for riparian flooding to any discrete level and the 2005 Flood Prevention Act codified the private prevention duty. State-level ministerial planners appreciate the signaling function of the EU Floods Directive: flood risk maps, according to several interviewees (FLO-05, FLO-06, FLO-09, FLO-08, and FLO-12) can help justify more clearly the limits of public accountability and strengthen private risk prevention duties all-too-readily forgotten in political struggles over damage removal and pay-outs when disasters hit. A more recent LAWA strategy paper equally argues that "the Directive ought to be used to improve private prevention activities by owners and municipalities" (LAWA, 2008, p. 4).

BOX 6.1: SPECIFICATION AND LIMITATION OF PUBLIC ACCOUNTABILITY FOR FLOOD PREVENTION

Statement 1: [talks about their Land's decision to declare two small cities as inundation areas after results of risk mapping and the reaction of Departments for Economy and land use] *"they wrote a statement saying inner cities are inappropriate a selection for inundation areas. [R.P.: because people live there?] Yes. So I said: there is no question of appropriateness (laughs), the water will be coming! . . . It would be extremely unfair not to let people know the water could be coming their way"*! (FLO-11)

Statement 2: *"they [mayors and property owners] might be angry, that the risk maps describe risks so clearly . . . [but] the problem is the creation of damage potentials in areas at risk of regular inundation . . . people enjoy the benefits of living at the water, but expect the state and general public to pay for damage of their risk-taking of living in inundation areas . . . We are very restrictive in financing any damage costs especially – in the case of damage one cannot simply recur to the general public"*! (FLO-09)

Statement 3: *"All we can say is: folks, it is your business. There is no state protection against every centimeter of water in your basement"!* (FLO-08)

Statement 4: *"Everyone living in risk areas must engage in prevention . . . And that needs to be communicated, there is no way around it"*! (FLO-12)

Statement 5: *"I admit that I am currently struggling with the question what to do in [a city in Northern Germany]. Every time they have a flood: a big public outcry, because the historical city center is being inundated . . . down at the Mosel they would laugh about the water levels! . . . and what they design in terms of protection there . . . I don't even know how to pay for it; it will be a fortune, 30 million I think, for twenty houses! At the same time, they had . . . I think up to seven meters of water in the historical city center down in Passau. Just to compare the dimensions . . . and damage potentials . . . I have to say quite frankly: I cannot use the national flood protection program for that, they will laugh at me"!* (FLO-12)

The role of risk analysis, in this context, is three-fold. At its most basic, the risk maps – and the requirement to publish them for all to access – help making risks transparent to the public, in some places for the very first time. To assess "where things could happen and to also tell the affected population" counts as the main goal of the Floods Directive according to most interviewees (here FLO-11). Informing people more clearly to what extent their property is affected in different probability scenarios is discussed as a matter of fairness (Statement 1). As Statements 1 and 2 indicate, such transparency has been controversial where property owners have taken risk maps to devalue their (blue-on-the-map) properties or, in the case of municipal planners, to restrict land use.

Second, amongst critique that risk mapping "destroys our property values" (FLO-02), the clear and persistent communication of risk analysis results is seen as chief strategy to manage the institutional risks arising from flood events. Risk maps are perceived as helpful for reminding people that their decision to live in flood prone areas comes with risks they must manage privately (see also Statement 3). The transparency created by common risk analysis, interviewees hope, ought to nudge private owners into taking informed decisions about prevention without calling for public money. Several interviewees also see risk analysis as a means to limit the political impulse to promise financial support after flood events (FLO-09 and FLO-12).

Third, however, risk analysis does not only help push aside accountability for adverse outcomes; it is also seen as a method for specifying the conditions under which the state(s) do(es) assume responsibilities for flood prevention by means of comparative assessment. Policymakers use risk-based differentiation to detail the parameters of blame for flooding events. This becomes obvious in Statement 5, which uses comparative language to highlight where a state or municipality ought to intervene and fund prevention measures and where such intervention seems inappropriate due to lower risk levels. Risk analysis, from this perspective, helps differentiating lower and local risk scenarios which are to be dealt with privately and locally *without* state or Federal level support.

6.3.2 Resolving collective action problems: coordination through shared risk evidence

Individual states' desire to signal limits of accountability toward private owners and budget-seeking municipalities alone does not explain why risk analysis emulated in a rather coordinated and substantial manner in German flood prevention policies. The strong sense of urgency for overcoming collective action problems among both Federal and state-level decision makers contributed to an instrumentally leaning adoption pattern of the EU's (vague) Flood Risk Management Directive. In Germany's multi-level flood prevention setting, risk analysis and risk-based modeling count as important enabling tools for desired (but difficult) policy coordination among autonomous actors with potentially competing interests. While Statement 6 (see Box 6.2) describes coordination between member states about how to deal with border-crossing flood risks as the main goal of the Floods Directive, Statement 7, by a Federal level official, identifies coordination of flood risk management to be a persistent "problem" *within* Germany, too. Decision makers across the administrative levels within the Federal Republic welcome the EU Directive as a pathway toward more effective coordination in this historically much-fragmented realm of executive federalism.

Typical for instrumentalist interpretations of risk analysis (Majone, 2010; cf. Section 3.1), policymakers suggest that flood risk assessment helps them rationalize decisions for or against specific prevention measures because it renders the relative efficiency and effectiveness of measures comparable across political boundaries. Statements 8 and 9, for instance, evidence a genuine desire to improve risk modeling to enable identification of *optimal* catchment-wide prevention decisions in the future. The Rhine catchment actors, for example, designed the simulation tool FloRiAn (see Section 6.2.2) deliberately to compare the cost-benefit ratio of different flood prevention measures in the Rhine catchment and to enable rational prioritization: "with this tool, we want to evaluate measures . . . to see what they actually brought. Not only in monetary terms . . . x Euros in terms of avoiding damages. But also x people are better protected or x industrial sites less affected" (FLO-03).

Hopes for increased cost-effectiveness in flood prevention also feature prominently in the support case for the National Flood Protection Program, a case of

BOX 6.2: EFFECTIVENESS AND EFFICIENCY GAINS THROUGH RISK-BASED COORDINATION OF FLOOD PREVENTION

Statement 6: "*It should not happen that states plan measures upstream which have a negative effect [downstream] or there is no cooperation . . . To improve coordination between states . . . the Directive . . . that was one main goal*". (FLO-03)

Statement 7: "*Of course Germany does do flood protection, also based on risk assessment, since decades. . . . But what did not work so well thus forth, and the Directive will hopefully bring change here . . . is simply a better coordination within Germany, . . . between Länder*". (FLO-07)

Statement 8: "*this would be a genuine quantum leap, more than that, I'd say . . . because as it stands we do not have a common targeting of financial resources across states towards a common priority . . . to use this financing tool, this is the idea, to highlight . . . the idea of effectiveness across a whole water basin district*". (FLO-07)

Statement 9: "*. . . to be able to ask: which measures are beneficial in this scenario. To be able to show a proper risk assessment and effectiveness assessment for discrete measures ex-ante . . . An analysis where you put measures in at the top and the result at the bottom tells you which effect it would have . . . And then we could approach things differently . . . with a cost-benefit assessment . . . to use such a modelling and scenario assessment . . . if we could include dams in the Swiss Jurassic and [model] their steering capacities down the Rhine . . . we'd have a relatively large effect for little effort . . . and could, potentially, do without other measures which, which are perhaps expensive or create a lot of resistance*". (FLO-05) vertical policy cooperation between the Bund and state-level actors. As the Federal authorities argue: "The most important goal must be to select and combine appropriate projects *coherently* across a riparian catchment so that the highest possible share of people benefits" (Bundesministerium für Umwelt, Naturschutz und nukleare Sicherheit, 2019, highlight added). Federals hope that the use of risk analysis in the national funding stream will increase what Majone called "procedural rationality": rather than preventing all flooding, the task of vertical cooperation is to identify measures with a *transregional* prevention effect and an *optimal* cost-benefit ratio and to thus create a basis for rational cross-border decision making (also see Statement 9).

Policymakers agree that the de-politicizing and "objectifying" credentials ascribed to risk analysis (Sections 3.1 and 3.3) have been central in the development of the Program. Some state-level decision makers report fierce struggles over appropriate funding criteria in the National Flood Protection Program, partly because national forerunners of flood risk management had already funded their own retention areas and so on and would no longer benefit from federal money, and argue that risk analysis was central for reaching agreement between states. Eventually, eligibility for national funding scheme demands any maintenance measures be justified in terms of their "national significance", based on risk analysis (Bund/Länder-Arbeitsgemeinschaft Wasser (LAWA), 2014, p. 5). As the Federal Ministry of the Environment specifies: "the funding of water gauge reduction measures with transregional effect directly tackles existing conflicts of interest between upstream and downstream communities and promotes the principle of solidarity" (Bundesministerium für Umwelt, Naturschutz und nukleare Sicherheit, 2019). The risk-analytical signaling of impartiality thus helped the Federal moderators manage conflicts of interests between upstream and downstream communities at state level and come up with a vertically coordinated funding approach in the first place. Just as idealized in rational choice accounts of risk regulation (Sunstein, 2002; Majone, 2010), the comparative simulation of risks in and across catchment areas is believed to prompt less politically biased flooding-related decision making.

6.3.3 Promoting a benchmark across levels: from the Rhine to the EU and back to Germany

Interview data evidences that the Flood Risk Management Directive and its requirements to do risk analysis set-off a triple dynamic of (1) forcing autonomous actors to coordinate their methodologies for assessing flood risks and eventually also discuss prevention priorities, (2) endowing central level government with a more powerful role in such coordination, and (3) enabling those actors who already had longstanding experience in risk-based policy coordination to promote their own policy as a benchmark for all.

The Floods Directive came with clear soft harmonization goals (Statement 10 by an EU level expert). Faced with the requirement to design risk maps, German Länder – notwithstanding their constitutionally guaranteed role in executing flooding policies – experienced "pressure" to "join forces" and to coordinate their methodologies so that territorial borders would be less visible on risk maps and in risk management plans (Statements 11 and 12). Policymakers in German states perceive the reporting regime for the Floods Directive – including the threat of EU level recommendations for improving one's analytical approach ("a letter from the Commission") but also the cyclical revision of risk maps and management plans every six years – as trigger for change toward more harmonized flood risk mapping within Germany (Statements 12 and 13). For Germany's Federal administration, pursuing its new role as national competent authority to report to Brussels, better coordination within the country seems inevitable "to avoid a letter from Brussels for dividing flood risk management by Länder borders" (FLO-07).

While Berlin may have had mainly instrumental goals of more effective policy coordination and coherent reporting in mind (Sections 6.3.2), the lack of own regulatory capacities left the Federal government with the promotion of a risk-analytical standard as a way of nudging autonomous state administrations into coordinating their approaches. Indeed, the LAWA (2008) guideline for transposing the EU Directive highlights that a more coordinated approach must be accommodated *within* the existing federal structures. As suggested more generally for quantification in public administration (Mennicken and Lodge, 2015, p. 8; cf. Section 3.3), Federal policymakers in German flood prevention have used risk-analytical quantification to advance their powers "to monitor and steer" in a domain – albeit for the sake of an instrumental belief in risk-based effectiveness gains – where they otherwise have little influence over decision-making. As the EU's risk mapping requirements have heightened the comparability of risk across jurisdictions due to unitarized risk reporting, it also enables – for the first time – nation-wide naming and shaming within Germany (FLO-01). According to a local decision maker, it is increasingly hard for municipalities to justify inactivity in prevention or the continuation of land use as usual if parts of their terrain are flagged as "dark blue on the maps" (FLO-01), especially when neighboring localities decide to change policies in response to similar results on the risk maps. Overall, the Federal government – endowed with its new central role as national competent authority – appreciates and uses the EU's dual requirement of risk mapping and catchment-wide coordination in its own meta-governance efforts: to pursue a common framework for flood prevention priorities within Germany without formally challenging Länder executive control of the domain.

In addition to strengthening the role of the Federal level in flood prevention, the EU's double coordination *and* risk assessment requirement gave catchment areas with experience in *coordinated* flood risk management – most importantly the

BOX 6.3: HARMONIZATION VIA CENTRAL REPORTING AND BENCHMARKING MECHANISMS

Statement 10: "*Harmonisation, I mean I've discussed it with member states, is a no-go. . . . I don't think that this would fly. . . . What we can do is extract experienced good practice from the implementation of member states and publish some case studies, good practices. And perhaps some member states . . . which don't have such a solid approach already, you know, they can take those good examples and adopt them and . . . other member states can maybe fine tune their approaches*". (FLO-EU)

Statement 11: "*The Floods Directive brings an element of harmonisation into things . . . connected to the methodology stuff, that we will eventually have comparable data*". (FLO-03)

Statement 12: "*Well, the reporting and coordination did lead to us joining forces . . . to have consistent maps, not to have water bodies ending at territorial borders anymore, to consider how measures affect the neighbour . . . to achieve, with the right level of pressure in the background, so to speak, that they choose the same assessment approaches [for floods]. Before the Floods Directive . . . we arrived at three different heights when we [three Länder in Northern Germany] applied our respective methodologies to [a city at the North Sea coast]*". (FLO-12)

Statement 13: "*There will certainly be a letter from the Commission, that there are differences [in risk mapping] which mainly follow territorial borders. We are already preparing for the next cycle of reporting, to make these differences, well, disappear through LAWA's work. . . . To ensure that . . . the boundaries of Länder won't be so visible anymore in reports*". (FLO-11)

Rhine – an advantage in EU-wide and member state internal searches for analytical best practices. Not without pride, ICPR representatives report about their influential role to shape the Flood Risk Management Directive in the first place:

> *FLO-04: It is fair to say that the EU's Floods Directive is based on ICPR experiences. R.P.: Really? I had no idea . . . FLO-03: Mhmmm (confirmative) . . . FLO-04: Yes, absolutely. This was one of the main elements to direct the development [of the Directive]. '93, '95 here along the Rhine [meaning the severe flood events] . . . And then 2002 [the year of the severe Elbe floods] triggered an EU-wide discussion about a Floods Directive. And in this context the Rhine, the experience with the action plan on flooding, was being used quite explicitly.FLO-03: Mhmmm (confirmative) . . . FLO-04: We were the only organisation in Europe which had such a thing, such a coordinated approach.*

This (perhaps complacent) narrative supports the expectation that instrument constituencies can accelerate the adoption of risk analysis in multi-level jurisdictions, especially when the sense of border-crossing crisis (as after large-scale floods in the early 2000s) prompts otherwise autonomous administrative authorities to engage in *coordinated* problem-solving. From the perspective of the Rhine valley actors, the EU Directive – which they had crucially shaped – could then also be embraced as a steppingstone toward a more rationally minded risk prevention strategy *within* Germany. Policy leaders along the Rhine invariably describe their coordination as "laboratory" for new analytical approaches and risk management solutions (FLO-04, similar meanings related by EU-01, FLO-03, FLO-05, and FLO-06). Their leadership role for policy coordination across the whole country is self-evident from their viewpoint: "of course, this (the Directive) will . . . accelerate things in our sense . . . give us an additional argument to assert our approach across Germany" (FLO-05). The Floods Directive seems to have supported promotional efforts among subnational actors – the Rhine Länder – already committed to risk-based and coordinated approaches for instrumental reasons and were now able to use the reporting, evaluation, and benchmarking mechanisms of the Directive to crack remaining hesitancy and mainstream their model across the country. The substantial Germany-wide turn to risk analysis in flood prevention, in that perspective, has resulted from the successful promotion of an analytical template by a pro-active and instrumentally minded regional forerunner (Länder in the Rhine catchment and their international organization in the ICPR) whose efforts have been powerfully embedded in a wider instrument constituency that included scientists and, since the mid-2000s, the EU Commission itself.

While some states dispute the unilateral leading role of the Rhine coordination in developing the analytical basis for coordinated flood risk management in Germany (FLO-12), eligibility and prioritization checks in the national flood protection program are indeed informed by the ICPR's advanced simulation tool, not least because the Federal government has actively promoted the ICPR model and explicitly praises the Rhine's pioneering role in evidence-based flood prevention (FLO-07 and FLO-08). Federal level actors report their excitement over the FloRiAn software and state their plans to "promote the tool also for other water basin districts and internationally, too" (FLO-08). Arguably, in its role as national competent authority to coordinate the German transposition of the EU flood risk assessment duties, the Federal Ministry for the Environment has itself become part of the instrument constituency which supports an instrumental and rather elaborate version of risk analysis. From an instrument constituency perspective, the expanding fellowship of the Rhine model, first in the EU Commission and later in Federal government, evidences an endogenous process of forging strategic actorness around risk analysis which contributes to its institutionalization in policy-making. Eventually, the initially rather implicit role of risk analysis in shaping how national moneys are being distributed might well be the beginning of a scientifically based (but also strategically promoted, see next subsection) harmonization spiral in historically highly fragmented German flood prevention.

6.3.4 Abolishing collective action problems? Risk-based pushes for Federal prevention duties

Last, not least, interpretations and uses of risk analysis in German flood prevention also relate to an ambivalent desire of Länder and Federal level to negotiate their respective competencies in the domain. The interview material and documented parliamentary hearings in the Bundestag suggest that there is an intensifying struggle over financial burden-sharing between Bund and Länder in which risk analysis becomes a tool for re-negotiating responsibilities for flood prevention in the multi-level polity. Parallel to states shifting the blame for low level and local flooding risks back to private and municipal actors, risk analysis has become intermingled with a (yet undecided) struggle between the Federal and state governments about who is in charge, and who needs to pay for high risk flooding events of national relevance.

BOX 6.4: RISK-BASED FUNDING IN THE NATIONAL FLOOD PROTECTION PROGRAMME AS POLITY POLICIES

Statement 14: *"There are . . . discussions around the National Flood Protection Program, for example along the Elbe, where we say: if we are debating more Federal level engagement in these measures . . . do we not also need to consider the funding side of things, whether we can do this together? It is early days still, and a precondition is that we find a basic agreement on how to select measures".* (FLO-08)

Statement 15: *"They do have Länder-specific funding guidelines . . . but they don't have this criterion of transregional or national significance, they only consider Länder-specific aspects. And this is where we come in, with the National Flood Protection Program, where we insisted strongly . . . to set criteria in a way that measures which will be included, that these must have . . . a transregional effect, that they have a significant effect, for example, on lowering water gauges downstream".* (FLO-07)

Statement 16: *"This [the national flood protection program] is about measures with transregional effect . . . the Federal Institute [of Hydrology] has calculated [that transregional measures at the Elbe] . . . can reach water gauge reductions of 26–45 cm . . . and it is particularly important then to include these [measures] in a national program and to also pay for it nationally".* (FLO-11)

Statement 17: *"Above all, the Federal level is able to have a transregional view . . . It's idiotic to stop at Länder borders in flood prevention. Well, and LAWA is nothing but a crutch we use to design things more consistently. If things would be . . . more centralised, like in France, we would be able to think and act across Länder borders and would be less exposed to local politicians' demands".* (FLO-11)

Statement 18: *"The Federal level and us, Länder, we were always expected to be solidaristic . . . to shoulder the billions of damages incurred in the East [talking about example of the 2004 and 2013 Elbe flooding]. Whilst at the same time the Federal level did nothing in terms of prevention. And we said: this is wrong! A national program only makes sense if the Federal level contributes in this area. So we tried to use the flood event [of 2013] to put pressure on the Federal level. They still have a . . . restrictive position [FLO-06: 'Mr. Schäuble wants to keep his budget clean'!]. But, as I said, we have the impression . . . that the Federal level will probably contribute financially after all".* (FLO-05)

Initially, the Federal government was a keen supporter of the national funding stream. Its design was part of the 2013 coalition agreement between Conservatives and Social Democrats, and the Ministry for the Environment has welcomed its inception as follows: "with the program we change onto a new track in German flood risk management and perceive the implementation of the solidarity principle, by means of balancing out the costs of upstream communities with the benefits of downstream communities, as a nationwide task" (Bundesministerium für Umwelt, Naturschutz und nukleare Sicherheit, 2019). As Statements 14 and 15 highlight, the Bund "insisted" on the creation of a common catalogue of risk-analytical indicators for funding national measures. Arguably, the power-seeking intentions discussed earlier – Berlin's wish to increase its ability to steer autonomous subnational decision-making in the domain via central reporting, naming, and shaming – helps explain such contentions.

However, rather than being founded on one-sided centralization intentions in Berlin, state-level impulses triggered the shift toward vertical coordination of funding through the National Flood Protection Program. Around 2013, state representatives came to an agreement that a Federal level program *only* could resolve dire collective action problems and conflicts of interest and thus ensure more effective transregional flood prevention at least for risks of national order (FLO-11, recalling LAWA discussions at the time). A policymaker from Lower Saxony reports, for example, how the state tried – in vain – to coordinate flood defense measures in the "Aller-Leine-Oker-Plan" in the 1960s. From a total of around 40 retention areas, only two were built up to 2013. Most interviewees at state level are thus rather skeptical as to the success of any non-coercive risk-based coordination. The hindrances of local resistance against measures of transregional relevance could only be remedied, interviewees argue, if the Federal level had more enforcement power and could demand "legal obligation of planned measures" based on risk assessment results (FLO-09). Several interviewees demand nothing short of a risk-oriented centralization of legislative and executive powers in the domain, at least for measures designed to counter transregional high-risk scenarios (see Statements 16 and 17). Indeed, in parallel to shifting blame for low-risk scenarios of local relevance back to private actors and municipalities – a more traditional interpretation of institutional risk management – states in Germany use risk analysis to also re-allocate responsibilities for high-risk scenarios of transregional (or national) relevance up to the Federal level. Risk analysis and its visualization in neatly comparable maps can thus help tackle the historical problem of unclear flood prevention duties, too.

From the Federal level perspective, this is arguably the dark side of taking on more meta-governance and central level coordination in the domain based on risk-analytical insights. Beyond what the new national program of 2014 already proposes, the states have more recently called upon Berlin to increase Federal budgets for flood risk management activities. For example, the Rhine Länder – instrumental for carving out a bigger national role in prevention funding in the first place (Statement 18) – argue that the Floods Directive's risk assessment plays into their hands "we have some more arguments for claiming money" from Berlin for prevention (FLO-05). In a 2015 hearing of the Committee for the Environment of the German Bundestag, Länder jointly appealed to the Federal level to increase its share in the National Flood Protection Program to 70 per cent (instead of 60 per cent). They justify their claim by highlighting that "only the most relevant measures of specific national significance" had been selected for the program in the first place and that this focus on *nationally* important measures justifies a higher share of *national* funding (Deutscher Bundestag, 2015). Its keen initial promotion of risk modeling for instrumental and nudging purposes thus backfires for Berlin as the results of the same risk modeling allow Länder to claim a national (financial) responsibility for high-risk flood scenarios of national scope.

States' push for a re-allocation of flood prevention and financing duties in the multi-level setting receives support from the Federal Audit Office which demands a driving seat for the Federal Ministry in the National Flood Protection Program alongside more powerful oversight over spending (Bundesrechnungshof, 2016). Such a move would end reliance on voluntary coordination in German flood prevention and introduce – based on risk-analytical consensus-finding about how to best ensure effective collective action – a distinct Federal competence in what has for centuries been an extremely fragmented case of executive federalism.

Notes

1 Interview partner FLO-11.
2 For ease of writing, I use the term flood prevention to include both more classic protective measures, such as dike maintenance and so on, alongside retention measures.
3 The first of these dike associations originated along the North Frisian coast in what is today's Schleswig-Holstein and Lower Saxony in the early Middle Ages, but there are similar associations for the non-tidal sections of major rivers.
4 For example, while the Rhine catchment usually sees winter and spring floods caused by heavy rainfalls and snow melting in the Alps, the Elbe typically brings summer floods

caused by the frequent extreme rainfalls in summer in the Czech Republic and the very East of Germany with their more Continental climate.

5 This is a standard method to describe statistical return periods of flooding events based on historical flood records. A flood with a 1 per cent AEP (= AEP 0.01) has a one in a hundred chance of occurring in any one year.

6 The Rhine flooding in 1993, for instance, caused around 500 million Euros of damage and affected around 100,000 inhabitants of Cologne alone. The 2002 Elbe flooding had even more disastrous effects with damage levels of around 15 billion Euros.

7 Arguably, the first supranational organisation and a pilot for the EU's common market (Bundeszentrale für politische Bildung, 2012), the Rhine Commission has extended its initial regulatory mandate for making the Rhine more navigable and profitable to protecting its habitats and coordinating flood prevention (ICPR, 2013).

8 For example, interviews expose that the Rhine group sees itself as a highly rational actor, and as forerunner for using risk analysis and CBA for prevention planning locally (FLO-03, FLO-04, FLO-05, and FLO-06). At the same time, catchments with large Eastern German shares – informed by the GDR heritage of centrally organised flood protection – tend to call for protection by the state (FLO-11 and FLO-12).

7

BREAKING FREE OF THE "LEGITIMACY TRAP"

Risk analysis as a collective defense strategy in work safety controls

> *We are always in a legitimacy trap: what are you up to and where do you move things? What is the outcome [of work safety inspections] in the end?*
>
> (WSY-12)

The book's last comparative case study addresses work safety[1] inspections, a domain which saw a later and less substantial turn to risk analysis than the previous two cases. While standard-setting in accident prevention has involved risk-based decision-making since the mid-2000s (Paul and Huber, 2015; Rothstein et al., 2019), state inspectorates only turned to risk analysis in 2014. The chapter, once more, starts by depicting the historical evolution of work safety inspections: their highly contested mandate, continuous regulatory competition with mutual trade associations' own control regime, and executive fragmentation. A striking under-funding of statutory labor inspectorates and a more recent watering down of their core mandate by coercive EU inspection requirements in neighboring domains, such as environmental and product safety, imperils the statutory work safety mandate further. I then describe how risk analysis was introduced in German work safety, in contrast to the other two cases, not via the EU venue, but through a voluntary bottom-up elaboration of a common, but relatively broad-brush, risk-analytical model. My interpretive analysis of policymakers' orientations toward risk analysis exposes how an initially purely instrumental template, trialed in some fore-runner states, got mainstreamed via horizontal coordination as legitimacy-seeking states sought to defend statutory inspections, as well as their subnational organization, against mounting criticism. Given the lasting squeeze on statutory work safety inspections, state inspectorates have also started promoting coordinated risk-analytical inspection programming as a tool for rendering their weak work safety mandates more visible politically, and even for ringfencing and expanding them in terms of resources.

7.1 Work safety in Germany: contested mandate and regulatory competition

The first regulatory interventions on behalf of work safety emerged in the most industrialized German states of Prussia and Saxony in the mid-19th century (Simons, 1984, p. 11). Prussia first passed a *Regulativ* in 1839 to address deteriorating working conditions in industrialized areas. Local police officers in particular often failed to enforce the new regulatory standards in practice, mainly because of lack of resources, lack of critical awareness for the issue, but also because local administrations heavily depended on factory owners and their tax payments and did not want to upset them with inspections (Simons, 1984, p. 16f). In this section, I detail how the historical reluctance to prioritize work safety in similar ways as food controls has nourished a constant struggle for state inspectorates to defend their mandate. This struggle intensified more recently when budgetary squeezes and regulatory competition with politically more salient neighboring domains jeopardized effective work safety controls, and the lack of a coordinated control strategy attracted vocal criticism.

7.1.1 Early regulation but reluctant enforcement

It took more than a decade to provide the legal grounds for statutory inspectorates: a 1853 amendment of the *Regulativ* enabled municipal districts in Prussia to establish facultative factory inspectorates but only few made use of this prerogative (Simons, 1984, p. 20f). While implementation remained a weak spot, the *Regulativ* was important as a blueprint for the rest of Germany. In 1869, the North German Confederation of Länder (*Norddeutscher Bund*) included Prussian-style factory inspections in its Industrial Code (*Gewerbeordnung*). Enforcement varied considerably across the territory: most states had local police forces check working hours and workers' age, the state of Baden used a volunteers' inspectorate, while the state of Saxony tasked existing self-regulatory steam boiler inspectors to (also) check compliance with work safety regulation in a newly founded state inspectorate. In 1878, the German Empire adopted a revised General Industrial Code which liberalized the market by abolishing the controls and representative powers of guilds. It replaced guilds' self-regulatory function with statutory provisions. As part of this, the Code adopted work safety regulations from the Northern German blueprint and expanded the mandate for state inspections: inspectorates were now obligatory, the control of "the protection of life and health" of workers explicitly mandated, especially dangerous industrial machinery became subject to licensing, and *all* work places covered by the Industrial Code were now to be checked for work safety issues (Simons, 1984, p. 32f).

Even though inspections were mostly concerned with the moral decency of (female) workers during night shifts and the health of military recruits who went through the hardships of child labor (Hennock, 2007), historians stress the path-breaking character of the Prussian *Regulativ* and its subsequent emulation across Germany. Indeed, the historically much cherished freedom of the German guilds to organize their economic production – including working conditions – as they see fit left little role for state intervention before. In effect, the landmark character of the General Industrial Code, including its legal origins in Prussia, respites from its role in forging a statutory mandate for work safety regulation and its enforcement (Simons, 1984; Hennock, 2007; Lehder, 2011). Yet, from a comparative perspective, it is important to note that work safety was perceived as less salient an issue than food safety, state intervention was much more contested and even seen as an illegitimate intervention in the freedom of trade and, accordingly, the resulting statutory inspection mandate was rather weak. There has also been no nationally relevant expert advocacy[2] which could have harmonized regulatory approaches based on a common scientific problem and/or solution definition.

Indeed, from the very start, the idea that central state authorities were to control workplaces found much less support than in food safety. Chancellor Bismarck ferociously opposed the introduction of statutory inspections and tried to halt respective passages in the Industrial Code. In this, he was joined by most Conservative and Liberal politicians at the time. When the Code was passed nonetheless due to increasing public pressure and the parliamentary initiatives of the Social Democrats, the Imperial government and Länder governments watered down work safety regulation with enforcement directives which prescribed a benevolent and advisory interpretation of the inspection mandate vis-à-vis regulatees (Simons, 1984, p. 41ff). Beyond several anti-regulation arguments[3] which must seem surprisingly familiar to contemporary regulation scholars, Bismarck's opposition to factory inspections reflected that his "social policy approach was not guided by an interest in welfare but by the goal of stabilising the social and political order" (Simons, 1984, p. 36, translation by author). He was convinced that accident prevention through extended statutory factory inspectorates would not contribute much to this goal as citizens would not perceive prevented accidents as a positive delivery by the state. This was an interesting discursive diversion from the strong and widely consensual perception in food safety that market failures required state-led correction – even if prevented food-borne illnesses were (and are) arguably just as invisible as prevented work accidents.[4]

7.1.2 Regulatory competition: mutual trade associations and interdisciplinary mandates

Instead of strengthening state inspections, Bismarck saw enormous strategic potential in compensating workers *after* they were injured or fell ill. Jointly with large manufacturing employers who increasingly saw private tort as an overly uncertain and socially destabilizing compensation practice, Bismarck invested heavily in creating a mandatory social insurance to meet the material interests of injured and ill workers ex-post (alongside schemes for otherwise ill, disabled, and old-aged workers) (Simons, 1984; Mares, 2003; Hennock, 2007). The creation of the first public accident insurance in 1884 is of lasting importance for German work safety regulation and its enforcement, as its basic institutional features have not changed much since:

- Since its foundation, the insurance has compensated workers through a fund to which all firms contribute fixed mandatory payments through no-fault compensation (Hennock, 2007, p. 88).
- Funds have been administered by the *Berufsgenossenschaften* (BGs), a set of powerful self-regulated[5] mutual trade associations with mandatory membership for all firms in an economic sector.
- BGs have also been granted the right to set preventative standards for work safety conditions. To date, the mutuals' accident prevention rules – though not legally binding – form a major part of the regulatory standards against which firms' compliance is being checked by inspectors (see our wider discussion in: Rothstein et al., 2019; Rothstein, Paul and Demeritt, 2020).
- Lastly, and most importantly from the perspective of state inspectors, BGs have also been tasked with inspecting firms in their respective sector to check compliance with accident prevention rules. The BG enforcement mandate has founded the "dual regime" of German work safety inspections where statutory inspections based on broad brush Imperial (today: EU and national) legislation overlap with BG enforcement of detailed sectoral by-law.

This historical pattern of dual inspections marks the German work safety regime to the present day and has considerable implications for the perceived effectiveness and legitimacy of state inspectorates. Their continuous regulatory competition with (the equally fragmented) social insurance inspectorates has fashioned a strong necessity to legitimize the role of state inspectorates. Whilst BG inspectors do not enforce state legislation and cannot use legal orders (*Anordnungen*) such as for the closure of premises (Rothstein et al., 2019), respective overlaps of mandates have been a constant source for critique. From its inception, the dual inspection regime has provoked debates about the need to facilitate efficient and effective inspections, avoiding regulatory overlaps and inconsistencies, through close coordination (Simons, 1984, pp. 49–89). Even the abolition of the dual inspection structure has been mooted repeatedly, most recently in the late 1990s when employer representatives demanded transferring the statutory mandate entirely to the *Berufsgenossenschaften* (Gerlinger, 2000). Critique further accumulated with an evaluation by the Committee of Senior Labour Inspectors of the EU which castigated the lack of consistent and effective priority-setting across the fragmented inspection regime in Germany (SLIC, 2006), which I specify later.

In addition to competition over mandates with the *Berufsgenossenschaften*, state inspectorates have also come under increasing pressure to defend their decisions because of an in-house watering down of their core mandate. Over the last decade, several other regulatory mandates got bundled together with traditional labor inspections – again rather unlike for the relatively ringfenced food safety domain. In some states, work safety remains a singular core task (Brandenburg and Bavaria), but in most it has been amalgamated with state-specific combinations of the following: environmental protection, consumer protection, product safety, hazardous goods, medical safety, radiation protection, or veterinary medicine. Interviewees argue that most of these mandates came in via EU regulation and with clear requirements for the frequency and shape of inspections. In their view, these more tightly mandated domains of common market concern have tended to crowd out resources for work safety in interdisciplinary departments (WSY-05). This is particularly problematic in a climate of heightening budget pressures – the numbers of state inspectors decreased from 3,521 in 2006 to 2,935 in 2013[6] (Deutscher Bundestag, 2018, p. 4). The extremely low annual inspection rate of 2.5 per cent[7] of all firms – especially when compared to food safety with its 43.7 per cent coverage[8] – suggests that statutory work safety inspectorates struggle rather existentially.

7.1.3 Executive fragmentation and potential venues for coordination

To understand how these convoluted pressures might shape orientations toward risk analysis and emulation patterns in Germany (Section 7.3), I detail the contemporary organization of state inspections and multi-level interlinkages next. Statutory work safety inspections are a case of strong executive federalism without any central level mandate and with varying municipal influence. Some smaller states (the city states of Berlin, Bremen, and Hamburg, and the small Saarland) entertain central inspectorates, while most bigger states have more decentralized work safety administrations. The most decentralized version applies in Baden-Württemberg where inspections – alongside many other executive functions of the Land – have been devolved to the level of 44 communal districts with only vague guidelines coming from the state government in Stuttgart (even though more recent developments just during the time of interviewing point to a centralization impulse in this Land, WSY-07, WSY-08). Most Länder follow a moderate decentralization model with regional directorates or municipal district (rather than municipal) governments overseeing inspections. A unique case is that of Schleswig-Holstein which delegated all statutory inspections to the mutual trade association of the public sector (the *Unfallkasse Nord*) in 2008. Organizational variety means that Länder inspection strategies vary considerably across Germany, as stated in an interview: "as we have organized work safety very differently across Länder, we also have different . . . well, approaches, let's say" (WSY-01). As will be discussed later, criticism of such variety – and lack of coordination – mounted more recently.

The current legislative landscape for work safety offers little reason to expect any centrally induced harmonization of enforcement soon. Like in the other two domains, the protection of workers' health is subject to concurrent legislation (art.

74/12 Basic Law). Unlike in the other two domains, there are neither levers for direct coercion and political control, nor is there any strong appetite by central level actors to gain more influence over decentral enforcement through forms of meta-governance. National legislative efforts since the Imperial Industrial Code were not concerned with the organization of work safety enforcement, but with the step-wise elaboration of work safety standards and the firm-internal governance of work safety in line with corporatist traditions (for a timeline of key legislation, see Lehder, 2011, pp. 13–18). Unlike in the food safety case with its harmonizing Control Regulation and administrative orders, there are no EU or Federal rules on how inspections should be organized. Unlike in flooding, there is also no EU Directive to provide a common analytical model as a foundation for soft harmonization of decision-making. A milestone Directive (89/391) from 1989, transposed with the 1996 Occupational Protection Act (*Arbeitsschutzgesetz*) into German law (Council of the European Communities, 1989; Bundesrepublik Deutschland, 1996), was perceived as a substantial regulatory paradigm change for Germany (Kalberlah, Bloser and Wachholz, 2005; Merdian, 2005; Larisch, 2009; BAuA, 2012) as it created (not statutory) duties of care for employers, similar to the cases of food safety and flood prevention. However, while the Control Regulation in food safety or the Flood Risk Management Directive both *require* risk analysis in administrative practice – the EU has so far not pushed for risk-based enforcement strategies in work safety. Equally, the broad norms of Convention 81 of the International Labour Organisation on the working conditions of work safety inspectors (such as their independence) have a limited harmonization potential as they do not prescribe any strategy for the organization and decision-making of inspectorates.

Fragmentation without coercive pressures makes voluntary emulation – be it normative or mimetic – the most likely form of diffusion for risk analysis in German work safety inspections. As in the other two cases, several mechanisms enable policy coordination between and across governance levels (cf. Chapter 4):

- First, as in food safety, the municipal *Gewerbeaufsicht* is subject to hierarchical ministerial control within states and the execution of their mandate is constitutionally overseen by the Federal government. Unlike in food safety, however, there are neither administrative orders nor higher level regulatory agencies which could pre-dispose inspectors' enforcement strategies with a new analytical approach.
- Second, the Interstate Committee for Occupational Safety and Safety Technology (*Länderausschuss für Arbeitsschutz und Sicherheitstechnik*, LASI) provides a platform for the horizontal coordination of enforcement practices. Like the LAWA in flood prevention – but without a seat for the Bund – the LASI adopts non-binding guidelines and principles for enforcement to harmonize inspection practices. In addition to this specialized exchange, the standing Conference of State Ministers of Labour and Social Affairs (ASMK) offers a high-level forum for horizontal coordination, typical of executive federalism.

- Third, at the European level, the Committee of Senior Labour Inspectors (SLIC) was created to foster horizontal harmonization between member states – with potential knock-on-effects for coordination *within* states (I proposed a similar line of argument for the EU Floods Directive and its harmonization pressure for German states). Whilst not wielding similar powers as an EU agency – EFSA and the FVO in food safety – the Committee conducts regular peer evaluations of the performance of labor inspection regimes in member states. Following the logic of soft governance by international organizations and the EU (e.g., Lodge, 2005; Martens and Jakobi, 2010), such benchmarking exercises might contribute to increasing pressure for coordination and harmonization within Germany. Importantly, a 2006 SLIC report castigated the fragmented German system for its seemingly unsystematic priority-setting. Yet, the SLIC report did not suggest risk analysis as a solution to the problems it diagnosed. Moreover, unlike in the case of flooding and food safety, the SLIC critique of fragmented decision-making in work safety controls was not about collective action problems or the structural need to coordinate, but merely about a lack of transparency about policy priorities.
- Fourth, the critical SLIC evaluation of 2006 led the responsible interstate ministerial conference (ASMK) to promote the adoption of a common work safety strategy (*Gemeinsame Deutsche Arbeitsschutzstrategie*, GDA), starting in 2008. While incorporating both state and social insurance inspectorates and giving an advisory role to the federal Ministry, GDA programs tend to be rather too broad to meaningfully constrain local enforcement. In addition, program priorities follow political negotiations between social partners rather than pursuing evidence-based coordinated problem-solving (Meffert, 2008, p. 49).

7.2 How risk analysis emerged in German work safety inspections

In contrast to the cases of food safety and flood prevention, the work safety administration experienced no EU-level coercion to introduce risk analysis to its decision-making. Instead, Länder voluntarily agreed upon risk-oriented inspection planning in 2014 within the LASI. The section describes how critical EU evaluation and a scandal lead to a country-wide search for best practices, found in forerunners' experience with risk-based priority-setting, and culminated in the elaboration of a common but rather superficial risk-analytical model in the Länder working group LASI. However, the scope for a common risk-based approach to priority-setting remains limited in work safety controls, unlike in food safety controls and flood prevention. While individually operating a common IT-based inspection planning tool, states seem unwilling to use this tool to coordinate inspection priorities let alone frequencies.

7.2.1 Before Länder coordination: risk analysis and the problem-solving drive of forerunners

There have been several instrumentally oriented forerunners to the LASI model. Interviewees report that Hessen, Schleswig-Holstein, Hamburg, and Brandenburg all used risk-based concepts before 2014, and North-Rhine Westphalia developed its own model alongside pushing for a LASI-oriented one (Section 7.2.2). Hamburg, first, developed a model of "system controls" in 2000, but representatives argue that the "basics of risk-based differentiation of firms have been around for a long time, historically, I think for 30 years or more" (WSY-10). At the time, this was driven by hopes of efficiency and effectiveness gains:

> *an approach . . . with fixed inspection intervals for all kinds of firms . . . is not feasible given our resources. . . . This is why [we chose] a differentiated concept to be able to control firms with high risk levels more densely than the medium risk ones and to visit low risk firms only during event-driven inspections.*
>
> *(WSY-10)*

> *So we asked ourselves: based on which criteria would we need to inspect them? Because . . . as inspection authority we cannot engage enough staff . . . to control each firm in a reasonable timespan. . . . This is simply a matter of resources.*
>
> *(WSY-11)*

A classic problem-solving approach seems to drive Hamburg's turn to risk analysis. This also becomes evident in the efforts vested in adapting blueprints from nuclear safety and environmental emissions to work safety controls: "We did try to enact this classic idea of risk, probability times impact, in our first inspection concept, let's say on a practicable level, by saying: well, the hazard potential of physical and chemical factors is one thing and the other thing is the organization of work safety within a company. This is why we developed the system controls approach, to be able to extend inspection frequencies in firms with high hazard potential depending on the results of system controls" (WSY-10). The 2008 version of Hamburg's system controls distinguished three hazard potentials (high, medium, and low) and three assessments of the ability of a firm to deal well with hazards (satisfactory, partly satisfactory, and insufficient system audit). Only firms with a high hazard potential and insufficient system audits were to be inspected regularly, firms with a high * partly sufficient or medium * insufficient combination of impact and probability could be inspected and all other firms were let of the hook (Amt für Arbeitsschutz der Freien und Hansestadt Hamburg, 2008).

Another risk-analytical inspection strategy emerged in Hessen in the 1990s. Like in Hamburg, instrumental problem-solving dominated the inner-administrative discourse in Hessen at the time (even if one interviewee also recalls incidences in the chemical industry which might have affected a legitimacy-oriented search for an appropriate-seeming inspection strategy, WSY-10). Much in line with what the

British Hampton Review suggests for cost-effective inspections in the UK (Chapter 4), the dominant question for Hessen was "how do I introduce rational priority-setting into inspections with limited resources? . . . to look where it is most necessary" (WSY-12). Under the banner of "IT-based priority-setting in inspections" (*Rechnergestützte Steuerung der Aufsicht*, RSA), eventually, Hessen's labor inspectorate programmed a module for risk-based inspection planning within an existing inspection software. Many states had then already used this so-called *information system for work safety* (IFAS[9]) for documentation purposes and the administration of inspectors' salaries but none, at the time, used it for inspection planning. This changed in Hessen when the desire to conduct inspections more cost-effectively lead policymakers to search for rationalization options (WSY-12). When realizing that the already widely used IFAS software could automate priority-setting, too, much effort went into programming and fine-tuning the RSA module within IFAS (WSY-10 describes the concept as much more elaborate than the one in Hamburg). As I will discuss later, though not intended at the time, and somewhat similar to the flood prevention case with its strong Rhine catchment leadership on risk modeling, the technical elaboration of an already widely shared IT solution by a small number of forerunners facilitated the relatively smooth mainstreaming of risk analysis via the LASI later on.

While Hessen's RSA module was also adopted in Schleswig-Holstein for a temporary period (until inspection duties were delegated to the BG in 2008), the more recent diffusion of the concept to Brandenburg, since 2000, also shaped the later mainstreaming across Germany. Unlike Hessen, Brandenburg uses the IFAS software "to do all of their steering of the [labour inspection] administration with this instrument, including cost and activity accounting" (WSY-12). As elsewhere in the forerunner Länder, efficiency and effectiveness considerations conditioned the choice of tool in Brandenburg: "we have to have a systematic approach to stay present across the state of Brandenburg. And, of course, we cannot visit the 66,000 or 70,000 firms we have regularly every year" (WSY-13). When policymakers in the state looked for blueprints of IT tools for risk-based inspection planning, in the late 1990s, they discovered the IFAS/RSA module from Hessen (after having tried another software which did not allow for an automation of priority-setting according to risk levels). The interviewee remembers playing around a bit with the setting of the different parameters for the algorithm (e.g., size of firm, hazard level in the sector, individual inspection results, and the number of available inspection hours) and was convinced it could deliver what their inspectorate needed: "this is doing exactly what we want, a steered, active control . . . we want to deploy our resources where the risks are highest and where we can make the most difference" (WSY-13). This is even more important, they suggest, in times of budget pressure where the inspectorate expects to half its staff between 2004 and 2020 (Landesamt für Verbraucherschutz, Arbeitsschutz und Gesundheit des Landes Brandenburg, 2013).

What Brandenburg's RSA model brought to the subsequent Germany-wide debate was a tight link of risk analysis to the automated deployment of pre-defined (limited) staff resources: "we press one button and can tell how much capacity we have left this year and how many firms we can inspect at max . . . And if the remaining number of potential inspections is small, where do we go?" (WSY-13). By contrast, in Hessen, the risk analysis "spit out" by the IFAS software and its RSA module has, in the past, not been used to automate priority-setting per se but to inform inspector's professional decisions about which firms to best visit (WSY-12). As we will see later, the experience and promotional agency of the forerunner states helped streamlining the RSA module across jurisdictions at a time when scandal-struck state inspectorates across Germany keenly searched for workable templates.

7.2.2 The coordinated turn to risk-oriented controls across Germany

A risk-analytical foundation of routine inspections across the whole country was initiated through horizontal cooperation in the 88th Conference of the Ministers of Labor and Social Affairs (ASMK). In 2011, the ASMK obliged the LASI to identify and agree upon "common guidelines for risk-oriented inspections" (Arbeits- und Sozialministerkonferenz, 2011, p. TOP 7.6, 145). The ASMK had already expressed the wish to coordinate work safety inspections more across states (and with the concurrent inspectorates of the *Berufsgenossenschaften*) and to jointly review inspection strategies in 2001. LASI first worked toward such coordination in 2006, in immediate response to the critical SLIC evaluation (see Section 7.1.3), by prompting a scoreboard. In this, states were questioned about their priority-setting for inspections and whether or not this contained "some basic elements of risk-based controls, even if they are not always the same" (WSY-11). Answers were voluntary and nothing much happened with the results of the scoreboard.

Indeed, it took a highly publicized scandal to move the agenda from goal expression and initial best practice exchanges to the design of a coordinated risk-based approach to work safety inspections across states. After 50 workers had been severely poisoned by polychlorinated biphenyl (PCB) in a recycling company in 2010, North Rhine Westphalia initiated a call upon the ASKM to promote "risk-oriented controls" across all Länder. This was precisely the task which the ASMK, in its 2011 autumnal meeting, delegated back to the LASI.

The LASI delivered its risk-oriented concept for inspections in 2014 with its "LV1" (LASI, 2014b). This non-binding guideline provides a common model for strategic priority-setting in inspection planning novel to all but the forerunner Länder. LASI suggests that "common risk assessment" will facilitate "risk-oriented inspections" across Germany (LASI, 2014b, p. 23). To achieve this shared strategic orientation, LV1 requires 25 per cent of all inspection activities to be pro-active and risk-based (reacting to accidents or complaints traditionally consumes the bulk of inspectors' time). This share is of course much lower than is the comprehensive risk-analytical priority-setting in food safety and flooding. According to the LASI's standard, (the partial) risk-oriented inspection planning pursues a three-step assessment procedure:

- In a first step, inspectorates classify each employer within their jurisdiction according to a *standardized basic classification* ("allgemeine länderübergreifende Grundeinstufung von Betrieben", LASI, 2014b, p. 23). As a basis for this assessment, Länder lead inspection managers sat together to agree upon a *common definition of basic hazard levels* for 615 economic branches (WSY-13) across four "hazard categories": mechanic and substance-related hazards, physical, and psychological strains on the employees. The classification ranges from negligible hazard (0) to low (1), medium (2), and finally, high hazard (3). High scores in singular categories or overall scores of 2 or 3 imply that a whole sub-sector will move onto the preliminary inspection list across all Länder. This basic classification scheme is founded on a blueprint from Hessen, which also already used economic subsector lists to classify firm's basic hazard level in the RSA (WSY-12). When LASI took up the template, the task was to sit down and adjust classifications with input from the 16. The joint classification of sub-sectors rests on accident statistics, data on occupational illnesses per sector, but also a qualitative discussion of inspectors' professional experience across economic sectors. All interviewees insisted that the classification process was "nothing scientifically proven. Not at all . . . it is more a gut feeling thing, to be honest, professional experience matters a lot here" (WSY-04). To rationalize the "gut feeling" of 16 Länder inspectorates, each Land gave individual assessments first and these were then averaged out to form a final *common* hazard score for each subsector (WSY-08). Länder hope that this basic risk assessment, though not touching upon firms' compliance behavior or the frequency of inspections at all, can already facilitate a common strategic inspection focus across the fragmented enforcement regime: "The summary of assessments enables work safety authorities to set priorities when selecting firms for inspection" (LASI, 2014b, p. 23). Accordingly, for instance, the inspection of sea fishing workplaces, mines, and quarries would need to be treated as a high priority whilst investment advisers or providers of web portals would be negligible for work safety inspectors (LASI, 2014a).
- In a second step, inspectorates *assess the size of companies in terms of "number of employees"* (LASI, 2014b, p. 23) to identify how many workers would potentially be affected by harm (i.e., of two firms with the same basic risk category the one with 10,000 employees as compared to the company with 10 employees would be prioritized in inspections). However, as the LASI guideline does not specify indicators for impact assessment for this category, Länder and local inspectorates retain much leeway for determining their inspection foci differently from one another. Indeed, the ASMK notes that Länder are meant to "complement" the common basic classification with "state-specific criteria" along with their own inspection concepts (Arbeits- und Sozialministerkonferenz, 2014, p. 176).

- In a final selection step, Länder ought to consider authorities' work safety intelligence on *any given firms' "individual work safety situation"*. This is intended to inform authorities about firms' likelihood of compliance and makes active use of the blueprint on system controls from Hamburg. Such probability assessment shall be based on "inspection records, accidents or complaints" (LASI, 2014b, p. 23), but LASI does not detail assessment methods any further. Länder can draw on their own accident and complaint statistics and inspection records, but also on another non-binding LASI guideline (LV 54, LASI, 2011). This second guideline lays down a coordinated approach to system controls at workplaces suggesting inspectors assess "whether the respective employer entertains an adequate organization fit for the identification, planning and execution of necessary OHS measures in its entirety" (LASI, 2011, p. 41). The LASI's system-audit-approach is relatively fine-grained[10]; it contains a 15-pages long definition of various assessment criteria and their categorization into a traffic light model (LASI, 2011, pp. 19–33). Criteria include, for example, firms' organization of their own risk assessment duty, or the effective communication of work safety policies vis-à-vis staff and lead management. Overall, the cumulative assessment model evaluates of companies' work safety management as being either "adequate", "partially adequate", or "insufficient" (LASI, 2011, p. 15), similarly to the template from Hamburg. With a typical traffic light approach, the LASI guideline then suggests deprioritizing those firms with adequate work safety management systems – including with system audit certifications – while targeting firms with "partially adequate" or "insufficient" systems (LASI, 2011, p. 42).

7.2.3 Pushes for a common risk algorithm and its limits

In theory, a substantial bottom-up harmonization of inspection planning across states would be easy to roll out in Germany: with 14 Länder – in 2014 – already using IFAS as their common software for managing their firm cadastres and inspection reports, they could all "switch on the module and use it" at almost no cost, by simply programming the algorithm in line with the 2014 LASI guideline (WSY-12). In the fashion of a growing and increasingly self-aware instrument constituency, the two states which had already used the module for IT-based inspection planning in IFAS before – Hessen and Brandenburg – promoted their algorithms as blueprints for all others to test during a piloting phase in 2017/2018 (Brückner, 2017). The pilot project had the goal of testing how the LASI approach to risk-oriented inspection planning could be aided by the RSA module. With a final report on the outcomes of this pilot project pending at the time of writing, I rely on interviewee statements for an assessment of the relative success of this instrument constituency in triggering a comprehensive turn to risk-based inspections in this context.

From the outlook, the instrument constituency appears weaker than the risk analysis constituency in flood prevention, mainly because it lacked national and EU level support for promoting its tool and it did not have access to coercive backup of risk-analytical decision-making (unlike in the other two cases). However, there is evidence that the piloting of the RSA has led some Länder to reconsider their existing priority-setting approaches. An example is Lower Saxony whose inspection strategy for workplaces was previously driven by the fixed enforcement requirements in EU environmental regulation (cf. the crowding out argument made in section 7.1.2). When they fed the new RSA algorithm with their data and ran an automatic sampling of firms to be inspected, to their surprise, none of the high-risk firms they usually target for environmental safety reasons made it on the priority list: "we were much astonished and said: hey, why does it not show any of our [usual target] firms?" (WSY-05). Such moments of irritation ostensibly made transparent both the various priorities of different inspections models and crowding out effects by neighboring regulatory domains. The new visibility of work safety inspection priorities thus informed a debate about best practices in the LASI: "If they all run and calculate with the same model, I have a certain level of transparency about who's acceptant of what. And then I can, potentially, also discuss this politically among interested circles" (WSY-05, also WSY-01, WSY-12, and WSY-13).

However, the introduction of common risk analysis across a fragmented work safety inspection landscape in Germany comes with a number of caveats, limiting its potential to be a tool for coordinated problem-solving. First, the relevant guideline which demands risk analysis for inspection planning (LASI's LV1), though following an explicit mandate by the Länder Ministers' Conference (ASMK), is "no . . . binding administrative decree, of course, but a kind of internal steering tool to deliver some targets for Länder inspection strategies" (WSY-11). Second, the non-binding guideline only harmonizes the impact assessment side of risk analysis, with a joint method for assessing sub-sectors' basic risk, while leaving the likelihood of harm dimension relatively vague (though the LV 54 on system control offers another template for potential voluntary emulation). Third, risk-oriented inspections are to make up only a fourth of all inspection activities. Fourth, unlike the highly detailed AVV RÜb guidance on food safety or the close link between risk analysis and national spending in the flood prevention case, the LASI does not specify how risk analysis ought to be used to determine inspection priorities and frequencies.

7.3 "Joining forces" to escape the "legitimacy trap": explaining the horizontal emulation of risk-based work safety inspections in Germany

Although LASI's guidelines on risk analysis are merely advisory they are widely followed, and interviewees seem optimistic that they represent "a positive offer" (WSY-05) for harmonizing – within the limits discussed earlier – priority-setting in work safety inspections across Germany. Why such embrace of a common risk analysis model from below? Interviewees portray a three-step narrative on the adoption of risk analysis.

- First, LASI-wide risk analysis and its algorithmic use for inspection planning attracted individual states' support for mainly instrumental reasons. In the absence of perceived collective action problems, however (and unlike in food safety and flood prevention), their individual instrumental orientation has so far not united states in coordinated problem-solving endeavors.
- Instead, second, a critical evaluation by the EU's SLIC plus a serious case of undetected work-related illnesses led states to "join forces" and forge a unified risk-oriented approach around existing blueprints. Beyond individual legitimacy-seeking within each Land, horizontal coordination built on a common wish to defend statutory inspections and their subcentral organization in executive federalism against continuing fragmentation critique.
- In addition, third, state inspectorates have started promoting a coordinated risk-analytical inspection programming more pro-actively – up to automation calls by some – as a tool for rendering their weak mandates more visible politically or even to promote evidence-based increases of work safety inspection staff among their respective state governments.

7.3.1 Mainstreaming instrumental orientations without coordinated problem-solving

When North Rhine Westphalia demanded a coordinated approach across states from 2011 onward, it did so under the strong impression of the failure to detect non-compliance with work safety regulation at a large recycling firm. While legitimacy-seeking also sprung-off from this incident (Section 7.3.2), inspection strategists' justifications for adopting risk analysis sound like a perfect rehearsal of the typical instrumental drivers of risk-based regulation (cf. Box 7.1). Where 200 of the previously more than 700 inspectors in one state had been laid off in the last decade (WSY-01), the targeting of scarce resources in a risk-based manner has become a remedy for rationalizing one's activities (Statement 1). As the trend of scarce budgets for work safety inspections is shared across all Länder, interviewees argue, it did make sense to use the scandalization momentum in one Land at that time as a stimulus for jointly "rationalizing" priority-setting (Statement 2). Indeed, in a climate where some inspectorates saw more than a 50 per cent staff cuts since the 1990s (Herbst, 2004), risk-based planning was welcomed as a formalized procedure for economizing the use of slim and ever slimmer state budgets (Ministerium für Klimaschutz, Umwelt, Landwirtschaft, Natur- und Verbraucherschutz des Landes Nordrhein-Westfalen, 2013, p. 9). Fittingly, the LASI guideline justifies the coordinated turn to risk-oriented inspections across Germany with hope that "inspections are optimized and made more effective by identifying companies with a high potential of endangering [workers]" (LASI, 2014b, p. 22).

BOX 7.1: HOPES OF EFFICIENCY AND EFFECTIVENESS GAINS IN WORK SAFETY THROUGH RISK ANALYSIS

Statement 1: *"If you don't have the resources . . . you cannot visit every firm . . . Given the scarce resources and great number of firms to inspect, we need to aim for a transparent and reproducible approach . . . Not least as we have to convey why have we done certain things and refrained from doing others . . . This [work-induced illnesses at a large recycling firm] was the trigger for us to reflect: how can we do it here? But to also bring this to the ASMK, thinking it would be good to do such a thing in a Länder-coordinated way . . . simply to achieve a certain comparability and maybe even a benchmark between Länder".* (WSY-01)

Statement 2: [when asked why LASI decided to create a common model, rather than letting each Land deal with priority-setting and its response to scandals alone] *"Well, this problem affects us all, and the related issue of resources also affects all . . . and when we got to ask how to rationalize this all it was really Hessen and Brandenburg who were there first to say: we have got an instrument! It's already adopted, it works . . . we can set and manage priorities with it. Why invent something new where we already have something?"* (WSY-12)

Statement 3: [discussing the Land's laggard position in inner-German accident rates and the goal of halving accident rates by help of risk-based inspections] *"Well, this is where we want to improve and look for a method which is especially effective. Not to do anything anyhow, but to try and operate most intensively . . . in a targeted way . . . in those areas where accident and illness potentials exist. This is the main goal, actually, not to work at random but to focus on the problematic areas".* (WSY-06)

Statement 4: *"to have new hazards . . . feature in assessment . . . We are quick [to consider] the practicable . . . apparent things [in inspection priorities] . . . Wherever it stinks and rumbles, where one can fall onto one's feet or head; this is being considered as especially risky. All the softer aspects are rather outside of this [calculation]. So this [the LV1 basic hazard assessment, including psychological strains] is an attempt to correct things step by step".* (WSY-12)

In addition to efficiency-seeking interviews also evidence a normative isomorphic diffusion process, driven by policymakers' shared rationalist assumption that risk-based inspections will genuinely improve work safety. This seemingly confirms the thesis of the apolitical and technical expert civil service in Germany

(Chapter 4). There are three elements to the pursuit of evidence-based effectiveness gains through risk analysis from the viewpoint of state inspectorates:

- First, states whose work safety performance is weaker than others consider the approach, and the necessary scientific research to implement it, as a chance to catch up and optimize inspection activities (Statement 3). Indeed, lead inspection managers in Baden-Württemberg hope to half work accident rates by the help of risk-based inspections (WSY-06 and WSY-07).
- Second, the common model is also seen, by some (WSY-01, WSY-05, and WSY-12), as a chance to reconsider existing priorities and check their effectiveness in lowering work safety risks for workers. This concerns, on the one hand side, the integration of novel and/or less apparent types of work-related risks, mainly stress and other psychological strains, into priority-setting (Statement 4, also WSY-01 and WSY-05). By comparing across different categories of hazard in the basic Länder assessment, inspection managers hope, the traditional focus on mechanical and chemical safety can be widened. On the other hand side, in some Länder, the piloting of the RSA has triggered a critical re-examination of the extent to which work safety effectiveness may in fact be jeopardized by priority-setting approaches whose lens is dominated by neighboring regulatory concerns such as environmental safety (WSY-05).
- Third, one interviewee highlights positive effects of risk analysis in illuminating "blind spots" among specialist inspectors who would tend, they argue, to inspect what they know best (be it mechanical risks or chemical hazards) rather than setting priorities according to a transversal assessment of different risk factors (WSY-13).

With these interpretive orientations we observe the thin contours of instrumentally founded coordinated action in Germany's multi-level regime of work safety inspections. Interviewees invariably highlight the importance of increasing the visibility and comparability of risks across states for furthering the cost-effectiveness of work safety controls. Some even name benchmarking as their goal (Statement 1). But while such orientations remind us of those held by food safety inspectors and flood prevention planners, unlike in these other two domains most interviewees see no scope for more substantial coordination of work safety inspection planning. To the contrary, the RSA module's very appeal is perceived in that "everyone can set parameters as they see fit" (WSY-12; also WSY-10 and WSY-11). This discretion does not seem to be negotiable; the same policymaker who was positive about discussing the larger implications of the piloting phase for shared priorities, is also skeptical about the extent to which pushes for risk-analytical harmonization of inspection frequencies would fly: "we'd ask too much of the majority in LASI if we wanted to set any fixed [inspection] requirements" (WSY-05). As another interviewee highlights, the reluctance to go further with a coordinated automation of inspection priorities – and especially frequencies – across states hits the wall mainly because automation might require (upward) budgetary adjustments for work safety enforcement in most states:

> *We did have debates within LASI . . . whether we have to come forward with actual control frequencies . . . firms ought to [be controlled] at least . . . in my opinion this won't happen in LASI and not in the ASMK either. There is much resistance in LASI against tangible requirements. Because people say: I might be able to sell this to my own Minister, but I won't be able to sell it to my Finance Minister.*
>
> *(WSY-11)*

Another interviewee assumes most states will reject any such plan because "they do not want to be measurable" and are therefore warry of introducing any specific cross-Länder performance measures (WSY-13). Whereas in flood prevention, EU-induced risk maps made the variable performance of states and municipalities in prevention planning visible and thus created a new platform for the (soft) harmonization of administrative priorities, German work safety inspectors seem reluctant to self-impose such transparency and its knock-on effects on their autonomous actions. But this may not only be a story of unwillingness to give up autonomy. Unlike in food safety and flood prevention, interviewees do no convey any urgent sense of having to act jointly to solve collective action problems; even where they perceive strong *other* sources for coordinated action. We turn to these next.

7.3.2 Inoculation against fragmentation critique: joining forces to signal consistency

While coordinated problem-solving desires are at best half-hearted in German work safety, unlike in food safety controls and flood prevention, other institutionally embedded drivers explain why policymakers engaged in the horizontal emulation of risk analysis. Indeed, the extremely low inspection rates of 2.5 per cent of firms per year – with Baden-Württemberg inspectors stating they control most firms in their constituencies only once in 22 years (WSY-08), – paired with the tendency to cut back on inspection staff (all whilst inflating inspectorates' non-work-safety-related duties further) suggests that German work safety inspectorates struggle rather too existentially to pursue a meaningful problem-solving strategy with their adoption of risk analysis – collectively and perhaps also individually, depending on the respective budgetary situation.

In line with expectations of mimetic isomorphism, the display of an apparently already well-functioning template for risk-analytical decision-making in forerunner states facilitated a speedy agreement upon a common model within the LASI (Statement 2 above). Two further patterns of justification have shaped this emulation dynamic: (1) states' institutional risk management strategies individually and their collective attempt to defend executive federalism in the domain, and (2) individual states' attempt to ringfence and expand the weak regulatory mandate for statutory work safety inspections. This and the next section will consider these instances of legitimacy-seeking in more depth. Together, they show that legitimacy-seeking cannot be reduced to symbolic policies or window-dressing – as sometimes done also with respect to analytical tools (for RIA: Radaelli, 2010). Rather, the risk-based defense of a weak mandate offers a straw to state inspectors who are professionally much-committed to their efforts in preventing work accidents (just like food safety inspectors) but whose instrumental goals are much frustrated by the adverse contextual conditions in which their mandate is situated.

Most interviewees justify the mimetic processes in the run-up to the LASI adoption of risk analysis with the hope of legitimacy gains. Without exception interviewees refer to the negative evaluation by the EU's SLIC – which mainly castigated fragmented and seemingly unsystematic priority-setting – and the scandal around work-related illnesses at a recycling company as key drivers for agreeing upon a shared systematic approach to work safety controls across Länder borders. Inspectorate heads describe their situation as "being chased" (WSY-05) and hope to inoculate themselves against criticism of regulatory, or even "organizational failure" (WSY-12) with the LASI agreement on risk analysis. First and foremost, the institutional risk management strategy described in Statement 5 – giving reasons for decisions ex-ante and thereby avoiding blame ex-post – feature on an individual state level. Indeed, as a chief inspector explains, risk-based inspections have been embraced by individual states not only with a problem-solving orientation in mind but also as a way of making transparent what inspectorates do, why, and what they cannot do as a consequence of increasingly scarce resources. This classic explication of the limits of state accountability for regulatory failure is directed toward the democratically elected leaders and the general public in each individual Land (WSY-02, WSY-05, and WSY-12).

Yet, interviewees also highlight that risk analysis offers them a *collective* defense strategy against potential claims to relocate inspection mandates – either to the central state or to the mutual trade associations (as mooted in the past, see Section 7.1). Because the SLIC's criticism of the German inspection regime targeted its very fragmentation (Statement 6), states considered risk analysis as an invitation to be "join forces" (WSY-12) in a common approach that could signal effective coordination to critics. The century-old competition over inspection mandates with the *Berufsgenossenschaften* arguably amplifies the perceived need to join forces around a systematic approach. State-level interviewees conceive of risk-based inspections as effective means for "speaking with one voice" – also vis-à-vis the mutual trade associations – and thus counter any attack of executive federalism in work safety inspections (WSY-12). A shared, ostensibly evidence-based strategy would help Länder, another interviewee suggests, to firmly stand their ground against potentially conflicting interests of the Federal Ministry of Labour or the *Berufsgenossenschaften* (WSY-05).

In work safety controls, more than elsewhere perhaps, we meet the continuation of historical attempts of states to counter "possible demands for relocating . . . Länder responsibilities to the central state" or indeed sectoral organizations in this domain (Kropp, 2010, p. 130). As policymakers in this domain experience higher

BOX 7.2: RISK ANALYSIS AND INSTITUTIONAL RISK MANAGEMENT IN WORK SAFETY

Statement 5: *"This is about transparency towards the political system, Land parliament, members of parliament, and so on. But also towards the general public. To be able to say: I have done this because we agreed it that way, we thought it to be right and important. And also: I refrained from doing other things because we agreed it that way . . . The trigger was [recycling company X], when everyone asked us: "Why have you not been there?". And now we can simply say: but we have a concept! Whether this concept is correct in every instance is open for discussion, but I have to be able to communicate it!"* (WSY-02)

Statement 6: *"Of course, this is also a political question, in the sense of 'what have you all learned from [the case of the recycling company]?' . . . The pressure to coordinate things and to have a more harmonised approach across Länder was there already and one of the . . . claims . . . political claims that emerged from the evaluation back then [SLIC evaluation 2006] . . . was to organise a coherent enforcement approach among Länder . . . So we brought the other Länder onto their toes and brought it [our RSA approach] into big politics, so to speak, via the ASMK".* (WSY-12)

Statement 7: *"And all that one wants to regulate in a coherent manner now is a walk on eggshells, of course, because one cannot actually regulate things in a legally-binding manner. So the trick is, in my opinion, to agree upon an approach which, let's say, involves such a compelling . . . a positive offer so that it, well, actually imposes itself, triggers voluntarily compliance . . . this is the most important thing for me, that we can sell it [the LASI risk-oriented inspection approach] positively in the end, and say: 'folks, this suits you, suits us all'".* (WSY-05)

levels of pressure on their mandates – both individually and collectively – and from several sources, horizontal emulation of risk analysis and the related signal of coordinated action offers them a straw to cling onto. In the absence of coercive pressures – unlike in food safety and to a lesser extent also in flood prevention – it is hence the very conflation of (1) a scandalization of failure to detect work safety risks, (2) rather fundamental criticism of fragmented inspections, (3) dire budgetary pressures in most states, and (4) the competition over the inspection mandate with mutual trade associations that lets Länder perceive voluntary (but not very substantial) analytical harmonization as a "positive offer" (Statement 7).

7.3.3 Empowering work safety inspectorates: toward risk-based increases of political salience

The German work safety case displays a twist to the usual tale of legitimacy-seeking through risk analysis or other policy-analytical tools. When one interviewee, in the opening prompter to this chapter, speaks of the "legitimacy trap" (WSY-12), they do not only imply the usual blame-shifting and mandate defense activities discussed earlier. In addition, interviews discuss the extent to which the perceived "structural disadvantage" of work safety inspections (WSY-12) can be cushioned, or even overcome, by risk-based rationalization of inspection activities. Länder in unison perceive the common risk-analytical approach as a tool for increasing the political salience of their activities in the perception of politicians and the general public, and eventually also ringfencing and expanding resources for their core mandate.

The argumentative thread runs as follows: in addition to the influential budgetary squeezes, four factors contribute to a low political salience of work safety inspections (also see Box 7.3):

BOX 7.3: INCREASING THE POLITICAL SALIENCE OF WORK SAFETY INSPECTIONS VIA RISK ANALYSIS

Statement 8: "*It is enormously difficult to prove the positive effects [of inspections] . . . So we are always in a legitimacy trap: 'what are you up to and where do you move things? What is the outcome [of work safety inspections] in the end?'. And in addition, we find ourselves in the awkward position . . . that we have Federal Law but enforced by the Land. Which means that for Länder this is only costing money without Länder parliaments having an adequate legislative say . . . So this [work safety] is no issue for a debate in any Landtag or Committee unless something [e.g., a larger accident] happens.* (WSY-12)

Statement 9: "*The problem in the work safety domain is the autonomy of Länder. The Federal level cannot meddle with enforcement or moneys or whatever. So it matters much to provide convincing arguments [to one's own Länder Minister] showing that the issue is and remains important*". (WSY-13)

Statement 10: "*So work safety is always facing environmental safety more or less helplessly and has to stand by its own re-orientation [and crowding-out]. And this is why we now insist on a systematic separation of these two domains. So that we [as inspection planners] have steering capacities over work safety . . . And the precondition is to make transparent with what resources we will operate . . . If the inspectorates are managed by the Environmental Ministry, the inspectorate head will of course do environmental safety*". (WSY-09)

Statement 11: "*So the refocusing on work safety tasks and the possibilities for prioritization in the domain is also the attempt, well, I'd say to become more visible. To specify our tasks for others . . . because it otherwise rather gets lost . . . It is a disadvantage of work safety, to have product safety completely steered by the EU, regulated with clear requirements. Emission protection has its fixed quota [for inspections] . . . This puts work safety into an open relationship where everyone thinks they can help themselves*". (WSY-12)

- More generally speaking, first, the public salience of work safety would be perceived as being particularly low, especially when compared to environmental regulation or food safety. As one interviewee states: "all that happens outside the company's fence, which . . . can affect the general public, has a higher political salience than things happening behind the fences and disappearing behind the company secret" (WSY-12).
- The effects of this partial ignorance are aggravated, second, by the deregulatory drive starting in the 1990s which had authorities with a more traditional policing role falling out of fashion (WSY-12 and WSY-13). While this process was certainly milder in Germany compared to the NPM forerunner countries in the Anglophone world (cf. Chapter 4), increasing scrutiny of inspectorates and their performance did amplify, in interviewees' perception, the need to legitimize one's mandate. Risk analysis, and especially its ability to signal cost-effective priority-setting, is therefore seen as a way of "selling controls as our core brand; if we play this card, I think, not only do we retain legitimacy for our existence [previous subsection], but we can *come forward much more strongly*" (WSY-13, highlight added).
- Third, the low steering capacity of Länder, who oversee the enforcement of work safety regulation but do not set standards in the domain, results in a low visibility and salience of work safety issues in Länder Ministries and Parliaments (Statements 8 and 9). In this setting, it would matter even more to present "convincing arguments" to state Ministers for them to put work safety issues onto their agenda and budgetary plans. A common risk-analytical approach is seen as such a convincing argument because it enables a systematic focus on high-risk areas all while signaling cost-effectiveness to the political system.
- Last, the revelation powers of risk analysis regarding work safety risks appeal particularly where the organizational integration with regulatory domains with a higher "common market relevance" (emissions, nuclear safety, product safety, and WSY-12) lower the visibility pf work safety controls further. Where they come with strong EU regulation and fixed control intervals neighboring regulatory duties pull away even more staff and budget from work safety up to the extent where others simply "help themselves" (Statements 10 and 11). One interviewee argues that the LASI risk analysis model has given them more headway in negotiating inspection capacities with their environmental safety colleagues in a mixed department (WSY-05). It gave work safety inspectorates a tool at hand, for the first time, to illuminate what they are doing in a systematic way (cf. chapter prompter by WSY-12) – despite lack of licensing requirements, fixed inspection rates or reporting duties – and to justify their activities as being evidence-based and cost-effective.

In such attempts to increase the visibility and political salience of work safety inspections, risk analysis has, for some at least, also become a weapon in their fight for stronger mandates, higher budgets and more staff (see Box 7.4). In distinctive contrast to the deregulatory drive usually associated with the turn to risk-based

BOX 7.4: RISK ANALYSIS AS A TOOL FOR EXPANDING RESOURCES FOR WORK SAFETY INSPECTIONS

Statement 12: *"The difference between our concept and the other Länder is that the other Länder calculate on the basis of existing staff and we start from the risk potential . . . of firms . . . So we are trying, via this way, via existing firms [and their respective risk levels], to get more staff".* (WSY-08)

Statement 13: [talking about the likely results of pre-setting inspection frequencies by risk level in the RSA module] *"I think we will reach results in Germany, on average, where the consequence would be an increase in staff rather than a decrease. . . . I don't think that risk-oriented controls can result in savings on staff".* (WSY-05)

Statement 14: *"This is, let's say, a political feedback loop within departments . . . There is a political rationale behind this, of course, because they [the inspectorates trying to claim more staff with the RSA module] can now say . . . well, you [Land x] have agreed on this [the risk-oriented model in the LASI and ASMK] . . . you have taken the decision and now you don't give us the budget"*! (WSY-11)

Statement 15: *". . . so that we can also say to a member of parliament, if they asked: well, we can no longer control these risk firms at some point . . . You have to ask yourself, in parliament, well, can we afford this: to visit a high risk firm every 5, 6, 7 or 8 years, and is there still an effect actually"*? (WSY-13)

enforcement, for instance in the UK's efficiency-seeking model (Hampton, 2005; Tombs and Whyte, 2013; cf. Chapter 4), among German states "the idea of the colleagues who push for that [risk-based inspections] and who also want to standardize [inspection frequencies] is the very opposite: they want to . . . evidence *staff expenditure* . . . prove *additional* staff requirements" (WSY-05, highlight added).

The colleagues alluded to here sit in Stuttgart and aim to re-allocate mandates in Baden-Württemberg's work safety inspection regime. As the state has the most decentralized regime and – some argue: relatedly so (WSY-11) – the highest work accident rates across Germany, a 2016 coalition agreement involved an initiative for "empowering" work safety. The state's average control rate of 22 years per firm (remember, once more, that food business operators in Germany have an average inspection frequency of once every two years!) is perceived as too low to create an effective regulatory environment for compliance and the state Ministry has set a goal of halving accidents (WSY-07). The instrumentally informed wish to increase the (notoriously low) effectiveness of controls concurs with the demand of more resources for work safety enforcement (WSY-06, WSY-07, WSY-08, and WSY-09).

Policymakers in Baden-Württemberg argue, not without pride, that their RSA programming "works differently" from other states in that the empirically observed variable risk levels in firms are associated with effective inspection rates, with staff requirements for risk-based controls calculated on that basis (Statement 12). They suggest this would be a genuine evidence-based approach as firms' risk levels determine staffing levels. The risk-based algorithm, interviewees report, tells the Ministry that it needs to claim 200 extra full-time inspectors to control premises effectively, "quite a lot, right?" (WSY-07). Lead inspectors of other states agree that the RSA module, when programmed this way (rather than have fixed staff resources integrated into the algorithm), all Länder would need to hire more inspectors (Statement 13). This narrative, or course, puts one of the core sellers of risk analysis in international regulatory reform, namely the promise of significant personnel reductions – up to a third according to the British forerunner (Hampton, 2005) – on its head.

The responsible strategists in Stuttgart seem aware of the limits of their risk-based claims for expanding the work safety mandate (in addition to divorcing it from environmental issues, as seen before) and argue that the 200 extra staff figure serves as a basis for negotiation of less significant (but still counter-tendential) staff increases with the Finance Department (WSY-07). Overall, however, similarly to flooding, where the Federal support of risk mapping was founded on hopes of effective collective action but triggered demands on central level funding for high risks, risk analysis in work safety enforcement can arguably help inspectorates push for a credible commitment by their state governments and parliaments. This is because risk analysis creates (1) a feedback loop between actors' initial signing-up for the LASI model and the financial consequences of implementing risk-based inspections in practice (Statement 14), and (2) an evidence-based trigger for parliamentary action on (too) low work safety control rates (Statement 15).

The likely success the risk-analytical expansion of the political (and fiscal) relevance of work safety enforcement, while welcomed in the professional community of inspectors, is seen skeptically by most. One interviewee describes a climate of ongoing deregulation and cut-backs in the German states' public administration and calls risk-based justifications of staff increases – through agreeing with them based on the risk evidence – "utopian" or "an element of Don Quixote" (WSY-05). Another is rather defeatist when concluding that "where public authorities are completely underfunded the best concept is in vain" (WSY-11). Indeed, the second edition of the influential SLIC evaluation, in 2017, congratulated Germany on its now more coherent and strategic enforcement approach but also censured the substantial underfunding of public inspectorates and the lowest inspection rate in the EU. Some diagnose a "factual enforcement deficit" in German work safety in this context and argue that "the most risk-oriented system cannot compensate staff deficits" (Räbel, 2018).

In this setting, the risk-analytical expansion of work safety mandates (and staff) might be an uphill struggle. Yet, if a recent reaction of state Ministers to the 2017

SLIC critique – they demand staff increases for the pro-active part of work safety enforcement and a new joint organizational structure for cross-Länder priority-setting lead by LASI (Arbeits- und Sozialministerkonferenz, 2018, p. 80) – were to become hard-wired, mandate and budgetary expansion might become a more realistic outlook. If this were the case, risk analysis in work safety controls would have morphed from (1) individual and collective mandate defense in a context of high legitimacy pressures to (2) coordinated analysis-based urges on state governments to attribute more salience to the domain and substantiate mandates for state-level enforcement with cash.

Notes

1 The more encompassing term is occupational health and safety, but I prefer to use the simpler term work safety as a shorthand for both health and safety issues in the reminder of the book.

2 As Bauerdick (1991) shows, for example, sector-specific advances of standards and their self-regulated enforcement did occur – as in the case of the *Dampfkesselüberwachungsvereine* (steam boiler inspection associations, the historical precedent of today's still influential *Technischer Überwachunsgverein* TÜV). Yet, these sectoral regulations did not develop into the encompassing national standard-setting and enforcement regime that emerged, during the same time frame, in the food safety domain.

3 Bismarck claimed that the competitiveness of German industry would suffer, that factories would make (less exploitable) workers redundant and provoke mass unemployment, that working conditions were not as serious an issue, and that inspectors should focus on implementing child labour regulation properly before expanding the regulatory mandate to include all workers (Simons, 1984, pp. 33–38).

4 One speculation about reasons for this variation involves the different transaction relationships on the food vs. the labour market. Paying for food on a market is bound up with the notion of consumer rights to safe and non-fraudulent food products – much frustrated by market asymmetries which need tight regulation. Inversely, on labour markets – at least in rational choice theory – workers' wages and potential 'risk premiums' operate as compensation for workers' time, physical and psychological effort but also for the potential health risks they face on the job (Viscusi, 1983).

5 Some argue that this transfer of regulatory duties from state authorities to para-public bodies which self-regulate work safety issues on behalf of their economic sectors fits with Bismarck's general reluctance to intervene state-hierarchically in trade freedom (Simons, 1984; Bauerdick, 1991; Hennock, 2007). Yet, as Mares (2003, p. 85) shows, Bismarck's favoured solution of centralising regulatory control over social insurance in an Imperial Insurance Office (Reichsversicherungsanstalt) – similar to the Imperial Health Office in food safety – was also eradicated in joint opposition of large industrial manufacturers (who preferred corporatist self-regulation) and the Zentrumspartei (which favoured strong federalism and preferred a corporatist solution to administrative centralisation).

6 In the same period, the number of staff working on prevention in the BG system rose slightly from 5,356 to 5,463 (Deutscher Bundestag, 2018, p. 5). Whilst BGs also must justify spending vis-à-vis their member firms, they are in the more comfortable position of managing budgets with retroactive cost coverage (through contribution adjustments) rather than global tax-financed budgets.

7 A recent report records that 3,186 inspectors in charge of 3,344,253 premises (covering 31,993,102 full time workers) in 2015 controlled 83,284 premises – some of them several times (BAuA, 2016).

8 In food safety, 2,400 to 2,500 inspectors controlled 532,151 premises in 2015, some of them several times (BVL, 2016).

9 https://ehs.kisters.de/software/verwaltung-arbeitschutz/

10 For a detailed description of methods of categorisation with indicators and scenario descriptions for all aspects of work safety management in firms, see appendices of LASI guideline 54 (2011).

8

MAPPING AND UNDERSTANDING THE VARIED APPEALS OF RISK ANALYSIS IN MULTI-LEVEL ADMINISTRATIONS

This section draws together findings on the variable appeals of risk analysis in Germany from Chapters 5–7 in a cross-sectoral perspective. I discuss variation in: legacies and context (Section 8.1), variable adoption patterns for risk analysis across policy domains (Section 8.2), and interpretive patterns around risk analysis and its uses (Section 8.3) to explore how contextual variation within the same polity shapes case-specific combinations of instrumental, legitimacy-seeking, and power-seeking orientations and inform variable adoptions of risk analysis across different policy domains (see comparative Table 8.1 and Figures 8.1–8.3 for each respective domain at the chapter's end). The comparative discussion builds the foundation for situating the book's finding in a wider research landscape, in the concluding Chapter 9.

8.1 Variation in policy legacies and multi-level interactions

While the policy domains under scrutiny in this book are all cases of long-established executive federalism (and were selected for this very reason, Section 1.4), they vary considerably as to (1) perceptions of policy problems and collective action requirements, (2) the relative strength and contestation of subcentral mandates for policy-making and enforcement, as well as (3) the relative desire and ability of higher levels of the multi-level administration to influence subcentral decision-making or to tilt decision-making structures altogether. Such contextual variation – spelled out synoptically below (cf. first row of summary Table 8.1) – represents a chief analytical anchor for the interpretivist comparison of variable adoption patterns for risk analysis across policy domains.

Food safety controls, first, emerged in direct response to the perception of stark and unacceptable problems caused by industrialized food production. Strong discontent with blatant market asymmetries (e.g., the case of adulterated flour or wine) and the perception of collective action requirements enticed a comparatively early impetus for central state regulation, as did the early regulatory advocacy by a strong, concentrated, and scientifically minded profession of food chemists. A comparatively high inspection rate of more than 40 per cent of all premises, especially when compared to work safety (just over 2 per cent), provides for a strong contemporary mandate, too. While concurrent legislation and executive federalism have left much enforcement authority to subcentral levels, both historically and contemporarily, central state actors made repeated use of executive orders to harmonize enforcement of food safety legislation coercively, usually without much contestation by subcentral actors. Indeed, the historical interaction of traditionally autonomous enforcement by Länder and municipalities, centrally organized scientific information-gathering, framework regulation by the central government, and central-level coercive frameworks to ensure the consistency of enforcement set the path for present day German food safety governance. More recently, modern day food scares such as the "mad cow" disease (BSE) have created severe legitimacy pressure for the regulatory authorities in Europe. Yet, the moment of scandalization also reinforced the historical patterns of tandem scientific rationalization and tight coordination of food safety inspections, not least by institutionalizing a highly integrated regulatory regime across the EU across otherwise autonomous member states.

In contrast to the food safety case, until recently, German *flood prevention* has not experienced any major Eureka moment during which calls for tighter regulation and/or more coordination between subcentral authorities and across governance levels would have arisen. An extreme fragmentation of executive responsibilities – involving several hundreds of municipal administrations and self-regulated dike associations – has dominated the policy domain since its inception. Unlike food safety issues, flooding was rarely discussed as a policy problem of national importance as disasters tended to be perceived as locally contained and prevention strategies as requiring local answers to distributional issues. A history of broad umbrella legislation and the lack of a clear regulatory mandate for flood prevention and damage compensation – there is no legal obligation for state actors to fund any measure – has further contributed to the extreme fragmentation of the domain. Major border-crossing floods in the 1990s and 2000s have changed perceptions of policy problems and coordination requirements though. They strengthened the view among EU and Federal policymakers that harmonized flood risk assessment methods are required to solve flood-related collective action problems, and especially conflicts of interests in flood prevention between riparian upstream and downstream communities, more effectively and efficiently. This perception concurred with the formation of an instrument constituency around risk analysis – both among European scientific experts of flood prevention and among a forerunner catchment district at the Rhine.

Like the food safety case, *work safety controls* emerged in direct response to a growing problem perception around the detrimental health and social effects of industrialized work patterns. Yet, the regulatory progress involved few centralizing impulses and met much more resistance than in the food safety case. Historically, the existing problem perception in the domain met a strong reluctance to put state actors in charge of controlling working conditions too strictly – prominently by Bismarck himself, who favored a compensatory social insurance regime over strict prevention and controls (Rothstein, Paul and Demeritt, 2020). This institutional choice resulted in a dual regulatory regime, where state inspectorates overlap with inspections by the social insurance funds, has created regulatory competition and fragmentation between statutory and non-statutory regulators, has lowered the political salience of statutory controls, and has informed a continuous need for state inspectorates to legitimize their activities, unlike in food safety where inspectorates stand strong as much-valued and endowed advocates of consumer interests. Recent critique by the EU's peer review committee for work safety inspections (SLIC), for example, castigated the lack of executive coordination and some business-friendly actors even mooted the abolition of state inspectorates and a complete transfer of powers to the mutual trade associations. The pressure to legitimize enforcement priorities in work safety has risen even more since the 1990s due to an expansion of common market regulatory tasks, which tend to pull away resources and political attention from core labor inspections in mixed departments. Certainly, this expansion of the portfolio and a simultaneous soaring reduction of staff over the last two decades has augmented efficiency pressures in the domain. However, extremely low annual inspection rates (only 2.5 per cent of firms are inspected) and low political salience and lack of a nation-wide problem perception – unlike in the other two cases (food has been of national concern from Imperial times and flood prevention has recently hit the spheres of national relevance, too) suggest that the statutory mandate for work safety controls is rather too existentially threatened for inspectorates to *afford* genuine problem-solving in the first place. At the same time, unlike for the cases of food safety controls (with strong EU coercion powers and Federal use of executive orders) or flood prevention (with more recent softer EU and Federal impulses to harmonize policies), the work safety domain does not display any strong top-down harmonization pressure on enforcement either.

From a historical institutionalist position, the displayed variation in institutional legacies and context will shape the relative dominance of any of the three argumentative orientations – instrumental, legitimacy-seeking, and power-oriented – in empirical adoptions of risk analysis. For example, where a strong collective problem perception has coincided with regulatory advocacy of scientific experts since centuries (like in food safety), a focus on the instrumental promises of risk analysis seems likely. By contrast, the work safety domain, being troubled by continuous legitimacy pressures and lack of political salience of their regulatory mandate, is a candidate for legitimacy-seeking adoptions of risk analysis. But while such ideal-typical matching is a fruitful starting point for comparative analysis and explains part of the variation (cf. Section 8.3), it is not sufficient from an interpretivist perspective. As I argued in the Introduction, to focus on contextual variation, from an interpretivist perspective, does not equal predictive modeling of the allures of analytical tool. As "meanings are *actualized* in a specific context-in-use" (Wagenaar, 2011, p. 110), we require a deeper ideographic comparison of actors' complex meaning-making as set against their strategic-selective perceptions of the contexts described earlier and their own envisioned role in these contexts (Section 1.3). Context certainly shapes the availability and relative argumentative weight of instrumental, legitimacy-, and power-oriented perceptions of analytical tools and pre-structures policymakers' meaning-making processes during adoption. However, how and why policymakers at different levels of the public administration "actualize" certain contextual aspects when they adopt a new policy tool, how they mute or ignore other aspects, or even seek to rework the underlying decision-making structures with a new tool, and how different actors' interpretations of risk analysis interact across the different levels of the administration, is a contingent process which needs qualitative empirical investigation.

8.2 Varied patterns of adopting risk analysis

Patterns of adopting risk analysis vary rather significantly, and it seems systematically by context, across our three policy sectors (second row of Table 8.1). In *food safety controls*, risk analysis was coerced onto member states and eventually Länder enforcement authorities with the EU's 2006 control regulation. While Brussels' text remained relatively vague as to the details of risk-based food controls and only harmonized some basic characteristics of risk assessments, an inner-German executive order (AVV RÜb of 2008) has provided a highly detailed specification of the EU regulation, including common assessment formula, lists of indicators, detailed guidance on using risk analysis in priority-setting, and even inspection frequencies per risk level. Such standardized assessment is further strengthened by the programming of a common risk-analytical model in a widely shared software solution which has automated inspection planning in local authorities.

German *flood prevention* also had risk analysis coming in via the EU venue, with a 2007 Directive, even if local forerunners in risk-analytical modeling in the Rhine catchment have been instrumental in promoting risk analysis at the EU level. Like the control regulation in food safety, the EU floods directive stayed vague on risk analysis beyond some general definition of probability and impact and did not prescribe any specific measures. Yet, it did impose tight six annually reporting structures both for risk mapping and for risk management. The vague EU template was, again, specified to an immense detail in the Bund-Länder coordination forum LAWA which provided a (non-binding) common assessment formula and detailed guidance on using risk analysis in prevention planning. Unlike the executive order did for food safety, however, LAWA stopped short of prescribing specific links between risk analysis and regulatory decision-making (e.g., types of prevention measure suiting what kind of risk level). Instead, the national government in Berlin set up risk-based funding criteria in a newly established National Flood Protection Program, thus creating financial incentives for coordinated priority-setting in a highly decentralized setting.

Unlike the other two cases, Länder and local authorities in the field of *work safety controls* experienced no coercive pressure to adopt risk analysis from higher governance levels. While a few local forerunners had introduced risk analysis for instrumental reasons in the early 2000s, Länder only adopted a single risk analysis template in 2014 after negotiations in the inter-Länder working group LASI. The LASI's risk-oriented approach to work safety controls has emulated existing blueprints from Hessen and Baden-Württemberg. It details a basic cross-Länder hazard assessment scheme but, unlike risk-analytical templates in food safety controls and flood prevention, leaves much leeway for Länder and municipal inspectorates to specify other risk factors (especially the likelihood of firms' compliance). Länder use a common software (IFAS) and have piloted a risk-based algorithm based on LASI risk analysis since 2017, but there is no appetite for harmonized inspection planning and explicit resistance against a risk-based determination of cross-Länder inspection frequencies.

In summary, the initiation of common risk analysis ranges from strict EU coercion (backed by national executive orders) for food safety controls, via softer EU coercion in the flood prevention case all the way to voluntary horizontal coordination and emulation in work safety inspections. There is also a stepwise decrease of specification and rigor of the common risk analysis template in terms of its technical and organizational design – from the highly rigorous and detailed risk-analytical model in German food safety controls via moderately detailed flood risk mapping toward the rather broad-brush risk-oriented approach in work safety inspections, – and likewise a decreasing significance of its use in administrative decision-making. The finding of a parallel increase of (1) central coercive powers and (2) rigor/comprehensiveness of risk-analytical policy change – if read in isolation from the more nuanced multi-level adoption dynamics – could suggest a correlation between the two from a positivist account. Indeed, it seems to support the claim in the literature that analytical tools for decision-making are unlikely to emerge, in any nationally comprehensive manner, in fragmented polities and public administrations (see discussion in Introduction and Chapter 4).

However, the more detailed scrutiny and comparison of adoption patterns highlights that the cases with stronger EU coercion are also precisely the ones where rigorous and detailed risk-analytical templates have been promoted *within* Germany. Certainly, the food safety case could be interpreted as an extension of the claim that regulatory fragmentation hinders comprehensive analytical innovation (Rothstein, Borraz and Huber, 2013; cf. Demeritt et al., 2017): the long-standing legal-administrative unitarization of the domain has arguably facilitated the coercive (instrumental) adoption of a detailed risk-analytical model for automated priority-setting across Germany through an executive order, and thus countered executive federalism. This is not the case for flood prevention though; a case where federal coercive powers are almost non-existent and we nonetheless observe a high level of specification of the EU directive's vague risk analysis and, more recently, a mainstreaming of a regional forerunner's risk-analytical model via a national funding stream. Most puzzling from the fragmentation-skeptical perspective seems the work safety case where risk analysis emerges in the absence of any coercive pressures and has been mainstreamed across all Länder. While being certainly less rigorous, less uniform, and less binding than in the former two cases, there is nonetheless evidence for some risk-based harmonization of enforcement approaches in the domain, including pilots of algorithmic inspection planning. To understand these complex adoption patterns, we need to stop treating polity fragmentation as inhibitive independent context variable for policy(-analytical) tool change and explore, instead, how the institutional environment of variable multi-level settings becomes actualized (and re-worked) in policymakers' interpretations of the instrumental, legitimacy-seeking, and power-oriented attractions of risk analysis, and how potentially multiple orientations and their interaction across the multiple levels of the administration come to shape overall adoption processes.

8.3 Comparative meaning-making: explaining the variable appeals of risk analysis

My analysis of actors' justifications for adopting risk analysis in three domains exposes a complex variation of their appreciative interpretations (see the third row of summary Table 8.1). While evidencing a relatively neat ideal-typical matching within the ILP framework in line with contextual variation at first sight (see above), each case involves significant (sometimes rather subtle or hidden) interaction dynamics between instrumental, legitimacy-seeking, and power-seeking orientations toward risk analysis. Policymakers actualize meanings of risk analysis as problem-solving and as polity policies *strategically* and highly *selectively* against the backdrop of their specific institutional contexts. For overview purposes, Figures 8.1–8.3 visualize the resulting *adoption process*[1] per policy domain.

To start with, risk analysis in *food safety controls*, at first glance, appears to be mono-dimensionally related to instrumental interpretations. The dominance of a continuously strong problem perception of food market failures – a historical theme since Imperial times in Germany and repeated with BSE in the 1990s and 2000s – and evidence-based coordination in the EU has seemingly shaped an instrumental focus on collective problem-solving in the multi-level setting. It thus seems logical, from our ideal-typical expectations, that administrators consider the adoption of risk analysis desirable mainly because it can enhance the effectiveness of controls on a common market by creating a coherent prioritization approach among otherwise autonomous enforcement bodies. Interview data highlight that the dominant effectiveness focus is further backed by, less relevant but mutually reinforcing, hopes of efficiency gains.

However, a closer analysis of interviews with food safety inspectors also exposes that the adoption of risk analysis involves dynamics of legitimacy-seeking and power-orientation in the domain and that the latter in particular actively reifies a historical decision on polity policies: to endow the central government with a strong regulatory and coordination role over formally autonomous enforcement actors. As for legitimacy-seeking, while the sectoral context does not create a need

TABLE 8.1 The varied appeals of risk analysis in Germany across three policy domains

	Food safety controls	*Flood prevention*	*Work safety controls*
Legacy of mandate	Strong mandate since Imperial times; high political salience; early unitarization as response to perception of severe collective action problem; uncontested central level coordination of subcentral executive actions	Weak/unspecific mandate coupled with high executive fragmentation; late coordination attempts in response to perceived collective action problems after devastating cross-border flood events; recent EU and national efforts in evidence-based coordination; strong instrument constituency	Weak/contested mandate; low political salience; competing mandate of mutual trade associations; dire budgetary pressures; no meaningful coordination attempts by EU or national level; increasing critique of fragmentation (including by EU actors)
Adoption pattern	Single detailed RA template coercively adopted by Länder with AVV RÜb as detailed specification of EU regulation; includes common assessment formula and detailed guidance on using RA; used in priority-setting and for automating inspection planning; common software solution with risk-analytical algorithm and unified inspection frequencies	Single detailed RA template, broad-brush EU requirements became specified to immense detail by LAWA; template includes common assessment formula and detailed guidance on using RA but leaves room for discretion for prevention planning; tight reporting structures for RA at EU level; risk-based funding criteria in National Flood Protection Program	Single RA template coordinated in LASI; determines basic common hazard assessment scheme but leaves much discretion for states to specify other risk variables; common software with risk-based algorithm exists but is not used consistently for inspection planning; explicit resistance against risk-based coordination of inspection frequencies

(*Continued*)

TABLE 8.1 (Continued)

	Food safety controls	*Flood prevention*	*Work safety controls*
Justification pattern	Dominant *instrumental* focus with desire of effective control of common food market in Europe requiring coordinated enforcement > RA facilitates consistent approach despite executive fragmentation Less relevant but reinforcing appeal of RA adoption: hopes of *instrumental* efficiency gains in times of tight budgets and *legitimacy-related* blame-shifting with inspectorates highlighting regulated firms' duty of care	*Instrumental* appeal of RA among forerunners along Rhine RA helps ind. state reject claims on public budgets and signal prevention/compensation duties of owners (*legitimacy-seeking*) Coordinated RA as *instrumental* facilitator of more cost-effective prevention planning across political boundaries, also against "irrational" local communities and collective action traps (elements of *central level meta-governance*) States use RA to claim more national level funding of high-risk prevention programs (*blame-* and *power-shifting*)	Initial *instrumental* appeal among forerunner states RA templates mainstreamed to other states to defend statutory inspections and their subcentral organization against continuing criticism of fragmentation and lack of strategy (*legitimacy-seeking*) Coordinated RA in inspection programming across Germany as tool for rendering mandates more visible politically (*collective legitimacy-seeking*), but also for ringfencing and expanding budget and staff for work safety inspections (*power-seeking*)
Overall adoption process (cf. Figures 8.1–8.3)	EU focus on *instrumentalism* (effectiveness gains on common market), amplified within Germany based on shared effectiveness goals across levels, enables *uncontested reinforcement of central steering* to counter executive fragmentation	EU *instrumental* turn to risk analysis (rising problem pressure), promoted by local forerunners, mobilizes inner-German rationalization in much fragmented setting and sets in motion struggles over *allocation of blame and power* for costly prevention measures across administrative levels	Availability of local *instrumental* risk analysis templates enables voluntary emulation, mobilized as states have shared interest in *defense* of weak work safety mandates (scandals, low salience and resources, fragmentation critique by EU) and morphing into attempt to *expanding* the mandate

Source: Author's compilation

ADOPTION PROCESS IN SHORT:

- EU initiative for RA as crisis response and effectiveness booster (**I** and **L**)
- *amplified* at Federal level by pre-existing focus on coordinated problem-solving and high political salience of the issue (**I**)
- *channeled* onto an automation track in line with legacy of uncontested central steering, unitarization of administrative actions, and rational consensus-seeking among autonomous actors (***rather silent* P**)

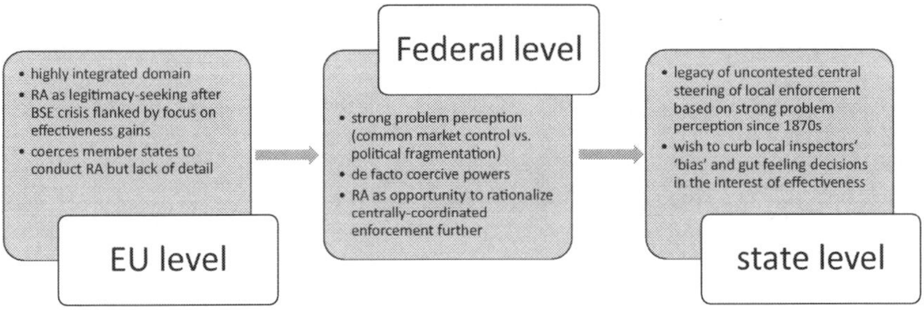

FIGURE 8.1 Adoption process of risk analysis in food safety controls

ADOPTION PROCESS IN SHORT:

EU initiative for risk analysis...

- *joins in* promotional efforts of regional forerunner within Germany and builds on effectiveness hopes (**I**)
- *is amplified by* Federal level perception of collective action problems and need to coordinate prevention more among states (**I**)
- *morphed into* meta-governance through central level financial incentives for transregional priority-setting (**P**)
- *mobilizes* blame-shifting strategies among states both towards private actors and municipal level (**L**)
- *set in motion* struggles over more Federal level financial involvement (**P**)

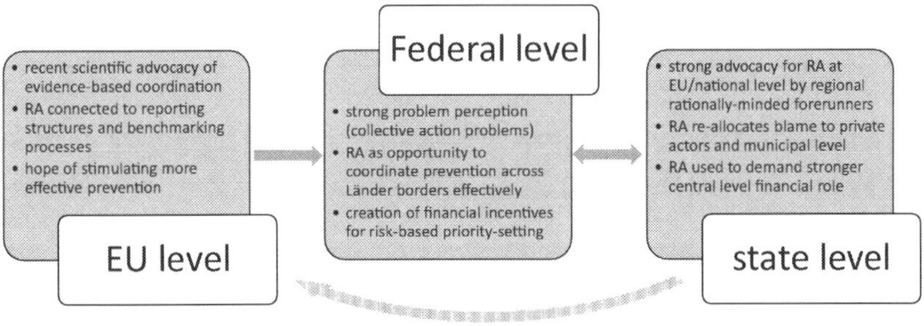

FIGURE 8.2 Adoption process of risk analysis in flood prevention

for inspectorates to defend their mandate against criticism (unlike in work safety), inspectorate leads, in interviews, nonetheless describe some more marginal blame-shifting desire toward regulatees in line with the food business operators' legal duty of care. This strategy is situated within the overarching effectiveness goals as it serves the wish of stimulating better compliance with food safety law among businesses themselves. Yet, some interviewees report that a fees-based system of food safety enforcement – with non-compliant regulatees needing to pay for inspection time – might increase adversarialism in the domain and may well re-direct the now

ADOPTION PROCESS IN SHORT:

- state level initiative for voluntary agreeement on common RA after series of scandals and fragmentation critique **(L)**
- *enabled by* existence of blueprints (including a shared software module) among rationally-minded forerunners **(I)**
- *supported by* shared wish to defend state level mandate and render work safety issues more visible politically **(L)**
- *culminating in* risk-based claims for higher budgets and more staff for state inspectorates **(P)** which are perceived as pre-requisite for effective control in the underfunded domain **(I)**

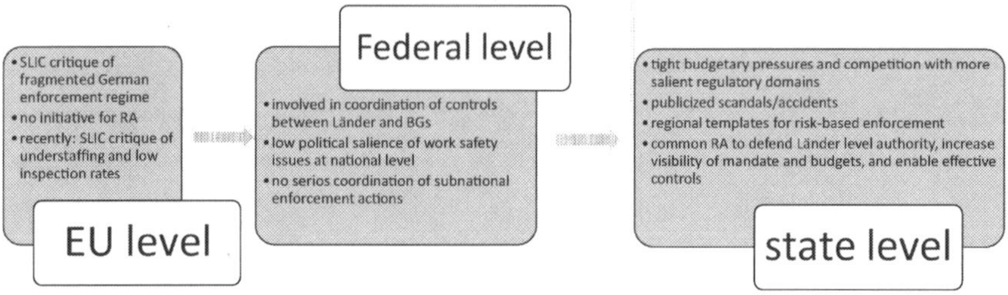

FIGURE 8.3 Adoption process of risk analysis in work safety controls

predominant instrumental use of risk analysis in Germany toward classic institutional risk management and legitimacy-seeking.

As for power-seeking, the contextual setting in the food safety domain creates no need for the central government to pursue power-seeking – the tight central level steering and coordination requirements for decentral enforcers have been a standard operating procedure since Imperial times and have recently been reinforced at EU level. In this context, risk analysis *reinforces* the central level monitoring and steering of subcentral enforcement activities. Again, the risk-based tightening of the central grip over local "autonomous" enforcement – all the way to automating inspection priorities – was discussed by interviewees as a matter of effectiveness-seeking rather than a powering strategy per se. As the desired effective control of the common food market in Europe is widely perceived to require consistent collective action, a de facto unitarization of subcentral approaches around risk analysis becomes an effectiveness-oriented remedy for fragmented controls in executive federalism. As actors at the different levels of administration share a strong problem perception (backed up by the political salience of the theme) and are united by the wish to enforce food safety regulation effectively and coherently in consumers' best interest, we observe a widely uncontested and far-reaching harmonization of risk-based controls which curtails Länder and local authorities' autonomy in enforcement considerably. Risk analysis seems to be just another way for central level actors to wield direct steering and meta-governance powers in a century-old attempt to create legal-administrative unity across fragmented jurisdictions. As this path has been so deeply sedimented in the domain since the very inception of a regulatory mandate for food safety in Germany, the related questions of the (re-confirmed) allocation of power over enforcement remain rather invisible.

An interpretive examination of the adoption process for risk analysis in *flood prevention* provides a counter point to such hidden and reifying polity policies. Similar to food safety, but much more recently in the early 2000s, an intensified problem perception after devastating border-crossing flood events and the increasing scientific advocacy for risk-analytical planning – including by inner-German forerunners along the Rhine – has infused an instrumental perception of risk analysis into the domain. Interviewees fittingly describe EU flood risk mapping as a welcome remedy for collective action problems and as facilitator of more efficient and effective prevention planning across political boundaries. In this effectiveness-seeking context, the ability of risk analysis to render risks comparable and transparent across states also helps Länder reject claims on public budgets for prevention and compensation and shift blame to private owners and municipal planning authorities.

From a comparative perspective, both food safety controls and flood prevention feature strong perceptions of collective action problems which actors believe risk analysis can help them manage more effectively. This explains the attention to detail in carving out risk analysis models by the AVV RÜb and the LAWA. In food safety, the instrumental turn to risk analysis is about enabling disparate authorities to unite their enforcement approaches – as they have done for centuries – for effective common market regulation. In flood prevention, risk evidence is meant to help dissolve conflicts of interest between riparian communities in managing border-crossing risks. While in both cases, risk analysis is perceived as a tool for creating a lingua franca for actors to "join forces" (food safety interviews), the flood prevention case with its rather recent coordination experiences is more prone to raising un-answered questions of competence allocation in the multi-level administration.

Indeed, unlike in the food safety case where the effectiveness-driven interactions across administrative levels are highly routinized, the flood prevention case highlights how struggles over administrative powers and accountability can be set in motion by a common analytical strategy in domains that have seen little coordinated problem-solving thus far. In this context, the initially instrumental case for risk-based policy coordination – through wide promotion by a rationally minded instrument constituency that included the Rhine cooperation – has morphed into a case of polity policies. On the one hand, the central government in Berlin perceives risk analysis as a welcome tool for central monitoring and steering, convinced that only some central level incentive – such as the National Flood Protection Program – can enable the desired effective coordination of flood prevention measures across borders (and thus amplified the soft EU initiative for coordination within Germany). On the other hand, states have more recently discovered risk analysis as a handy instrument for re-allocating blame to higher administrative levels in an increasingly costly domain. They claim more national level funding of regional high-risk prevention measures or even an outright centralization of flood prevention duties for measures of transregional relevance. Actors in the domain have not yet settled upon the right balance between national steering (and funding) and locally autonomous planning and enforcement and risk analysis might well play a decisive role in determining such balance based on its differentiation powers. The domain might well be on the track of a problem-based executive unitarization, and risk analysis seems to be the calculative platform for determining which flooding scenarios should go Federal, which should stay within the realms of states and which should frankly remain issues of private prevention.

The analysis of interviews with *work safety* inspectorates exposes a vastly different dynamic of adopting and justifying risk analysis. Given the low salience of work safety control problems and lack of a distinct collective action perspective in the domain – unlike in food safety controls and the more recently hyped coordinated flood risk management – administrators in German work safety are rather unlikely to adopt risk analysis for purely instrumental reasons. In addition, the absence of any harmonizing pressure from the center – again unlike in the much-centralized food safety domain but also the more softly harmonizing flood prevention regime – political control agendas by central level actors were also unlikely to emerge. Instead, when scandals hit and fragmentation critique rose, states decided to mainstream the risk analysis template by some effectiveness-minded local forerunners as a model for priority-setting across the country. They hoped that risk-based differentiation would enable institutional risk management and thus help defend statutory inspections, but also their subcentral organization, against continuing criticism of fragmentation and lack of coordination. Seeking to tackle their notoriously contested mandate head-on, Länder inspectorates have also engaged in the voluntary emulation of risk-analytical inspection programming as a tool for rendering their weak work safety mandates more visible politically, and even ring-fencing and expanding them in terms of budget and staff.

And yet, as long as work safety inspections are blatantly underfunded and lack political salience – unlike flood prevention has since the early 2000s – the rather existential threats to the statutory work safety mandate are likely to dwarf any instrumental problem-solving focus, even if inspectors themselves – in interviews – gather around a normative desire for risk-based effectiveness gains. In some Länder, therefore, risk analysis has set in motion – similarly to the flood prevention case but so far less successful – a discussion over more central steering and investment as a perceived structural requirement for more effective controls. Länder level attempts to wield the results of risk analysis as a weapon for claiming more money for controls from their own regional governments (given inner-departmental competition for resources with ostensibly more salient regulatory domains) might be aided by the EU's critique of low inspection rates in Germany.

Note

1 The term *adoption process* connects the dots between contextual factors (Section 8.1), empirical adoption patterns (Section 8.2), and policymakers' selective sense-making around risk-analytical innovation (combinations of ILP) in these different settings (Section 8.3).

9

CONCLUSION

Analyze and rule: findings and future research venues

Risk has become a new lens through which to view the world.[1]

So why do analytical tools appeal to actors in public administrations and how do variable contexts shape this appeal? How do fragmented decision-making structures – often said to hamper analytical turns – affect the appeal of analysis? This chapter summarizes the book's findings and discusses future research venues. It does so in three steps, aided by a ballistic metaphor:

- First, the book exposed how the inescapable co-existence of instrumental problem-solving orientations with actor's valuation of analysis in positional struggles over legitimacy and power furnishes a high interpretive versatility of analytical tools in practice, turning them into veritable "magic bullets". Findings also highlight, however, the need to explore more closely why some interpretations of analytical tools materialize in actual policy-making and polity policies while others do not.
- Second, the book reappraised and substantiated the role of context in shaping specific interpretive patterns around analytical tools. The targets which analytical tools are meant to "hit", from the perspective of policymakers, shift both with the specific decision-making context (cross-nationally and cross-sectorally) and over time (diachronic perspective). In particular, the study highlights that analytical tools flourish not "against the odds" in fragmented administrations, as assumed in parts of the literature (Introduction and Chapter 4), but precisely *because* of these "odds".
- Third, the comparative analysis also revealed that actors' strategically selective wielding of risk analysis in polity policies can stabilize or transform decision-making structures in a domain beyond wishful thinking. The targets that are

domain contexts are not set in stone: when "hit" by actors' interpretations of risk analysis these targets might well be set off their position and change their coordinates. These material effects on decision-making structures in public administrations – captured in the slogan "analyze and rule" – render the examination of analytical tools, their appeal, their strategic uses, but also their increasing technical elaboration a fruitful research agenda for comparative political science and policy studies.

9.1 Semiotic magic bullets: the interpretive versatitlity of analytical tools

The book has shown that the strong appeal of analytical tools builds on their interpretive versatility. The co-existence of actors' problem-solving orientations with their ideas about how analysis suits their positional struggles in a domain renders analytical tools attractive from vastly different perspectives. Whilst these two visions of the allures of analytical tools seem to be irreconcilably scattered across different literatures (see Introduction), my conceptualization of analytical tools in Chapter 2, and risk analysis in Chapter 3, synthesized the various accounts. I argue that instrumental problem-solving, legitimacy-seeking, and power-seeking must be understood as interpretive frames for the desired performance of analytical tools which co-exist in any one actor's, as well as in collective, sense-making in a domain. Meaning-making over policy substance – ideas over the "best" approach for problem-solving – co-evolves with actors' ideas over who should legitimately be in charge of decision-making and/or whose authority in a domain should be expanded, curtailed, or controlled more closely, and why. At the same time, the interpretive versatility of analytical tools does not imply wildly unstructured bundles of meaning: to the contrary, my analysis of three cases within Germany evidence quite structured interpretive patterns around analytical "turns" in a domain.

9.1.1 The co-existence of problem-solving and polity policies in analytical "turns"

At its basic, the comparative policy analysis in this book confirmed that public administration actors embrace analytical tools with a large variety of orientations in mind. None of the three policy domains studied here is fully determined by actors' instrumental perceptions of analytical tools (even the highly instrumentally leaning actors in food safety use risk analysis to re-confirm the distribution of power in the domain); in fact, none features just one ideal-typical frame for interpreting the assumed merits of risk analysis (cf. Figures 8.1-8.3, in the previous chapter). On the one hand, my analysis validates a common assumption in mainstream definitions of analytical tools: they *are* relevant pre-decision aids from the perspective of actors seeking to optimize their decision-making (cf. Howlett, 2011; Turnpenny et al., 2015 and see Introduction). My study has shown that instrumental orientations are well and alive, albeit to variable degrees in different sectoral contexts. This is most obvious in the case of food safety controls where a long-established pattern of evidence-based *collective* problem-solving is being reinforced with the adoption of instrumentally oriented risk analysis, all the way to automating inspection planning. Instrumental orientations also matter in flood prevention where local forerunners have promoted their effectiveness-seeking strategies, and especially a common risk-analytical IT simulation, successfully as a template for national flood prevention efforts. Even for the case of work safety controls, the case with the lowest evidence of risk-based problem-solving orientations and the least rigorous common risk-analytical model in practice, I found evidence of instrumentally oriented advocacy of risk analysis. This speaks to a more universal trend of "doing more with less" in times of austerity and perceived regulatory crises that extends well beyond the much-studied benchmark cases of "core marketizer" NPM reformers (Pollitt and Bouckaert, 2011). As resource pressure and related modernization agendas have been widespread phenomena, risk analysis and its instrumental promise of cost-effective problem-solving clearly enjoy purchase outside the US or the UK, too.

On the other hand, my study problematizes the orthodox assumption that analytical tools are neutral "option generators" for decision-making (Viscusi, 1983; Sunstein, 2000, 2002; Majone, 2010; Howlett, 2011; Turnpenny et al., 2015). A purely instrumental account obscures which problems analytical tools are perceived to be an answer to and therefore underestimates their appeal. My analysis explored how actors promote and adopt analytical tools in response to their perceptions of decision-making structures in a domain and what's problematic about them – be it the autonomy of regulatory agencies or the complex interdependencies of actors in multi-level settings. My conceptual work labelled such orientations as instances of *polity policies* to highlight that the relationship between analytical tools and policy-making does not stop with problem-solving in the narrow sense but involves attempts to re-work decision-making structures themselves.

Findings in the book confirm Jessop's claim that governance – including the introduction of seemingly technical analytical models – "cannot be reduced to questions of how to solve issues of a specific techno-economic, narrowly juridico-political in character, tightly focused social-administrative, or otherwise neatly framed problem" (Jessop, 2016, p. 178). My cases clearly evidence that actors negotiate their own positions within a domain when they reflect upon the merits of an analytical tool. This is most evident in the work safety and flood prevention cases. In the former, risk analysis is mostly about defending and ringfencing a weak inspection mandate in a domain; in the latter, very vocal struggles over the relationship between subcentral autonomous flood prevention actions and central level involvement in priority-setting and funding of high risk measures have unfolded around risk analysis. Even the strongly instrumentally framed risk analysis in food safety controls displays an underbelly of confirming pre-existing agreements over how authority and power are distributed in the domain (strong central steering).

The cases show that analytical tools have a much more explicitly political role to play than is ascribed to them in mainstream theories of policy and institutional change or policy tools (Hood, 1983; Sabatier, 1988; Hall, 1993; Sabatier and Jenkins-Smith, 1993; Howlett, 2011). In line with more constructivist interpretations of policy tools in general (Peters, 2002; Lascoumes and Le Galès, 2004, 2007; Voß and Simons, 2014) and of risk analysis and other forms of quantification in particular (Porter, 1995; Scott, 1998; Desrosières, 2002; Rothstein, Huber and Gaskell, 2006; Black, 2010; Stone, 2012; Mennicken and Lodge, 2015), I have shown that actors' perceptions of the ability of an analytical tool to "rule" – to legitimize their own role and mandate and/or expand their influence in a given domain and multi-level setting – is crucial. My findings thus help substantiate existing insights in EU studies, research on international bureaucracies, but also the more general claims on policy instrumentation and instrument constituencies: analytical tools speak to actors' desire to re-structure policy domains (Lascoumes and Le Galès, 2007), advance their own "strategic agency" in a field (cf. also: Jankauskas and Eckhard, 2019; cf. Radaelli and Meuwese, 2010), influence how perks and powers are distributed in a domain (Peters, 2002), and create powerful collective identities and new institutions (Voß and Simons, 2014; Simons and Voß, 2017).

Overall, then, to assume a dichotomy or schism between the two "camps" – instrumental problem-solving and polity policies – would be deeply flawed. My findings offer support for recent claims within critical policy studies that any "rift" between rationalist and constructivist views on the role of evidence in policy-making is "obsolete" (Straßheim, 2017, p. 238; also see: Carmel and Kan, 2019; Paul, 2020). Like other types of evidence, the turn to risk analysis in the public administration is never only about the "quest for 'ultimate', 'objective' truth as key to problem solving" but neither is it solely about somewhat 'biased' political or symbolic uses of evidence (Straßheim, 2017, p. 237f). Rather, an interpretive perspective highlights that both problem-solving and polity policies (with a focus on legitimacy-seeking and/or power-seeking) are co-existent interpretive frames through which actors come to appreciate analytical tools. Their semiotic versatility makes analytical tools magic bullets which can hit several targets at the same time.

9.1.2 Patterned interactions between analysis-based problem-solving and polity policies

But while their interpretive versatility is part of the promise of analytical tools, the result is clearly no unstructured bundle of neutrally co-existent meanings which evenly and independently shape the policy domain. Findings of the book suggest we explore more closely how different actors' interpretations of an analytical tool interact, join forces, mobilize additional support for the case of an analytical tool, co-evolve in interdependence with one another, or are being challenged or re-worked; but also how these interpretations and re-interpretations of what analysis can bring to the respective policy domain shapes *actual* policy and polity policy decisions in a domain (on that latter point, cf. Section 9.3).

Within-case analysis enabled me to explore interactions of different actors' appreciative orientations in any one case – within and across administrative levels – and to chart dynamic development in how the promotion of an analytical tool travels through a policy domain. For example, the book's comparative analysis highlights that the use of risk analysis in collective problem-solving endeavors can morph into questions about how decision-making in a domain ought to be organized. In flood prevention, the initially instrumental interpretation of flood risk mapping by the EU Commission and the Rhine forerunners – and the successful promotion of risk analysis as a tool for all by this instrument constituency – morphed into a tug-of-war between the German central government and the 16 states about the Federal role in funding state-level prevention measures for high risk scenarios of national relevance. Such questions of power distribution and legitimate administrative action in executive federalism have arguably been done and dusted in food safety controls since the 19th century. In work safety, vice versa, states' initial collective focus on breaking much critiqued and highly underfunded inspectorates free of a "legitimacy trap" turned into some individual state's endeavor to claim more resources from their own Ministry and Parliament for effective problem-solving. It seems then that, depending on how well decision-making structures are suited, from the perspective of different actors, to deal with policy problems and collective action problems, analysis-based polity policies play out more in the background or the foreground of a domain. Where such structures are themselves under negotiation (as in flooding) or even highly contested (as in work safety), analytical tools become central battle horses in positional struggles. While this study offered a first step into exploring such dynamics in comparative perspective, it remains unclear whether domains with similar contextual conditions – for example, a highly contested mandate for inspections – develop similar interpretations and uses of risk analysis.

My analysis also highlights how some actors' meaning making *materializes* in institutional decisions while side-lining or overwriting others' interpretations. I studied the organizational design and uses of risk analysis in the three domains alongside actors' interpretations to explore how meaning-making materializes in policy and institutional action. Findings warrant more systematic comparative research on how legacies of a domain, dominant perceptions of policy problems (especially collective action problems), existing decision-making structures, and actors' relative positions to one another shape interaction patterns between collective problem-solving orientations and positional struggles over legitimacy and power in administrations' turn to analytical tools (see next section).

On the one hand, the materialization of meanings in policy-making is always a question of relative resources and powers (Jessop, 2016; Carmel, 2019). For example, the promotional efforts of a strong international and interdisciplinary instrument constituency, which commended risk analysis as a rational problem-solving tool in flood prevention, literally overrun those states in Germany which had not yet coordinated their prevention policies closely and had no experience with risk-based prioritization. The powerful combination of the Rhine states' advanced practical expertise in applying risk analysis to coordinate among them with the EU Commission's instrumental commitment to the concept of risk – but also the latter's power to coerce risk mapping onto member states – swept over German flood prevention policies and potentially triggered a transformation of decision-making structures (see Section 9.3). Rather than stopping at collective problem-solving, the workings of the instrument constituency created the very conditions for re-negotiating a structural balance between (1) the autonomy of subcentral flood preventers vs. (2) the role of central coordination, steering and – maybe most importantly – funding of prevention on the basis of risk-analytical modeling. To explore the conditions for promotional efforts to materialize and contribute to the adoption of an analytical tool beyond rhetoric, for example in the structuring of access to funding, a more systematic examination of the role of instrument constituencies therefore seems fruitful, too.

On the other hand, we need to understand how the inbuilt calculative and (re-) presentational capacities of the analytical tool itself (Chapter 3 for risk analysis) help advance actors' strategic meaning-making and prioritize some interpretations over others. The book discussed both conceptually and empirically how and why actors' come to cherish the specific capacities of risk as an analytical concept. Here, the more generic claims of "rigor", "transparency", and "fairness" – usually associated with analysis – rely on the ability of risk analysis to differentiate phenomena and by extension administrative action. For example, while risk-based differentiation helps all actors define "the parameters of blame" for their own organizational actions in acts of self-defense, just as suggested in regulation studies (Black, 2010; Rothstein, Huber and Gaskell, 2006; cf. Chapter 3), it plays a more differential role in re-organizing who is to blame and who should be in charge in the multi-level setting (see Chapter 4). Risk-based intergovernmental blame-shifting attempts materialize in the multi-level administration in a double sense: they shift accountability for low-risk scenarios to lower and for high-risk scenarios to central administrative levels. Indeed, the EU's requirement of common risk mapping in flood prevention enabled state-level actors to point to the newly visualized risks on their maps to increase the pressure on Berlin to co-fund prevention measures of high transregional significance.

As analytical tools provide versatile lenses through which actors "view the world" (both in terms of policy problems and the structural context of policy-making) (Hutter, 2005, p. 1; cf. Paul, 2017b), scholars of policy-making and governance also need to understand the specific credentials of different analytical heuristics better. The interaction of different forms of analysis – risk analysis, CBA, RIA, and so on – and their specific calculative patterns with administrative actors' sense-making around (but also use of) analytical tools deserves more comparative exploration.

9.2 Moving targets: the contextualized appeal of analytical tools

If we understand analytical tools as semiotic magic bullets, then they are bullets which shoot on moving targets, in two senses. First, variable underlying structural conditions shape both how actors understand policy problems and potential solutions (relevant for their specific problem-solving orientation) and how they perceive of their own role vis-à-is others in decision-making processes (relevant for their specific view on polity policies). The section summarizes how different underlying structural conditions in the well-studied benchmark cases of analytical "turns" vs. the case studied here – the EU-German multi-level administration – shape the appeal of analytical tools, and discusses implications for future research. Second, analytical tools also "hit" targets which shift over time. Findings in this book highlight the value of a prospective *diachronic* examination of the attractions of analytical tools and their dynamic materialization in policy-making and polity policies. I develop these two points in more detail next.

9.2.1 How decision-making contexts shape interpretations of analytical tools

A comparative discussion of the (well-researched) Anglo-American "benchmark" cases with the (less well understood) EU-German case, explored in this book, highlights that variable structural contexts do not necessarily shape the overall proclivity (more or less) of a specific administration to turn to analytical tools, as suggested in parts of the literature (Radaelli, 2005; Rothstein, Borraz and Huber, 2013; Demeritt et al., 2017). Rather, context shapes variable sets of perceptions of *why* analytical tools appeal. In that respect, the relative concentration of executive powers, accountability structures, and variable commitment to the NPM agenda set important landmarks, just as proposed in the literature. However, the formal and informal coordination requirements and constitutional norms of legal-administrative unity and equal living conditions in Germany's executive federalism also condition the rise of analytical tools, but they do so in specific ways which require more scholarly attention.

In a nutshell, in forerunner countries like the US and the UK, analytical tools have emerged from a mutually supportive interaction of a public interest culture *with* a concentration of executive powers and heightened principal-agent accountability concerns. While the former promotes an ideational focus on cost-effective problem-solving, the latter set of conditions create high pressure for agencies to justify executive decisions vis-à-vis their principals in the central government (legitimacy-seeking) and the principal's wish to control executive decisions of these autonomous actors (power-seeking). By contrast, the specific conditions for policy-making in multi-level settings – in the German case with a strong focus on coordination and a unified legal-administrative framework – shape different interpretations of how analysis aids problem-solving and polity policies.

So, what about problem-solving orientations, first? Individual actors in multi-level administrations also turn to risk to develop cost-effective prioritization (e.g., work safety controls in Hessen or Brandenburg, flood prevention along the Rhine), just as in the benchmark cases and for similar reasons (Section 9.1). In addition to this standard account of rational problem-solving, however, the *shared* instrumental interpretation of risk analysis in German executive federalism relied on its perceived credentials as "unbiased" and "objective" *enabler of collective action.* As the ability to solve country- and EU-wide collective action problems is of particular concern in settings with highly autonomous subnational administrations – and may even be sharpened with Germany's constitutional norms of legal-administrative unity or equal living conditions – the perceived value of risk analysis as a "rational" foundation for identifying a common approach growths. In my cases, actors' desire to overcome collective action problems and/or ensure legal-administrative consistency across jurisdictions makes analytical tools important devices for establishing the typically German "rational consensus" (Richardson, 1982; Howlett and Tosun, 2018). Of course, this dynamic might well divert in competitive federalist administrations where norms of cooperation are weaker and relative administrative unity no declared goal.

Overall, executive fragmentation does indeed present an institutional entry barrier to comprehensive risk-based problem-solving across a whole country (e.g., Rothstein, Borraz and Huber, 2013; Demeritt et al., 2017). Yet, this barrier is not unsurmountable. On the one hand, fragmentation can itself stimulate analysis-based coordination processes among formally autonomous administrative entities in the fashion of the rationalist consensus, debated earlier (cf. example of the EU's Corona risk map). On the other hand, as fragmentation is a constant source for actors to reflect upon their role vis-à-vis others in a domain, analytical tools become central in negotiating and reworking actors' relative positions of legitimacy and power in a domain. Rather than throwing out the baby with the bathwater, when discussing executive fragmentation as impediment for the flourishing of analytical tools, we need to investigate how the wish to overcome executive fragmentation for coordinated or collective problem-solving purposes increases the appeal of risk analysis. Beyond the German case, the EU Commission's (2020) recent attempts to develop a common approach to (the highly uneven) pandemic-related mobility restrictions across member states around a shared risk-analytical framework for COVID-19 infections, suggests a wider applicability of my findings.

Second, as for their framings as polity policy, the book's findings also confirm that analytical tools flourish not "against the odds" in fragmented administrations, as commonly assumed in parts of the literature (Introduction and Chapter 4), but precisely *because* of these "odds". A key finding of the book is that analytical tools appeal in multi-level settings because administrative actors perceive them as useful for navigating the complex decision-making settings in which they act, in relation to both legitimacy-seeking and power-seeking. In German executive federalism, the ubiquitous requirement to confirm or rework a balance between constitutional requirements of legal-administrative unity (and related pressures for unitarization) and the constitutional autonomy of states makes risk analysis especially attractive. In my sample, the role of risk analysis in polity policies ranges from the effectiveness-oriented reinforcement of long existing patterns of central steering and coordination in food safety controls, the in-vivo consolidation of the allocation of mandates for effective flood prevention in the context of a fragmented and nebulous mandate, all the way to existential legitimacy-seeking efforts in the case of politically side-lined work safety inspections.

As I argued in Chapters 3 and 4, these strategies work – at least on the semiotic level but also in terms of changing material conditions (see next section) – because risk-based differentiation and visualization enable actors to substantiate and re-work mandates, the exact division of authority, and blame for failure, across different administrative levels. In flood prevention, for example, risk analysis supports central level monitoring and steering goals but also subnational actors' attempts to shift responsibility for managing low risks back to municipal or private actors while equally engaging the national level more prominently in high-risk scenarios. In previous research on EU border controls, I have already observed a similar risk-based shifting up and down of enforcement competencies (Paul, 2017a). This suggests that scholars need to attend more systematically not only to how analytical tools may be adopted to strengthen one particular actor in a domain (e.g., there is much focus on the EU Commission), but also to how different actors' views on how analysis serves their positional struggles interact, compete with one another, and come to co-shape a domain.

9.2.2 How the appeal of analytical tools shifts over time

The second kind of shift of the very targets for analytical "bullets" is temporal. A key observation in this study is that actors in multi-level administrations may see a need to address positional struggles in a domain *first* for an instrumental problem-solving focus to develop grip in the future. This dynamic is most visible for work safety inspectorates which seek to forge stronger and more visible mandates which would enable, in their view, effective problem-solving. In flood prevention, too, hopes of effective cross-regional coordination lead actors to re-distribute mandates and authorities across the multiple levels of governance around risk-based differentiation. Such temporally staggered interpretive orientations of analytical tools deserve more scholarly attention.

Whilst this book's synchronous comparison of three sectors did not allow for sector-internal comparisons over time (diachronic analysis), the historical contextualization of findings provide some first cues about moving targets over time. For example, the current consolidation efforts in the flood prevention case as to the "right" allocation of authority over prevention measures for them to be effective reads like an early version of food safety controls in Germany. In other words, the question of how to best solve collective action problems in multi-level settings and enable effective problem-solving despite executive fragmentation through specific coordination structures – a question troubling contemporary German flood prevention actors – has already been answered in the food safety domain during the times of Bismarck. The adoption process in work safety also makes use of a future horizon of effective problem-solving, with some inspectorates taking pains to program an algorithm for priority-setting with a sole focus on effectiveness and demanding more staff based on such rational risk-based calculations. This strategically envisioned future of a routinized use of risk analysis to improve the health and safety of workers through effective inspections might, of course, never materialize. The conditions under which it could ought to be a focus of future research also for the sake of those who would benefit from "effective" administrative action, in this case workers in highly under-inspected workplaces.

Of course, coordinated problem-solving is no linear or natural end point for dynamically changing interactions between analysis-based problem-solving and polity policies in multi-level settings. If we trust diagnoses from recent critical studies on evidence and policy-making, namely, that the questions of power over decision-making which evidence-based policy-making seeks to eliminate tend to reappear further down the line (Straßheim and Kettunen, 2014, p. 260), an instrumental focus on coordinated problem-solving might well crumble when actors' underlying perceptions change or their positional struggles surface more prominently. Again, the conditions under which retreats from analysis-driven policy coordination might occur – for example, when there is a decrease in perceptions of collection action problems, a loss of relevance of scientific advocacy in contributing to "rationalist consensus-seeking" (including the silencing of scientific evidence as "Fake News"), budgetary squeezes, or a weakening of the willingness to coordinate in the multi-level setting – are so far not well understood. I hope that this book's attempt in systematizing the co-existence of problem-solving and polity policies in actors' perceptions of, and euphoric turns to, analytical tools will stimulate respective research agendas.

Overall, the reflections in this section lend support to the Jessopian notion of "strategic selectivity". Clearly, structures constrain actors' sense-making processes not just around public policy governance at large (e.g., what counts as risky behavior in different political economies of food production: Borraz et al., 2020), but also for the seemingly more mundane analytical tools. For example, unlike their British homologues in Whitehall, the German government cannot easily work around the constitutional distribution of executive power and cannot – in most policy domains – simply coerce states and municipalities to adopt risk-analytical inspection planning. At the same time, my study also confirms that contextualized meaning-making always involves "scope . . . for actions to overwhelm, circumvent, or subvert structural constraints" (Jessop, 2016, p. 55). This is obvious, for instance, in actors' attempts to re-distribute accountability for funding flood prevention upward to the Federal level based on differential risk analysis or in the analysis-based efforts of state-level work safety inspectorates to forge a stronger mandate and ringfence budgets for their activities. Overall, interpretations of analytical tools are simultaneously structured by contextual conditions and are cherished as devices for re-working these very conditions.

9.3 Analyze and rule: analytical tools as game-changers in public administrations

Yet a different question – and one going beyond the original aims of this book – is whether the re-working of context conditions in multi-level settings really succeeds because of analytical "turns", and if so under which conditions? My IPA focused on administrators' reported *perceptions* of why risk analysis is attractive to them. It does not assume a straightforward linearity of interpretations, intentions, and change. And yet, the study provides noteworthy observations on how actors' semiotic wielding of risk analysis contributes to stability and change of the underlying decision-making structures. The book hence connects research on analytical tools to insights from critical governance analysis (see Introduction) according to which our research must "[synthesize] the discursive conditions of what actors think is possible with the material social action of creation that can challenge these conditions of possibility, even accidentally" (Carmel, 2019, p. 25). In this final section, I provide some examples of how actors' interpretations and uses of analytical tools as *polity policies* – as means to re-organize decision-making structures – can turn into actual game-changers in the public administration.

First, my findings highlight that analytical tools can *stabilize* the interactions and structures within a multi-level administration. The best example for a stabilizing effect of risk analysis concerns its perception and use in food safety controls. A risk-based algorithm, using the platform of the EU Control Regulation but going much beyond its requirements for common risk analysis, reinforces the existing allocation of power between central steering and local autonomous enforcement and curtails the remaining scope for the latter further. This example suggests that risk analysis and a related algorithmic inspection software can sustain the infamous institutional stability of the German public administration through smaller scale analytical adaptations (Ellwein, 2001; Seibel, 2001) or "procedural reconstitution" (Döhler, 2006, p. 219). We also find stabilizing effects of an analytical tool in work safety where the risk-based attempt to defend a weakly endowed mandate seems to bear fruits, at least from the viewpoint of the 2017 SLIC report which praises improved coordination and strategic design of enforcement activities in Germany. Future research will have to specify more systematically the conditions under which the stabilization of existing positions and distributions of power through the adoption of analytical tools succeeds or fails in different settings.

My cases also evidence, second, that risk analysis can turn into a game changer. Because the allocation of authority and power is always also itself at stake in policy-making (Jessop, 2016; Carmel, 2019), and because such positional struggles can be expected to be pronounced in complex decision-making structures, it cannot surprise that analytical tools can shift the grounds for decisions over who should be in charge of policy-making in a domain and why. My German cases show that where there is no strong consensus among actors on the "right" allocation of authority and mandates across the multiple levels of executive federalism, the re-distribution of such powers can itself become the key target in promotions of an analytical tool and wield material consequences in a domain. In German flood prevention, for example, central level actors in Brussels and Berlin keenly expanded central monitoring and steering of local prevention activities in the guise of coordinated risk mapping. The EU bureaucrat's desire to entice soft harmonization or the Federal Ministry of the Environment's "insisting" on better coordination within the country did not remain in the realm of wishful thinking. Central reporting structures for risk analysis and risk management, and risk-based financial incentives for coordinated flood prevention have indeed engendered harmonization effects already. For example, the National Flood Protection Program incentivizes Länder to plan prevention measures more solidaristically across political borders in return for getting access to national funds. With common risk mapping, the weight of national prescription of what is appropriate and effective prevention planning – accumulating to more than one hundred tangible measures worth 5.4 billion Euros until 2030 – has measurably increased in a domain that had been extremely decentralized and uncoordinated so far. This makes risk analysis an effective tool of meta-governance (cf., e.g., Jessop, 2016) for the central state in a domain where it so far lacked hierarchical steering competencies. Just like in Scott's (1998) account of the French metric system's historical function in furnishing central administrative powers (Introduction), risk analysis can contribute to unitarization or even centralization of administrative actions in contemporary multi-level administrations.

And yet, the book's analysis also recognized that transformative effects do not usually unfold *because* of, or in line with, any one actor's intentions. Speaking with Jessop (2016, p. 55), once more: "because subjects are never unitary, never fully aware of the conditions that affect (their) strategic action, never fully equipped to engage in strategic reflection and learning, there are no guarantees that they will largely realize their strategic goals. Indeed, for the most subjects, this is unlikely". This is certainly true of actors' strategic interpretation of analytical tools in this study. For example, the makeup of decision-making in flood prevention might transform much beyond the original intentions of the Federal level, because sub-central level actors spun the "initial" meaning of risk analysis. The spinning went from better policy coordination among autonomous states and municipalities toward the re-allocation of accountability for high-risk scenarios of transregional scope to the central level. This powerful role of analytical tools in confirming or transforming actors' relative influence in a policy domain, ought to become a more systematic focus in research on multi-level administrations beyond immediate problem-solving foci.

If anything, the 2020/21 pandemic governance highlights the need to keep on studying the role of analytical models in multi-level policy-making along the lines projected in this book. Has the coordinated use of color-coded Corona "risk maps" within Germany since summer 2020 contributed to rational consensus-finding among state Minister Presidents? Has the public visibility of yellow dots turning red and dark red on this map – representing the soaring infection rates in the over 400 autonomous municipal districts over the autumn – helped justify the extension of exceptional Federal executive authorities for the Ministry of Health in October 2020? Will we even observe a more lasting unitarization or even centralization of governance in public health based on analytical groundwork, as already demanded by some Länder (Der Spiegel, 2020)? Why has the EU Commission adopted and adapted Germany's analytical approach (cf. Figure 1.1 in Introduction)? Will doing so enable closer coordination of lock-down measures across EU member-states?

How will Corona risk maps change Brussels' so far limited role in governing the pandemic? For example, do member states follow the Council of the European Union's (2020) proposal that mobility should *not* be restricted for green dots on the maps? Whatever answers future research on analytical tools will provide, the COVID-19 crisis illustrates their great relevance beyond scholarly spheres.

Note

1 (Hutter, 2005, p. 1).

APPENDIX

TABLE A1 Primary sources and materials per case

	Food safety controls	*Flood prevention*	*Work safety controls*
Key legislation	EU Regulation 882 (2004) on official controls amended by EU Regulation 625 (2017) General Administrative Decree AVV RÜb (2008, last amended 2017) EU Regulation 178 (2002) on general food law (transposed with German General Food Law 2005)	EU Directive 2007/60/EC on flood risk management German Flood Prevention Law 2005	*No binding legislation on risk analysis*
Additional documents	AVV RÜb appendix 1 with model risk analysis (not coercive but widely emulated) LAV Document 08-VA-AGQM-01 Länder guidelines on risk-based controls	LAWA guidelines on flood protection 1995 LAWA strategy paper on transposition of directive (2008) LAWA recommendations on flood risk mapping and management 2010	ASMK (2011) tasks LASI with working toward common risk-based principles for controls (TOP 7.6) LASI LV 1 (2014b) LASI excel worksheet on basic risk categorization (2014a)

	Food safety controls	*Flood prevention*	*Work safety controls*
	PowerPoint presentation on risk-oriented approach in North Rhine Westphalia National control plan und Länder specific control plans	LAWA internal excel worksheet on National Flood Protection Programme including funding criteria (2014) Bundesrechnungshof report on National Flood Protection Programme (2016) Several implementation guidelines by Ländern	SLIC reports (2006, 2017) annual ASMK procedures (2012–2018) Länder guidelines on risk-oriented controls Internal PowerPoint presentations on the application of risk-based control approach in several Länder
Interviews conducted between 2013 and 2017	9 interviews/11 interviewees with 2 Länder, Bund, EU FSY_EU (conducted by Mara Wesseling) FSY 1_Land A[1] FSY 2_Land A (municipal level) FSY 3_Federal level FSY 4_Federal level FSY 5_Land B FSY 6_Federal level FSY 7–8–9_Land B (municipal level) FSY 10_Land A (municipal level)	11 interviews/14 interviewees with 5 Länder, Bund, 1 Riparian Catchment, EU FLO_EU FLO 1_Land A (municipal level) FLO 2_Land A (municipal level) FLO 3–4_Catchment A FLO 5–6_Land B FLO 7–8_Federal level FLO 9_Land C FLO 10_Land C (municipal level) FLO 11_Land D FLO 12_Land E FLO 13_Land A (municipal level, conducted by Vera Linke)	8 interviews/14 interviewees with 6 Länder, EU OHS-EU OHS 1 Land A OHS 2_3_4 Land A (with municipal level) OHS 5 Land B OHS 6_7_8_9 Land C (with municipal level) OHS 10_11 Land D OHS 12 Land E OHS 13 Land F
Questionnaire on adoption process for RA	13 Länder (missing: Bayern, Niedersachsen, Thüringen; collected in 2015 via the head of a professional association of food safety inspectors)		
Published work from HowSAFE project which discusses case	Borraz et al., 2020 Paul, 2016	Demeritt et al., 2017 Paul, Bouder and Wesseling, 2016 Paul, 2016	Paul und Huber, 2015 Paul, 2016 Rothstein et al., 2019 Rothstein, Paul and Demeritt, 2020

1 Codings of interviews do not match across cases (Land A in work safety is not Land A in flood prevention, etc.).

BIBLIOGRAPHY

Abels, G. and Kobusch, A. (2010). *Regulation of food safety in the EU: Changing patterns of multi-level governance.* Available at: http://regulation.upf.edu/dublin-10-papers/2F3.pdf.

Acciai, C. and Capano, G. (2020). Policy instruments at work: A meta-analysis of their applications. *Public Administration,* n/a(n/a), p. e12673. doi:10.1111/padm.12673.

Alder, K. (2002). *The measure of all things: The seven-year odyssey and hidden error that transformed the world.* New York: Free Press.

Allemeyer, M.L. (2006). *'Kein Land ohne Deich . . . Lebenswelten einer Küstengesellschaft in der Frühen Neuzeit.* Göttingen: Vandenhoeck & Ruprecht.

Amt für Arbeitsschutz der Freien und Hansestadt Hamburg. (2008). *OHS in Hamburg. The inspection concept.* Hamburg. Available at: www.hamburg.de/aufsichtskonzept-arbeitsschutz/

Ansell, C.K. and Vogel, D. (2006). *What's the beef? The contested governance of European food safety.* Cambridge, MA: MIT Press.

Arbeits- und Sozialministerkonferenz. (2011). *Ergebnisprotokoll der 88. Konferenz der Ministerinnen und Minister, Senatorinnen und Senatoren für Arbeit und Soziales der Länder.* Leipzig.

Arbeits- und Sozialministerkonferenz. (2014). *Ergebnisprotokoll der 91. Konferenz der Ministerinnen und Minister, Senatorinnen und Senatoren für Arbeit und Soziales der Länder.* Mainz. Available at: https://asmkintern.rlp.de/fileadmin/asmkintern/Beschluesse/Beschluesse_91_ASMK_Extern/ergebnisprotokoll_91_asmk_neu.pdf.

Arbeits- und Sozialministerkonferenz. (2018). *Ergebnisprotokoll der 95. Konferenz der Ministerinnen und Minister, Senatorinnen und Senatoren für Arbeit und Soziales der Länder.* Münster. Available at: https://asmkintern.rlp.de/fileadmin/asmkintern/Beschluesse/Beschluesse_95_ASMK_Extern/Externes_Ergebnisprotokoll_ASMK_2018.pdf.

Atkinson, G. (2015). Cost-benefit analysis: A tool that is both useful and influential? In: A.J. Jordan and J.R. Turnpenny, eds., *The tools of policy formulation: Actors, capacities, venues and effects.* Cheltenham, UK: Edward Elgar Publishing, pp. 76–99.

Aven, T. (2003). *Foundations of risk analysis: A knowledge and decision-oriented perspective.* Chichester, UK: John Wiley & Sons.

Bähr, H. (2010). *The politics of means and ends: Policy instruments in the European Union.* London: Routledge.

Baldwin, G.R. and Veljanovski, C.G. (1984). Regulation by cost-benefit analysis. *Public Administration*, 62(1), pp. 51–69. doi:10.1111/j.1467-9299.1984.tb00544.x.

Baldwin, R. and Black, J. (2016). Driving priorities in risk-based regulation: What's the problem? *Journal of Law and Society*, 43(4), pp. 565–595. doi:10.1111/jols.12003.

Balla, S.J. (1998). Administrative procedures and political control of the bureaucracy. *The American Political Science Review*, 92(3), pp. 663–673. doi:10.2307/2585488.

Baumgartner, F.R. (2014). Ideas, paradigms and confusions. *Journal of European Public Policy*, 21(3), pp. 475–480. doi:10.1080/13501763.2013.876180.

Beck, U. (1992). *Risk society: Towards a new modernity*. London: Sage.

Behnke, N. (2015). Stand und Perspektiven der Föderalismusforschung. *Aus Politik und Zeitgeschichte*, (28–30), pp. 9–16.

Behnke, N. (2020). Föderalismus in der (Corona-)Krise? Föderale Funktionen, Kompetenzen und Entscheidungsprozesse. *Aus Politik und Zeitgeschichte*, (35–37). Available at: www.bpb.de/apuz/314343/foederalismus-in-der-corona-krise.

Bekkers, V., Fenger, M. and Scholten, P. (2017). *Public policy in action: Perspectives on the policy process*. Cheltenham, UK: Edward Elgar Publishing.

Béland, D. and Howlett, M. (2016). How solutions chase problems: Instrument constituencies in the policy process. *Governance*, 29(3), pp. 393–409. doi:10.1111/gove.12179.

Bemelmans-Videc, M.-L., Rist, R.C. and Vedung, E.O., eds. (2011). *Carrots, sticks, and sermons: Policy instruments and their evaluation*. New Brunswick: Transaction Publishers.

Benz, A. (2001). Verflechtung der Verwaltungsebenen. In: K. König and H. Siedenkopf, eds., *Öffentliche Verwaltung in Deutschland*. Baden-Baden: Nomos, pp. 165–184.

Benz, A. (2009). *Politik in Mehrebenensystemen*. Wiesbaden: VS Verlag für Sozialwissenschaften.

Benz, A., Detemple, J. and Heinz, D. (2016). *Varianten und Dynamiken der Politikverflechtung im deutschen Bundesstaat*. Baden-Baden: Nomos.

Bernstein, P.L. (1996). *Against the gods: The remarkable story of risk*. New York: Wiley.

Bjørnholt, B. and Larsen, F. (2014). The politics of performance measurement: "Evaluation use as mediator for politics". *Evaluation*. doi:10.1177/1356389014551485.

Black, J. (2005). The emergence of risk-based regulation and the new public management in the UK. *Public law*, 2005(Autumn), pp. 512–549.

Black, J. (2010). The role of risk in regulatory processes. In: R. Baldwin, M. Cave and M. Lodge, eds., *The Oxford handbook of regulation*. Oxford: Oxford University Press.

Black, J. and Baldwin, R. (2010). Really responsive risk-based regulation. *Law & Policy*, 32(2), pp. 181–213. doi:10.1111/j.1467-9930.2010.00318.x.

Blanc, F. (2014). *Inspection reforms: Why, how and with what results?* Paris: OECD. Available at: www.oecd.org/regreform/Inspection%20reforms%20-%20web%20-F.%20Blanc.pdf.

Blatter, J. and Haverland, M. (2012). *Designing case studies – Explanatory approaches*. Basingstoke: Palgrave Macmillan.

Bora, A. (2007). Risk, risk society, risk behavior, and social problems. In: G. Ritzer, ed., *The Blackwell encyclopedia of sociology*. Oxford: Blackwell, pp. 3926–3932.

Borraz, O. et al. (2020). Why regulators assess risk differently: Regulatory style, business organisation, and the varied practice of risk-based food safety inspections across the EU. *Regulation & Governance*. First Online. doi:10.1111/rego.12320.

Börzel, T.A. (2002). Föderative Staaten in einer entgrenzten Welt: Regionaler standortwettbeweerb oder gemeinsames regieren jenseits des nationalstaats? In: A. Benz and G. Lehmbruch, eds., *Föderalismus: Analysen in entwicklungsgeschichtlicher und vergleichender Perspektive*. Wiesbaden: VS Verlag für Sozialwissenschaften, pp. 363–388.

Boswell, C. (2008). The political functions of expert knowledge: Knowledge and legitimation in European Union immigration policy. *Journal of European Public Policy*, 15(4), pp. 471–488.

Boswell, C. (2015). The double life of targets in public policy: Disciplining and signaling in UK asylum policy. *Public Administration*, 93(2), pp. 490–505. doi:10.1111/padm.12134.

Boswell, C. (2018). *Manufacturing political trust: Targets and performance measurement in public policy*. Cambridge: Cambridge University Press.

Bouder, F., Slavin, D. and Löfstedt, R. (2007). *The tolerability of risks, a new framework for risk management*. London: Earthscan.

Bourdieu, P. (1991). *Language and symbolic power*. Cambridge: Polity Press.

Breuer, S. (1990). Rationale Herrschaft. Zu einer Kategorie Max Webers. *Politische Vierteljahresschrift*, 31(1), pp. 4–32.

Brückner, B. (2017). Risikoorientierte Steuerung der Aufsichtstätigkeit. Presentation at the conference. *A+A Forum Arbeitsschutzverwaltung*. 19 October 2017, Düsseldorf.

Brunsson, N. (1989). *The organisation of hypocrisy: Talk, decisions and actions in organisations*. Chichester: John Wiley & Sons.

Bubeck, P., Kreibech, H., Penning-Rowsell, E., Klijn, F. and Botzen, W. (2012). *Explaining differences in flood risk management approaches in Europe and the USA – A comparative analysis, in 2012*. Rotterdam: Taylor & Francis.

Bund/Länder-Arbeitsgemeinschaft Wasser (LAWA). (1995). *Leitlinien für einen zukunftsweisenden Hochwasserschutz [Guidelines for forward-looking flood protection]*. Stuttgart. Available at: www.lawa.de/documents/Leitlinien_d59.pdf (Accessed March 2013).

Bund/Länder-Arbeitsgemeinschaft Wasser (LAWA). (2008). *Strategie zur Umsetzung der Hochwasserrisikomanagement-Richtlinie in Deutschland [Transposition strategy for the flood risk management directive in Germany]*. Kiel. Available at: www.bmu.de/fileadmin/Daten_BMU/Download_PDF/Binnengewaesser/hochwasserschutzprogramm_bericht_bf.pdf.

Bund/Länder-Arbeitsgemeinschaft Wasser (LAWA). (2010a). *Empfehlungen zur Aufstellung von Hochwassergefahrenkarten und Hochwasserrisikokarten [Recommendations for the establishment of flood hazard maps and flood risk maps]*. Dresden: LAWA. Available at: www.lawa.de/documents/hwgk15062010_1552299609.pdf (Accessed March 2013).

Bund/Länder-Arbeitsgemeinschaft Wasser (LAWA). (2010b). *Empfehlungen zur Aufstellung von Hochwasserrisikomanagementplänen [Recommendations for the establishment of flood risk management plans]*. Dresden: LAWA. Available at: www.lawa.de/documents/EmpfHWRMPl_25_260310_d20.pdf (Accessed March 2013).

Bund/Länder-Arbeitsgemeinschaft Wasser (LAWA). (2014). *Nationales Hochwasserschutzprogramm: Kriterien und Bewertungsmaßstäbe für die Identifikation und Priorisierung von wirksamen Maßnahmen*. Kiel: Bund/Länderarbeitsgemeinschaft Wasser [LAWA].

Bundesamt für Verbraucherschutz und Lebensmittelsicherheit. (2016). *Jahresbericht 2015 der Bundesrepublik Deutschland zum mehrjährigen nationalen Kontrollplan nach Verordnung (EG) Nr. 882/2004*. Berlin. Available at: www.bvl.bund.de/SharedDocs/Downloads/01_Lebensmittel/06_mnkp_dokumente/mnkp_Jahresbericht_2015.pdf?__blob=publicationFile&v=5.

Bundesamt für Verbraucherschutz und Lebensmittelsicherheit and Robert Koch Institut. (2017). *Gemeinsamer nationaler Bericht des BVL und RKI zu lebensmittelbedingten Krankheitsausbrüchen in Deutschland 2016*. Berlin. Available at: www.rki.de/DE/Content/Infekt/Ausbrueche/LM/Jahresbericht_2016.pdf?__blob=publicationFile.

Bundesanstalt für Arbeitsschutz und Arbeitsmedizin. (2012). *Das Risikokonzept für krebserzeugende Stoffe des Ausschusses für Gefahrstoffe. Von der Grenzwertorientierung zur Maßnahmenorientierung.*

Dortmund. Available at: www.baua.de/de/Publikationen/Broschueren/A82.html (Accessed February 2013).

Bundesanstalt für Arbeitsschutz und Arbeitsmedizin. (2016). *Sicherheit und Gesundheit bei der Arbeit 2015 – Unfallverhütungsbericht Arbeit*. Dortmund. Available at: www.baua.de/DE/Angebote/Publikationen/Berichte/Suga-2015.pdf?__blob=publicationFile&v=5.

Bundesministerium für Ernährung, Landwirtschaft und Verbraucherschutz. (2013). *Food safety strategies*. Berlin. Available at: www.bmelv.de/SharedDocs/Downloads/EN/Publications/FoodSafetyStrategies.pdf?__blob=publicationFile.

Bundesministerium für Umwelt, Naturschutz und nukleare Sicherheit. (2019). *Nationales Hochwasserschutzprogramm – BMU-Cluster*. Berlin. Available at: www.bmu.de/FQ81 (Accessed August 2019).

Bundesrechnungshof. (2016). *Bericht an den Haushaltsausschuss des Deutschen Bundestages nach § 88 Abs. 2 BHO Aufgabenwahrnehmung des Bundesministeriums für Umwelt, Naturschutz, Bau und Reaktorsicherheit beim Nationalen Hochwasserschutzprogramm*. Potsdam. Available at: www.bundesrechnungshof.de/de/veroeffentlichungen/produkte/beratungsberichte/langfassungen/langfassungen-2016/aufgabenwahrnehmung-des-bundesmi-nisteriums-fuer-umwelt-naturschutz-bau-und-reaktorsicherheit-beim-nationalen-hochwasserschutzprogramm-pdf.

Bundesrepublik Deutschland. (1996). *Gesetz über die Durchführung von Maßnahmen des Arbeitsschutzes zur Verbesserung der Sicherheit und des Gesundheitsschutzes der Beschäftigten bei der Arbeit. ArbSchG*. Available at: www.gesetze-im-internet.de/bundesrecht/arbschg/gesamt.pdf.

Bundesrepublik Deutschland. (2008). *Allgemeine Verwaltungsvorschrift über Grundsätze zur Durchführung der amtlichen Überwachung der Einhaltung lebensmittelrechtlicher, weinrechtlicher, futtermittelrechtlicher und tabakrechtlicher Vorschriften (AVV RüB): Last amended in 2017 for EU Regulation 2017/625. AVV RüB*. Available at: www.verwaltungsvorschriften-im-internet.de/bsvwvbund_03062008_3158100140002.htm.

Bundeszentrale für politische Bildung. (2012). *Der geopferte Rhein*. Available at: www.bpb.de/gesellschaft/umwelt/hochwasserschutz/169948/der-geopferte-rhein (Accessed March 2018).

Buschhüter, E., van Dillen, A., Menn, K. and Paas, R. (2018). Das nationale hochwasserschutzprogramm. *Natur und Landschaft*, 93(2), pp. 50–53.

Cairney, P. and Weible, C.M. (2015). Comparing and contrasting Peter Hall's paradigms and ideas with the advocacy coalition framework. In: J. Hogan and M. Howlett, eds., *Policy paradigms in theory and practice: Discourses, ideas and anomalies in public policy dynamics*. New York: Palgrave Macmillan (Studies in the political economy of public policy), pp. 83–99.

Capano, G. and Lippi, A. (2017). How policy instruments are chosen: Patterns of decision makers' choices. *Policy Sciences*, 50(2), pp. 269–293. doi:10.1007/s11077-016-9267-8.

Carmel, E. (1999). Concepts, context and discourse in a comparative case study. *International Journal of Social Research Methodology*, 2, pp. 141–150.

Carmel, E., ed. (2019a). *Governance analysis: Critical enquiry at the intersection of politics, policy and society*. Cheltenham, UK: Edward Elgar Publishing.

Carmel, E. (2019b). Introduction to governance analysis: Critical enquiry at the intersection of politics, policy and society. In: E. Carmel, ed., *Governance analysis: Critical enquiry at the intersection of politics, policy and society*. Cheltenham, UK: Edward Elgar Publishing, pp. 2–23.

Carmel, E. (2019c). Regimes of governing practices, socio-political order and contestation. In: E. Carmel, ed., *Governance analysis: Critical enquiry at the intersection of politics, policy and society*. Cheltenham, UK: Edward Elgar Publishing, pp. 24–46.

Carmel, E. and Harlock, J. (2008). Instituting the "third sector" as a governable terrain: Partnership, procurement and performance in the UK. *Policy & Politics*, 36(2), pp. 155–171. doi:10.1332/030557308783995017.

Carmel, E. and Kan, H. (2019). Expertise, governing and migration in Europe. In: A. Weinar, S. Bonjour and L. Zhyznomirska, eds., *The Routledge Handbook of the politics of European migration*. London: Routledge, pp. 71–81.

Chandler, D. (2014). Beyond neoliberalism: Resilience, the new art of governing complexity. *Resilience*, 2(1), pp. 47–63. doi:10.1080/21693293.2013.878544.

Chandler, D. (2016). How the world learned to stop worrying and love failure: Big data, resilience and emergent causality. *Millennium*, 44(3), pp. 391–410. doi:10.1177/0305829816636673.

Cheong, L. et al. (2016). Evaluating the impact of visualization of wildfire hazard upon decision-making under uncertainty. *International Journal of Geographical Information Science*, 30(7), pp. 1377–1404. doi:10.1080/13658816.2015.1131829.

Cohen, M.D., March, J.G. and Olsen, J.P. (1972). A garbage can model of organizational choice. *Administrative Science Quarterly*, pp. 1–25.

Commission of the European Communities. (2012). *The European commission impact assessment board*. Prague.

Commission of the European Communities. (2015). *Better regulation guidelines (staff working document)*. SWD (2017) 350. Brussels. Available at: https://ec.europa.eu/info/sites/info/files/better-regulation-guidelines.pdf.

Commission of the European Communities. (2020). *European commission statement on the coordination of measures restricting free movement in the European Union related to the coronavirus pandemic*. Press release. Brussels. Available at: https://ec.europa.eu/commission/presscorner/detail/en/statement_20_1871.

Committee of Senior Labour Inspectors (SLIC). (2006). *SLIC Evaluation report on the German inspection system*. Available at: www.vdgab.de/Ablage/SLIC-Bericht_deutsch.pdf.

Committee of Senior Labour Inspectors (SLIC). (2017). *SLIC Evaluation report on the German inspection system*. Available at: http://www.arbeitswelt.hessen.de/sites/awh/files/dateien/slic_report_2017_19_06_2019.pdf.

Council of the European Communities. (1989). *Council Directive 89/656/EEC of 30 November 1989 on the minimum health and safety requirements for the use by workers of personal protective equipment at the workplace (third individual directive within the meaning of Article 16 (1) of Directive 89/391/EEC). 89/656/EEC*. (1989). Available at: http://eur-lex.europa.eu/LexUriServ/LexUriServ.do?uri=OJ:L:1989:393:0018:0028:EN:PDF.

Council of the European Union. (2000). *Directive establishing a framework for community action in the field of water policy*. (2000/60/EC). Available at: http://eur-lex.europa.eu/LexUriServ/LexUriServ.do?uri=CONSLEG:2000L0060:20011216:EN:PDF (Accessed March 2013).

Council of the European Union. (2002). *Regulation laying down the general principles and requirements of food law, establishing the European food safety authority and laying down procedures in matters of food safety* (Regulation 178(2002) final). Available at: http://eur-lex.europa.eu/LexUriServ/LexUriServ.do?uri=OJ:L:2002:031:0001:0024:EN:PDF.

Council of the European Union. (2004). *Regulation on official controls performed to ensure the verification of compliance with feed and food law, animal health and animal welfare rules* (Regulation 882(2004) final). Available at: http://eur-lex.europa.eu/LexUriServ/LexUriServ.do?uri=OJ:L:2004:165:0001:0141:EN:PDF.

Council of the European Union. (2007). *Directive on the assessment and management of flood risks* (2007/60/EC). Available at: http://eur-lex.europa.eu/LexUriServ/LexUriServ.do?uri=OJ:L:2007:288:0027:0034:EN:PDF.

Council of the European Union. (2017). *Regulation on official controls and other official activities performed to ensure the application of food and feed law, rules on animal health and welfare, plant health and plant protection products* (Regulation 2017/625 final). Available at: http://eur-lex.europa.eu/legal-content/DE/TXT/?uri=uriserv:OJ.L_.2017.095.01.0001.01.DEU&toc=OJ:L:2017:095:TOC.

Council of the European Union. (2020). *COVID-19: Council adopts a recommendation to coordinate measures affecting free movement.* Available at: www.consilium.europa.eu/en/press/press-releases/2020/10/13/covid-19-council-adopts-a-recommendation-to-coordinate-measures-affecting-free-movement/.

Davoudi, S. (2012). Resilience: A bridging concept or a dead end? *Planning Theory & Practice*, 13(2), pp. 299–307.

Defra. (2004). *Making space for water: Developing a new Government strategy for flood and coastal erosion risk management in England. A consultation exercise.* London: Department for Environment, Farming, and Rural Affairs. Available at: www.look-up.org.uk/2013/wp-content/uploads/2014/02/Making-space-for-water.pdf.

Dehousse, R. (2004). La méthode ouverte de la coordination, quand l'instrument tient lieu de politique. In: P. Lascoumes and P. Le Galès, eds., *Gouverner par les instruments.* Paris: Presses de Sciences Po.

Delogu, B. (2016). *Risk analysis and governance in EU policy making and regulation: An introductory guide.* [Cham] Switzerland: Springer.

Demeritt, D. et al. (2015). Mobilizing risk: Explaining policy transfer in food and occupational safety regulation in the UK. *Environment and Planning A*, 47, pp. 373–91. doi:10.1068/a140085p.

Demeritt, D. et al. (2017). *Making space for failure? Rationalising risk-based flood management in Europe* (HowSAFE Working Papers, No. 8). London: King's College.

Department for Business, Enterprise and Regulatory Reform [BERR]. (2007). *Regulators' compliance code: A statutory code of practice for regulators.* London.

Department for Work and Pensions [DWP]. (2013). *New code curbs unnecessary council safety checks.* Available at: www.gov.uk/government/news/new-code-curbs-unnecessary-council-safety-checks (Accessed: 20 December 2016).

Der Spiegel. (2020). *Merkel verteidigt Föderalismus gegen Forderung Söders.* Published 19 October.

Desrosières, A. (2002). *The politics of large numbers – A history of statistical reasoning.* Cambridge, MA: Harvard University Press.

Deutscher Bundestag. (2015). *Bund soll mehr für Hochwasserschutz zahlen (Bericht aus dem Umweltausschuss).* Available at: www.bundestag.de/dokumente/textarchiv/2015/kw10_pa_umwelt-360140 (Accessed August 2019).

Deutscher Bundestag. (2018). *Antwort der Bundesregierung auf die Kleine Anfrage der Abgeordneten Beate Müller-Gemmeke, Markus Kurth, Sven Lehmann, weiterer Abgeordneter und der Fraktion BÜNDNIS 90/DIE GRÜNEN.* Berlin.

Di Palma, G. (2013). *The modern state subverted: Risk and the deconstruction of solidarity.* Colchester: ECPR Press.

DiMaggio, P.J. and Powell, W.W. (1983). The iron cage revisited: Institutional isomorphism and collective rationality in organizational fields. *American Sociological Review*, 48(2), pp. 147–160. doi:10.2307/2095101.

Disco, C. (2002). Remaking "Nature": The ecological turn in Dutch water management. *Science, Technology & Human Values*, 27(2), pp. 206–235.

Döhler, M. (2002). Institutional choice and bureaucratic autonomy in Germany. *West European Politics*, 25(1), pp. 101–124. doi:10.1080/713601587.

Döhler, M. (2006). Regulative Politik und die Transformation der klassischen Verwaltung. *Politische Vierteljahresschrift: Sonderheft*, (37), pp. 208–227.

Döhler, M. (2015). Das Politikfeld als analytische Kategorie. *der moderne staat – dms: Zeitschrift für Public Policy, Recht und Management*, 8(1), pp. 51–69.

Döhler, M. and Wegrich, K. (2010). Regulierung als Konzept und Instrument moderner Staatstätigkeit. *der moderne staat – Zeitschrift für Public Policy, Recht und Management*, (1), pp. 31–52.

Douglas, M. and Wildavsky, A. (1983). *Risk and culture: An essay on the selection of technological and environmental dangers*. Berkeley: University of California Press.

Dunlop, C.A. and Radaelli, C.M., eds. (2015). Impact Assessment in the European Union: Lessons from a research project. *European Journal of Risk Regulation*, 5(1), pp. 27–42.

Dunlop, C.A. and Radaelli, C.M., eds. (2016). *Handbook of regulatory impact assessment*. Cheltenham, UK: Edward Elgar Publishing.

Dunlop, C.A. et al. (2012). The many uses of regulatory impact assessment: A meta-analysis of EU and UK cases. *Regulation & Governance*, 6(1), pp. 23–45. doi:10.1111/j.1748-5991.2011.01123.x.

Dunsire, A. (1978). *Control in a bureaucracy*. New York: St Martin's Press.

Ellwein, T. (2001). Geschichte der Öffentlichen Verwaltung. In: K. König and H. Siedenkopf, eds., *Öffentliche Verwaltung in Deutschland*, 2nd ed. [first published 1997]. Baden-Baden: Nomos, pp. 39–53.

Ewald, F. (1986). *L'etat providence*. Paris: Bernard Grasset.

Fischer, F. (2003). Beyond empiricism: Policy analysis as deliberative practice. In: M.A. Hajer and H. Wagenaar, eds., *Deliberative policy analysis: Understanding governance in the network society*. Cambridge: Cambridge University Press, pp. 209–227.

Fischer, F. and Forester, J., eds. (1993). *The argumentative turn in policy analysis and planning*. Durham, NC: Duke University Press.

Fjørtoft, T.N. (2020). More power, more control: The legitimizing role of expertise in Frontex after the refugee crisis. *Regulation & Governance*. First Online. doi: 10.1111/rego.12373.

Gemeinsames Verbraucherschutzinformationssystem Niedersachsen (GeViN). (2007). *Leitfaden zur Risikobeurteilung von Betrieben im Fachbereich Lebensmittel in Niedersachsen*. Hannover.

Genschel, P. and Jachtenfuchs, M., eds. (2013). *Beyond the regulatory polity? The European integration of core state powers*. Reprint Edition. Oxford University Press.

Gerlinger, T. (2000). *Arbeitsschutz und europäische integration: Europäische Arbeitsschutzrichtlinien und nationalstaatliche Arbeitsschutzpolitik in Großbritannien und Deutschland*. Opladen: Leske + Budrich.

Gilardi, F. (2002). Policy credibility and delegation to independent regulatory agencies: A comparative empirical analysis. *Journal of European Public Policy*, 9(6), pp. 873–893. doi:10.1080/13501760220000 46409.

Gray, P. (2005). The politics of risk and young offenders' experiences of social exclusion and restorative justice. *British Journal of Criminology*, 45(6), pp. 938–957. doi:10.1093/bjc/azi018.

Grek, S. (2009). Governing by numbers: The PISA "effect" in Europe. *Journal of Education Policy*, 24(1), pp. 23–37. doi:10.1080/02680930802412669.

Groenleer, M.L.P. (2014). Agency autonomy actually: Managerial strategies, legitimacy, and the early development of the European union's agencies for drug and food safety regulation. *International Public Management Journal*, 17(2), pp. 255–292. doi:10.1080/10967494.2014.905416.

Grüne, J. (1994). *Anfänge staatlicher Lebensmittelüberwachung in Deutschland: der 'Vater der Lebensmittelchemie' Joseph König (1843–1930)*. Stuttgart: Franz Steiner Verlag.

Guidi, M. (2014). Delegation and varieties of capitalism: Explaining the independence of national competition agencies in the European union. *Comparative European Politics*, 12(3), pp. 343–365. doi:10.1057/cep.2013.6.

Haines, F. (2011). *The paradox of regulation: What regulation can achieve and what it cannot*. Cheltenham, UK: Edward Elgar Publishing.

Haines, F. (2013). Three risks, one solution? Exploring the relationship between risk and regulation. *The ANNALS of the American Academy of Political and Social Science*, 649(1), pp. 35–51. doi:10.1177/0002716213490884.

Hall, P.A. (1993). Policy paradigms, social learning, and the state: The case of economic policymaking in Britain. *Comparative Politics*, 25(3), pp. 275–296. doi:10.2307/422246.

Hall, P.A. and Taylor, R.C.R. (1996). Political science and the three new institutionalisms. *Political Studies*, 1996(XLIV), pp. 936–957.

Hampton, P. (2005). *Reducing administrative burdens: Effective inspection and enforcement*. administrative. London: HM Treasury.

Hartmann, T. and Albrecht, J. (2014). From flood protection to flood risk management: Condition-based and performance-based regulations in German water law. *Journal of Environmental Law*, 26(2), pp. 243–268.

Havinga, T. (2014). National variations in the implementation and enforcement of European food hygiene regulations: Comparing the structure of food controls and regulations between Scotland and the Netherlands. *Recht der Werkelijkheid,* 35(3), pp. 32–53.

Hay, C. (2004). Theory, stylized heuristic or self-fulfilling prophecy? The status of rational choice theory in public administration. *Public Administration*, 82(1), pp. 39–62. doi:10.1111/j.0033-3298.2004.00382.x.

Health and Safety Executive. (1989). *Annual report 1988/89*. London: Health and Safety Executive.

Heidbreder, E.G. (2013). Regulating capacity building by stealth: Pattern and extent of EU involvement in public administration. In: P. Genschel and M. Jachtenfuchs, eds., *Beyond the regulatory polity? The European integration of core state powers*. Oxford University Press.

Heidbreder, E.G. (2017). Strategies in multilevel policy implementation: Moving beyond the limited focus on compliance. *Journal of European Public Policy*, 24(9), pp. 1367–1384. doi:10.1080/13501763.2017.1314540.

Heidenreich, M. and Bischoff, G. (2008). The open method of co-ordination: A way to the Europeanization of social and employment policies? *Journal of Common Market Studies*, 46, pp. 497–532.

Heinelt, H. (2007). Do policies determine politics? In: F. Fischer, G.J. Miller and M.S. Sidney, eds., *Handbook of public policy analysis: Theory, politics, and methods*. Boca Raton: CRC Press, pp. 109–119.

Heinelt, H. (2016). *Governance und politisches Entscheiden: zur intersubjektiven Erschliessung der Grundlagen politischer Entscheidungen*. 1. Auflage. Baden Baden: Nomos.

Heinelt, H. and Knodt, M. (2011). *Policies within the EU multi-level system: Instruments and strategies of European governance*. Baden-Baden: Nomos.

Heintz, M.D., Hagemeier-Klose, M. and Wagner, K. (2012). Towards a risk governance culture in flood policy – Findings from the implementation of the "floods directive" in Germany. *Water*, 4(4), pp. 135–156.

Hennock, E.P. (2007). *The origin of the welfare state in England and Germany, 1850–1914: Social policies compared*. Cambridge: Cambridge University Press.

Herbst, A. (2004). *Transparenzstudie zur aktuellen Konzeption und Tätigkeit der staatlichen Arbeitsschutzaufsicht (Gewerbeaufsicht) in 16 Bundesländern*. Hamburg: Verein Arbeit & Gesundheit.

Hesselberger, D. (1995). *Das Grundgesetz. Kommentar für die Politische Bildung*. Bonn: Bundeszentrale für Politische Bildung.

Hierholzer, V. (2010). *Nahrung nach Norm. Regulierung von Nahrungsmittelqualität in der Industrialisierung 1871–1914*. Göttingen: Vandenhoeck & Ruprecht.

Hogan, J. and Howlett, M., eds. (2015). *Policy paradigms in theory and practice: Discourses, ideas and anomalies in public policy dynamics.* New York: Palgrave Macmillan (Studies in the political economy of public policy).

Hood, C. (1983). *The tools of government.* London: Palgrave Macmillan.

Hood, C. (1991). A public management for all seasons? *Public Administration*, 69(1), pp. 3–19. doi:10.1111/j.1467-9299.1991.tb00779.x.

Hood, C. (2007). Intellectual obsolescence and intellectual makeovers: Reflections on the tools of government after two decades. *Governance*, 20(1), pp. 127–144. doi:10.1111/j.1468-0491.2007.00347.x.

Hood, C. and Rothstein, H. (2001). Risk regulation under pressure problem solving or blame shifting? *Administration & Society*, 33(1), pp. 21–53. doi:10.1177/00953990122019677.

Hood, C., Rothstein, H. and Baldwin, R. (2001). *The government of risk: Understanding risk regulation regimes.* Oxford: Oxford University Press.

Hooghe, L. and Marks, G. (2001). *Multi-level governance and European integration.* Lanham, MD and Oxford: Rowman and Littlefield (Governance in Europe.).

Hooghe, L. and Marks, G. (2003). Unraveling the central state, but how? Types of multi-level governance. *American Political Science Review*, 97(2), pp. 233–243. doi:10.1017/S0003055403000649.

Howlett, M. (2011). *Designing public policies: Principles and instruments*, 1st ed. Abingdon and New York: Routledge.

Howlett, M. and Tosun, J. (2018). Policy styles: A new approach. In: M. Howlett and J. Tosun, eds., *Policy styles and policy-making: Exploring the linkages*, 1st ed. London and New York, NY: Routledge, pp. 3–21.

Hutter, B.M. (2005). *The attractions of risk-based regulation: Accounting for the emergence of risk ideas in regulation* (CARR Discussion Paper, No. 33). London School of Economics.

International Commission for the Protection of the Rhine (ICPR). (2013). *Nine states – One River Basin (web site of the ICPR).* Available at www.iksr.org/index.php?id=58&L=3&cHash=455fdab52ce6eafbf6f72632159564bf (Accessed March 2013).

International Commission for the Protection of the Rhine (ICPR). (2015). *Rhine atlas, 2015.* Available at: www.iksr.org/en/public-relations/documentsarchive/rhine-atlas/ (Accessed August 2019).

International Labour Organization (2011). *A guide to selected labour inspection systems (with special reference to OSH).* Geneva: ILO Working paper. Available at: http://www.ilo.org/labadmin/info/pubs/WCMS_160576/lang--en/index.htm.

Jankauskas, V. and Eckhard, S. (2019). International bureaucracies as strategic actors: How the better regulation reform strengthens the European commission. *Politische Vierteljahresschrift*, 60(4), pp. 681–699. doi:10.1007/s11615-019-00189-3.

Jann, W., Röber, M. and Wollmann, H., eds. (2006). *Public management – Grundlagen, Wirkungen, Kritik.* Berlin: Edition Sigma.

Janning, F. (2006). Koexistenz ohne Synergieeffekte? Über das Verhältnis von Policy-Forschung und Verwaltungswissenschaft. In: J. Bogumil, W. Jann and F. Nullmeier, eds., *Politik und Verwaltung.* Wiesbaden: VS Verlag für Sozialwissenschaften (PVS Sonderheft), pp. 77–96.

Jessop, B. (2008). *State power: A strategic-relational approach.* Cambridge: Polity Press.

Jessop, B. (2009). From governance to governance failure and from multi-level governance to multi-scalar meta-governance. In: B. Arts, A. Lagendijk and H. van Houtum, eds., *The disoriented state: Shifts in governmentality, territoriality and governance.* Dordrecht: Springer Netherlands (Environment & Policy), pp. 79–98. doi:10.1007/978-1-4020-9480-4_4.

Jessop, B. (2016). *The state: Past, present, future.* 1st ed. Cambridge and Malden, MA: Polity.

John, P. and Cole, A. (2000). When do institutions, policy sectors, and cities matter? Comparing networks of local policy makers in Britain and France. *Comparative Political Studies*, 33(2), pp. 248–268. doi:10.1177/0010414000033002004.

Kalberlah, F., Bloser, M. and Wachholz, C. (2005). *Toleranz- und Akzeptanzschwellen für Gesundheitsrisiken am Arbeitsplatz [Thresholds for tolerable and acceptable health risks at the workplace]*. Dortmund: Bundesanstalt für Arbeitsschutz und Arbeitsmedizin.

Katzenstein, P.J. (1987). *Policy and politics in West Germany: The growth of a semi-sovereign state*. Philadelphia: Temple University Press.

Kingdon, J.W. (1984). *Agendas, alternatives, and public policies*. Boston: Little Brown.

Klijn, F., Samuels, P. and Os, A.V. (2008). Towards flood risk management in the EU: State of affairs with examples from various European countries. *International Journal of River Basin Management*, 6(4), pp. 307–321.

Knipschild, K. (2003). *Lebensmittelsicherheit als Aufgabe des Veterinär- und Lebensmittelrechts. Risikoverwaltung im Europäischen Binnenmarkt. [Food safety as task of veterinary and food law. Risk administration in the European internal market]*. Baden-Baden: Nomos.

Krapohl, S. (2003). Risk regulation in the EU between interests and expertise: The case of BSE. *Journal of European Public Policy*, 10(2), pp. 189–207. doi:10.1080/1350176032000058991.

Krieger, K. (2011). *Putting varieties of risk-based governance in institutional context: The case of flood management regimes in Germany and England in the 1990s and 2000s*. London: King's College London.

Krieger, K. (2013). The limits and variety of risk-based governance: The case of flood management in Germany and England. *Regulation & Governance*, 7(2), pp. 236–257.

Kropp, S. (2010). *Kooperativer Föderalismus und Politikverflechtung*. Wiesbaden: VS Verlag für Sozialwissenschaften.

Kuhlmann, S. (2010). New public management for the "classical continental European administration": Modernization at the local level in Germany, France and Italy. *Public Administration*, 88(4), pp. 1116–1130. doi:10.1111/j.1467-9299.2010.01869.x.

Kuhlmann, S., Bogumil, J. and Grohs, S. (2008). Evaluating administrative modernization in German local governments: Success or failure of the "new steering model"? *Public Administration Review*, 68(5), pp. 851–863. doi:10.1111/j.1540-6210.2008.00927.x.

Land Niedersachsen. (2018). *Die Strategie Niedersachsens zur digitalen Transformation. Masterplan Digitalisierung*. Available at: https://niedersachsen.de/startseite/themen/digitales_niedersachsen/masterplan_digitalisierung/zweites_buch_digitalisierung_von_wirtschaft_und_gesellschaft/zweites-buch-digitalisierung-von-wirtschaft-und-gesellschaft-167943.html.

Länderausschuss für Arbeitsschutz und Sicherheitstechnik [LASI]. (2011). *Grundsätze der behördlichen Systemkontrolle (guidelines for OHS system audit)*. Available at: http://lasi-info.com/uploads/media/lv54_01.pdf.

Länderausschuss für Arbeitsschutz und Sicherheitstechnik [LASI]. (2014a). *Risikogrundeinstufung nach Branchen (interne Exceltabelle)*.

Länderausschuss für Arbeitsschutz und Sicherheitstechnik [LASI]. (2014b). *Überwachungs- und Beratungstätigkeit der Arbeitsschutzbehörden der Länder – Grundsätze und Standards [Inspection and consulting activities of the länder labour inspectorates – Principles and standards]*. Available at: https://lasi-info.com/uploads/media/LV_1_Grundsaetze_01.12.2016.pdf.

Landesamt für Verbraucherschutz, Arbeitsschutz und Gesundheit des Landes Brandenburg. (2013). *Brandenburger Wege (internal PowerPoint presention)*. Potsdam.

Larisch, J. (2009). *Arbeitsschutz und ökonomische Rationalität: Ansätze und Grenzen einer 'Verbetrieblichung' von Sicherheit und Gesundheitsschutz*. Berlin: Edition Sigma.

Lascoumes, P. and Le Galès, P. (2004). *Gouverner par les instruments*. Paris: Presses de Sciences Po. Available at: http://www.pressesdesciencespo.fr/fr/livre/?GCOI=27246100737700.

Lascoumes, P. and Le Galès, P.(2007). Introduction: Understanding public policy through its instruments – From the nature of instruments to the sociology of public policy instrumentation. *Governance*, 20(1), pp. 1–21. doi:10.1111/j.1468-0491.2007.00342.x.

Lasswell, H.D. (1970). The emerging conception of the policy sciences. *Policy Sciences*, 1(1970), pp. 3–14.

Lasswell, H.D. (1971). *A pre-view of policy sciences*. New York: American Elsevier.

Lasswell, H.D. (2003). The policy orientation. In: S. Braman, ed., *Communication researchers and policy-making*. Cambridge, MA: MIT Press, pp. 85–104.

Lehder, G. (2011). *Taschenbuch Arbeitssicherheit. [Pocket guide on occupational safety]*. 12th ed. Berlin: Erich Schmidt Verlag.

Lehmbruch, G. (2000). The institutional framework: federalism and decentralisation in Germany. In: H. Wollmann and E. Schröter, eds., *Comparing public sector reform in Britain and Germany. Key traditions and trends of modernisation*. Aldershot: Ashgate, pp. 85–106.

Lehmbruch, G. (2002). Der unitaristische Bundesstaat in Deutschland: Pfadabhängigkeit und Wandel. In: A. Benz and G. Lehmbruch, eds., *Föderalismus: Analysen in entwicklungsgeschichtlicher und vergleichender Perspektive*. Wiesbaden: VS Verlag für Sozialwissenschaften, pp. 53–110.

Linder, S.H. and Peters, B.G. (1989). Instruments of government: Perceptions and contexts. *Journal of Public Policy*, 9(1), pp. 35–58. doi:10.1017/S0143814X00007960.

Lodge, M. (2005). The importance of being modern: International benchmarking and national regulatory innovation. *Journal of European Public Policy*, 12(4), pp. 649–667. doi:10.1080/13501760500160151.

Lodge, M. (2011). Risk, regulation and crisis: Comparing national responses in food safety regulation. *Journal of Public Policy*, 31(1), pp. 25–50.

Lodge, M. and Wegrich, K. (2011). Governance as contested logics of control: Europeanized meat inspection regimes in Denmark and Germany. *Journal of European Public Policy*, 18(1), pp. 90–105.

Lowi, T.J. (1972). Four systems of policy, politics and choice. *Public Administration Review*, 32(4), pp. 298–310.

Maggetti, M. (2009). The role of independent regulatory agencies in policy-making: A comparative analysis. *Journal of European Public Policy*, 16(3), pp. 450–470. doi:10.1080/13501760802662854.

Majone, G. (1989). *Evidence, argument, and persuasion in the policy process*. New Haven, CT: Yale University Press.

Majone, G. (1997). The new European agencies: Regulation by information. *Journal of European Public Policy*, 4(2), pp. 262–275. doi:10.1080/135017697096342.

Majone, G. (2010). Strategic issues in risk regulation and risk management. In: *OECD reviews of regulatory reform*. Paris: Organisation for Economic Co-operation and Development, pp. 93–128.

Mansfield, B. (2012). Environmental health as biosecurity: "Seafood choices", risk, and the pregnant woman as threshold. *Annals of the Association of American Geographers*, 102(5), pp. 969–976. doi:10.1080/00045608.2012.657496.

March, J.G. and Olsen, J.P. (1989). *Rediscovering institutions: The organizational basis of politics*. New York: Free Press.

Mares, I. (2003). *The politics of social risk: Business and welfare state development*. Cambridge and New York: Cambridge University Press.

Margetts, H. and Hood, C. (2016). Tools approaches. In: B.G. Peters and P. Zittoun, eds., *Contemporary approaches to public policy. International series on public policy*. London: Palgrave Macmillan, pp. 133–154.

Martens, K. and Jakobi, A.P. (2010). *Mechanisms of OECD governance: International incentives for national policy-making?* Oxford: Oxford University Press.

Martens, K. and Niemann, D. (2013). When do numbers count? The differential impact of the PISA rating and ranking on education policy in Germany and the US. *German Politics*, 22(3), pp. 314–332. doi:10.1080/09644008.2013.794455.

Mau, S. (2017). *Das metrische Wir: Über die Quantifizierung des Sozialen*. Frankfurt am Main: Suhrkamp.

Mayntz, R. and Scharpf, F.W. (1995). *Gesellschaftliche Selbstregelung und politische Steuerung*. Frankfurt am Main: Campus.

Meffert, K. (2008). *Entwicklung von gemeinsamen Arbeitsschutzzielen und Handlungsfeldern. [Developing joint occupational health and safety objectives and fields for action]*. Berlin: DGUV.

Mennicken, A. and Lodge, M. (2015). Quantification, administrative capacity and democracy. *Risk & Regulation*, (30), pp. 6–9.

Mennicken, A. and Miller, P. (2012). Accounting, territorialization and power. *Foucault Studies*, (13), pp. 4–24.

Merdian, J. (2005). Die Bedeutung der Gefährdungsbeurteilung zum nachhaltigen Steuern und Lenken der betrieblichen Risiken im Arbeitsschutz. *Zeitschrift für betriebliche Prävention und Unfallversicherung*, 9(2005), pp. 581–584.

Micklitz, H.-W. and Tridimas, T., eds. (2015). *Risk and EU law*. Cheltenham, UK: Edward Elgar Publishing.

Miller, P. and Rose, N. (1990). Governing economic life. *Economy and Society*, 19(1), pp. 1–31. doi:10.1080/03085149000000001.

Ministerium für Klimaschutz, Umwelt, Landwirtschaft, Natur- und Verbraucherschutz des Landes Nordrhein-Westfalen. (2013). *Hochwasserrisiko-Management. Schritte zum zukunftsfähigen Umgang mit den Risiken durch Hochwasser in Nordrhein-Westfalen*. Düsseldorf.

Moran, M. (2000). The Frank Stacey memorial lecture: From command state to regulatory state? *Public Policy and Administration*, 15(4), pp. 1–13. doi:10.1177/095207670001500401.

Moran, M. (2003). *The British regulatory state: High modernism and hyper-innovation*. Oxford: Oxford University Press.

Müller, U. (2010). *Hochwasserrisikomanagement [Flood risk management]*. Wiesbaden: Vieweg Teubner Verlag.

Mythen, G., Walklate, S. and Khan, F. (2013). "Why should we have to prove we're alright?": Counter-terrorism, risk and partial securities. *Sociology*, 47(2), pp. 383–398. doi:10.1177/0038038512444811.

Neal, A.W. (2009). Securitization and risk at the EU border: The origins of FRONTEX. *Journal of Common Market Studies*, 47(1), pp. 333–356.

O'Malley, P. (2004). *Risk, uncertainty and government*. London: Glasshouse Press.

OECD. (2010). *Risk and regulatory policy: Improving the governance of risk*. Paris: OECD.

Oliver, A. (2017). *The origins of behavioural public policy*. New York: Cambridge University Press.

Oosterveer, P. (2002). Reinventing risk politics: Reflexive modernity and the European BSE crisis. *Journal of Environmental Policy & Planning*, 4(3), pp. 215–229.

Osborne, D. and Gaebler, T. (1992). *Reinventing government: How the entrepreneurial spirit is transforming the public sector*. Reading, MA: Addison-Wesley Publishing Company.

Palier, B. (2007). Tracking the evolution of a single instrument can reveal profound changes: The case of funded pensions in France. *Governance*, 20(1), pp. 85–107. doi:10.1111/j.1468-0491.2007.00345.x.

Paul, K.T. (2007). Food for thought: Change and continuity in German food safety policy. *Critical Policy Studies*, 1(1), pp. 18–41.

Paul, K.T. (2012). The Europeanization of food safety: A discourse-analytical approach. *Journal of European Public Policy*, 19(4), pp. 549–566.

Paul, R. (2012). Limits of the competition state: The cultural political economy of European labour migration policies. *Critical Policy Studies*, 6(4), pp. 379–401. doi:10.1080/19460171.2012.730764.

Paul, R. (2013). Strategic contextualisation: Free movement, labour migration policies and the governance of foreign workers in Europe. *Policy Studies*, 32(2), pp. 122–141. doi:10.1080/01442872.2013.767584.

Paul, R. (2015). *The political economy of border-drawing: Arranging legality in European labor migration policies*. New York and Oxford: Berghahn Books.

Paul, R. (2016a). Entgegen aller Wahrscheinlichkeiten? Erklärungsansätze für die Diffusion risikobasierter Regulierung im föderalen System Deutschlands. [Against all odds? Explaining the diffusion of risk-based regulation in Germany's federal system]. *der moderne staat – Zeitschrift für Public Policy, Recht und Management*, 9(2), pp. 325–352.

Paul, R. (2016b). Negotiating varieties of capitalism? Crisis and change in contemporary British and German labour migration policies. *Journal of Ethnic and Migration Studies*, 42(10), pp. 1631–1650. doi:10.1080/1369183X.2016.1162357.

Paul, R. (2017a). Harmonization by risk analysis? Frontex and the risk-based governance of European border control. *Journal of European Integration*, 39(6), pp. 689–706.

Paul, R. (2017b). Risk: New issue or new tool in regulation and governance research? In: K. T. Paul et al., eds., *Society, regulation and governance: New modes of shaping social change?* Cheltenham, UK: Edward Elgar Publishing, pp. 59–74.

Paul, R. (2020). Analyse and rule? A conceptual framework for explaining the variable appeals of ex-ante evaluation in policymaking. *der moderne staat – Zeitschrift für Public Policy, Recht und Management*, 13(1), pp. 124–142. doi:10.3224/dms.v13i1.11.

Paul, R., Bouder, F. and Wesseling, M. (2016). Risk-based governance against national obstacles? Comparative dynamics of Europeanization in Dutch, French, and German flooding policies. *Journal of Risk Research*, 19(8), pp. 1043–1062. doi:10.1080/13669877.2015.1074936.

Paul, R. and Huber, M. (2015). Risk-based regulation in continental Europe? Explaining the corporatist turn to risk in German work safety policies. *European Policy Analysis*, 1(2), 5–33.

Paul, R. and Mölders, M. (2017). Society, regulation and governance: New modes of shaping social change? An introduction. In: R. Paul et al., eds., *Society, regulation and governance: New modes of shaping social change?* Cheltenham, UK: Edward Elgar Publishing, pp. 1–12.

Paul, R. et al. (2017). Decide, defend and discipline: Explaining the varied appeals of risk-based inspection reforms in Europe. *HowSAFE Working Papers*, (11). Available at: www.kcl.ac.uk/sspp/departments/geography/research/hrg/projects/howsafe/Rothstein-et-al-2015-Varieties-of-Risk-Regulation-HowSAFE-WP1.pdf.

Peck, J. (2011). Geographies of policy: From transfer-diffusion to mobility-mutation. *Progress in Human Geography*, 35(6), pp. 773–797. doi:10.1177/0309132510394010.

Peters, B.G. (2002). The politics of tool choice. In: L.M. Salomon, ed., *Designing government – From instruments to governance*. New York: Oxford University Press, pp. 552–564.

Peters, B.G. (2005). Conclusion: The future of instruments research. In: P. Eliadis, M.M. Hill and M. Howlett, eds., *Designing government – From instruments to governance*. Montréal and Kingston: McGill-Queen's University Press, pp. 353–366.

Pollitt, C. and Bouckaert, G. (2011). *Public management reform: A comparative analysis – New public management, governance, and the neo-weberian state*. 3rd ed. Oxford: Oxford University Press.

Pollitt, C., van Thiel, S. and Homburg, V. (2007a). New public management in Europe. *Management Online Review*, 2007(October), pp. 1–6. Available at: hdl.handle.net/1765/11553.

Pollitt, C., van Thiel, S. and Homburg, V. (2007b). *New public management in Europe: Adaptation and alternatives*. 2007th ed. Basingstoke England and New York: Palgrave Macmillan.

Porter, T.M. (1995). *Trust in numbers. The pursuit of objectivity in science and public life*. Princeton: Princeton University Press.

Posner, E.A. (2001). Controlling agencies with cost-benefit analysis: A positive political theory perspective. *University of Chicago Law Review*, 68, pp. 1137–1200.

Powell, W.W. and DiMaggio, P.J. (1991). *The new institutionalism in organizational analysis*. Chicago: University of Chicago Press.

Räbel, B. (2018). Zur staatlichen Kontrolle des Arbeitsschutzes in Deutschland – Weniger schaffen mehr? *Sicherheitsbeauftragter und Sicherheitsingenieur*, December 13. Available at: www.sifa-sibe.de/aktuelles/meinung/zur-staatlichen-kontrolle-des-arbeitsschutzes-deutschland-weniger-schaffen-mehr/

Radaelli, C.M. (2005). Diffusion without convergence: How political context shapes the adoption of regulatory impact assessment. *Journal of European Public Policy*, 12(5), pp. 924–943.

Radaelli, C.M. (2009). Desperately seeking regulatory impact assessments: Diary of a reflective researcher. *Evaluation*, 15(1), pp. 31–48. doi:10.1177/1356389008097870.

Radaelli, C.M. (2010). Rationality, power, management and symbols: Four images of regulatory impact assessment. *Scandinavian Political Studies*, 33(2), pp. 164–188. doi:10.1111/j.1467-9477.2009.00245.x.

Radaelli, C.M. and Meuwese, A.C.M. (2010). Hard questions, hard solutions: Proceduralisation through impact assessment in the EU. *West European Politics*, 33(1), pp. 136–153. doi:10.1080/01402380903354189.

Raimondo, E. (2018). The power and dysfunctions of evaluation systems in international organizations. *Evaluation*. doi:10.1177/1356389017749068.

Renn, O. (2008). *Risk governance coping with uncertainty in a complex world*. London and Sterling, VA: Earthscan.

Repgow, E. von. (1984). *Der Sachsenspiegel*. München: Manesse-Verlag.

Reusch, H.K. (1986). *Zur Geschichte der Lebensmittelüberwachung im Großherzogtum Baden und seinen Nachfolgeterritorien (1806–1954)*. Marburg/Lahn: University of Marburg.

Rhodes, R. (1996). Governing without government. *Political Studies*, 44(4).

Rhodes, R. (2000). Governance and public administration. In: J. Pierre, ed., *Debating governance: Authority, steering, and democracy*. Oxford: Oxford University Press, pp. 55–89.

Richardson, J., ed. (1982). *Policy styles in Western Europe*. London: Allen and Unwin. doi:10.4324/9780203082010.

Room, G. (2011). *Complexity, institutions and public policy: Agile decision-making in a turbulent world*. Cheltenham, UK: Edward Elgar Publishing.

Room, G. (2016). *Agile actors on complex terrains: Transformative realism and public policy*. London: Routledge.

Rose, N. (1991). Governing by numbers: Figuring out democracy. *Accounting, Organizations and Society*, 16(7), pp. 673–692. doi:10.1016/0361-3682(91)90019-B.

Roth, A. (2009). *Die allgemeine Lebensmittelüberwachung als Instrument des Verbraucherschutzes [General food inspection as legal tool in consumer protection]*. Stuttgart: Deutscher Gemeindeverlag.

Roth, M. (2012). Lebensmittelüberwachung und Datenquellen. In: H. Dunkelberg, T. Gebel and A. Hartwig, eds., *Lebensmittelsicherheit und Lebensmittelüberwachung*. Weinheim: Wiley VCH, pp. 143–170.

Rothstein, H., Borraz, O. and Huber, M. (2011). From the "neurotic" to the "rationalising" state: Risk and the limits of governance. In: C.O. Meyer and C. de Franco, eds., *Forecasting, warning, and transnational risks: Is prevention possible?* pp. 187–207.

Rothstein, H., Borraz, O. and Huber, M. (2013). Risk and the limits of governance: Exploring varied patterns of risk-based governance across Europe. *Regulation & Governance*, 7(2), pp. 215–235. doi:10.1111/j.1748-5991.2012.01153.x.

Rothstein, H., Demeritt, D., Paul, R. and Wang, L. (2021). True to type? State traditions and COVID-19 governance in comparative perspective. In: P. Brown and J. Zinn, eds., *COVID-19 – From the perspective of the sociology of risk and uncertainty*. London: Routledge.

Rothstein, H., Huber, M. and Gaskell, G. (2006). A theory of risk colonization: The spiraling regulatory logics of societal and institutional risk. *Economy and Society*, 35(1), pp. 91–112. doi:10.1080/03085140500465865.

Rothstein, H., Paul, R. and Demeritt, D. (2020). The boundary conditions for regulation: Welfare systems, state traditions, and the varied governance of work safety in Europe. *Governance*, 33(1), pp. 21–39. doi:10.1111/gove.12411.

Rothstein, H. et al. (2019). Varieties of risk regulation in Europe: Coordination, complementarity and occupational safety in capitalist welfare states. *Socio-Economic Review*, 17(4), pp. 993–1020.

Sabatier, P.A. (1988). An advocacy coalition framework of policy change and the role of policy-oriented learning therein. *Policy Sciences*, 21(2/3), pp. 129–168.

Sabatier, P.A. and Jenkins-Smith, H.C. (1993). *Policy change and learning: An advocacy coalition approach*. Boulder, CO: Westview Press.

Sack, D. (2013). *Regieren und Governance in der BRD*. München: Oldenbourg.

Salamon, L.M. (2002). The new governance and the tools of public action. In: L.M. Salomon, ed., *Designing government – From instruments to governance*. New York: Oxford University Press, pp. 1–47.

Scharpf, F.W. (1985). Die Politikverflechtungs-Falle: Europäische Integration und deutscher Föderalismus im Vergleich. *Politische Vierteljahresschrift*, 26(4), pp. 323–356.

Scharpf, F.W. (1988). The joint-decision trap: Lessons from German federalism and European integration. *Public Administration*, 66(3), pp. 239–278. doi:10.1111/j.1467-9299.1988.tb00694.x.

Scharpf, F.W. (2006). The joint-decision trap revisited. *JCMS: Journal of Common Market Studies*, 44(4), pp. 845–864. doi:10.1111/j.1468-5965.2006.00665.x.

Schmid-Breton, A., Kutschera, G., Botterhuis, T. and The ICPR expert group 'flood risk analysis' (EG HIRI). (2018). A novel method for evaluation of flood risk reduction strategies: Explanation of ICPR FloRiAn GIS-tool and its first application to the Rhine River Basin. *Geosciences*, 8(10), p. 371.

Schneider, S. (2005). *Rechtliche Instrumente des Hochwasserschutzes in Deutschland [Legal tools of flooding protection in Germany]*. Berlin: Schmidt.

Scott, J. (1998). *Seeing like a state: How certain schemes to improve the human condition have failed*. New Haven: Yale University Press.

Seibel, W. (2001). Verwaltungsreformen. In: K. König and H. Siedenkopf, eds., *Öffentliche Verwaltung in Deutschland*. Baden-Baden: Nomos, pp. 87–106.

Seipel, S. and Lim, N.J. (2017). Color map design for visualization in flood risk assessment. *International Journal of Geographical Information Science*, 31(11), pp. 2286–2309. doi:10.1080/13658816.2017.1349318.

Sewekow, E., Schmidt-Faber, B. and Frost, M. (2010). Daten amtlicher Lebensmittelkontrolle in Deutschland–Analyse und Erfassung der Unterschiede. *Journal für Verbraucherschutz und Lebensmittelsicherheit*, 2010(5), pp. 313–331.

Shore, C. and Wright, S. (2015). Governing by numbers: Audit culture, rankings and the new world order. *Social Anthropology*, 23(1), pp. 22–28.

Shrader-Frechette, K.S. (1990). *Risk and rationality. Philosophical foundations for populist reforms*. Berkeley: University of California Press.

Simons, A. and Voß, J.-P. (2017). The concept of instrument constituencies: Accounting for dynamics and practices of knowing governance. *Policy and Society*, pp. 1–22. doi:10.1080/14494035.2017.1375248.

Simons, R. (1984). *Staatliche Gewerbeaufsicht und gewerbliche Berufsgenossenschaften: Entstehung und Entwicklung des dualen Aufsichtssystems im Arbeitsschutz in Deutschland von den Anfängen bis zum Ende der Weimarer Republik. [Statutory workplace inspection and mutual trade associations: Emergence and development of the dual inspection regime in german occupational safety from its origins to the end of the weimar republic]*. Frankfurt am Main: Haag + Herchen.

Steiner, C.K. (2006). Governance reform of German food safety regulation: Cosmetic or real? In: C.K. Ansell and D. Vogel, eds., *What's the beef? The contested governance of European food safety*. Cambridge, MA: MIT Press, pp. 181–209.

Stone, D. (2012). *Policy paradox: The art of political decision making*. New York: W.W. Norton & Co.

Stone, D. (2020). *Counting: How we use numbers to decide what matters*. New York, NY: Liveright.

Straßheim, H. (2017). Bringing the political back in: Reconstructing the debate over evidence-based policy. A response to Newman. *Critical Policy Studies*, 11(2), pp. 235–245. doi:10.1080/19460171.2017.1323656.

Straßheim, H. and Beck, S. (2019a). Introduction to the handbook of behavioural change and public policy. In: H. Straßheim and S. Beck, eds., *Handbook of behavioural change and public policy*. Cheltenham, UK: Edward Elgar Publishing, pp. 1–21.

Straßheim, H. and Beck, S., eds. (2019b). *Handbook of behavioural change and public policy*. Cheltenham, UK: Edward Elgar Publishing.

Straßheim, H. and Kettunen, P. (2014). When does evidence-based policy turn into policy-based evidence? Configurations, contexts and mechanisms. *Evidence & Policy: A Journal of Research, Debate and Practice*, 10(2), pp. 259–277. doi:10.1332/174426514X13990433991320.

Sum, N.-L. and Jessop, B. (2013). *Towards a cultural political economy. Putting culture in its place in political economy*. Cheltenham, UK: Edward Elgar Publishing.

Sunstein, C. (2009). *Laws of fear: Beyond the precautionary principle*. Cambridge: Cambridge University Press.

Sunstein, C.R. (2000). Cost-benefit default principles. *Michigan Law Review*, 99, pp. 1651–1723.

Sunstein, C.R. (2002). *Risk and reason: Safety, law, and the environment*. Cambridge: Cambridge University Press.

Szmukler, G. and Rose, N. (2013). Risk assessment in mental health care: Values and costs. *Behavioral Sciences & the Law*, 31, pp. 125–140. doi:10.1002/bsl.2046.

Tholoniat, L. (2010). The career of the open method of coordination: Lessons from a "Soft" EU instrument. *West European Politics*, 33(1), pp. 93–117. doi:10.1080/01402380903354122.

Thomann, E. (2019). *Customized implementation of European union food safety policy – United in diversity?* Basingstoke: Palgrave Macmillan.

Thomann, E., Trein, P. and Maggetti, M. (2019). What's the problem? Multilevel governance and problem-solving. *European Policy Analysis*, 5(1), pp. 37–57. doi:10.1002/epa2.1062.

Tombs, S. and Whyte, D. (2013). Transcending the deregulation debate? Regulation, risk, and the enforcement of health and safety law in the UK. *Regulation & Governance*, 7(1), pp. 61–79. doi:10.1111/j.1748-5991.2012.01164.x.

Trondal, J. (2013). The rise of a European public administration: European capacity building by stealth. In: P. Genschel and M. Jachtenfuchs, eds., *Beyond the regulatory polity? The European integration of core state powers*. Oxford: Oxford University Press.

Turnpenny, J.R. et al. (2015). The tools of policy formulation: An introduction. In: A.J. Jordan and J.R. Turnpenny, eds., *The tools of policy formulation: Actors, capacities, venues and effects*. Cheltenham, UK: Edward Elgar, pp. 3–29.

TÜV Rheinland and Risktec. (2018). *Risk-based decision making and ALARP*. Köln. Available at: www.risktec.tuv.com/wp-content/uploads/2018/11/Risktec-Essentials-Risk-based-Decision-Making-ALARP-brochure-i1.0-med-res-single-pages.pdf.

Unnerstall, H. (2010). *Legal framework for public participation in flood risk mapping: A comparative study of the responses of different European member states to some requirements of the floods directive*. UFZ Working Paper, Leipzig: Helmholtz Centre Department of Environmental and Planning Law.

van Asselt, M.B.A. and Renn, O. (2011). Risk governance. *Journal of Risk Research*, 14(4), pp. 431–449. doi:10.1080/13669877.2011.553730.

Vedung, E. (2011). Policy instruments: Typologies and theories. In: M.-L. Bemelmans-Videc, R.C. Rist and E. Vedung, eds., *Carrots, sticks, and sermons: Policy instruments and their evaluation*. New Brunswick: Transaction Publishers, pp. 21–58.

Viscusi, W.K. (1983). *Risk by choice: Regulating health and safety in the workplace*. Cambridge, MA: Harvard University Press.

Viscusi, W.K. (1995). *Fatal tradeoffs: Public and private responsibilities for risk*. Oxford: Oxford University Press.

Voß, J.-P. (2016). Realizing instruments: Performativity in emissions trading and citizen panels. In: J.-P. Voß and R. Freeman, eds., *Knowing governance: The epistemic construction of political order*. London: Palgrave Macmillan UK (Palgrave Studies in Science, Knowledge and Policy), pp. 127–153. doi:10.1057/9781137514509_6.

Voß, J.-P. and Freeman, R. (2016). Introduction: Knowing governance. In: J.-P. Voß and R. Freeman, eds., *Knowing governance: The epistemic construction of political order*. London: Palgrave Macmillan UK, pp. 1–33.

Voß, J.-P. and Simons, A. (2014). Instrument constituencies and the supply side of policy innovation: The social life of emissions trading. *Environmental Politics*, 23(5), pp. 735–754. doi:10.1080/09644016.2014.923625.

Vos, E. (2000). EU food safety regulation in the aftermath of the BSE crisis. *Journal of Consumer Policy*, 23(3), pp. 227–255.

Wagenaar, H. (2011). *Meaning in action: Interpretation and dialogue in policy analysis*. Armonk, NY: M.E. Sharpe.

Weible, C.M. and Sabatier, P.A. (2007). A guide to the advocacy coalition framework. In: F. Fischer, G.J. Miller and M.S. Sidney, eds., *Handbook of public policy analysis: Theory, politics, and methods*. Boca Raton: CRC Press, pp. 123–136.

Weiss, C. (1973). The politics of impact measurement. *Policy Studies Journal; Urbana, Ill.*, 1(3), pp. 179–183.

Weiss, C. (1993). Where politics and evaluation research meet. *Evaluation Practice*, 14(1), pp. 93–106. doi:10.1016/0886-1633(93)90046-R.

Weiss, C.H., Murphy-Graham, E. and Birkeland, S. (2005). An alternate route to policy influence: How evaluations affect D.A.R.E. *American Journal of Evaluation*, 26(1), pp. 12–30. doi:10.1177/1098214004273337.

Wiener, J.B. (2010). Risk regulation and governance institutions. In: *OECD reviews of regulatory reform*. Paris: Organisation for Economic Co-operation and Development, pp. 133–157.

Yanow, D. (2000). *Conducting interpretive policy analysis*. Thousand Oaks, CA: Sage (Qualitative Research Methods).

Yanow, D. (2006). Thinking interpretively: Philosophical presuppositions and the human sciences. In: D. Yanow and P. Schwartz-Shea, eds., *Interpretation and method. Empirical research methods and the interpretive turn*. New York: M.E. Sharpe, pp. 5–26.

Yanow, D. (2007). Interpretation in policy analysis: On methods and practice. *Critical Policy Analysis*, 1, pp. 110–122.

Yanow, D. (2014). Interpretive analysis and comparative research. In: I. Engeli and C.R. Allison, eds., *Comparative policy studies: Conceptual and methodological challenges*. London: Palgrave Macmillan UK, pp. 131–159.

Yanow, D. and Schwartz-Shea, P., eds. (2006). *Interpretation and method. Empirical research methods and the interpretive turn*. New York: M.E. Sharpe.

Ziblatt, D. (2008). *Structuring the state: The formation of Italy and Germany and the puzzle of federalism*. Princeton, NJ: Princeton University Press.

INDEX

Note: Page numbers in *italics* indicate a figure and page numbers in **bold** indicate a table on the corresponding page. Page numbers followed by 'n' indicate a note.

Made in the USA
Las Vegas, NV
01 November 2024

aa076f60-3e80-43df-89b5-8643f00beeb9R01